D0843197

This is the first study to consider the meaning of Anglicanism for ordinary people in nineteenth-century England. Drawing extensively on unpublished sources, particularly those for rural areas, Frances Knight analyses the beliefs and practices of lay Anglicans and of the clergy who ministered to them. Building on arguments that the Church of England was in transition from State Church to denomination, she argues that strong continuities with the past nevertheless remained. Through an examination of denominational identity, personal piety, Sunday church-going and Anglican rites of passage she shows that the Church continued to cater for the beliefs and values of many Christians. Far from becoming a minority sect, the Anglican Church in the mid-Victorian period continued to claim the allegiance of one in four English people.

THE NINETEENTH-CENTURY CHURCH
AND ENGLISH SOCIETY

'Religion descending in a cloud'. The frontispiece of Thomas Bankes'
The Christian's New and Complete Family Bible (1790). Reproduced by permission
of the Syndics of Cambridge University Library.

THE NINETEENTH-CENTURY CHURCH AND ENGLISH SOCIETY

FRANCES KNIGHT

*Lecturer in Christian Theology,
University of Wales, Lampeter*

CAMBRIDGE
UNIVERSITY PRESS

Published by the Press Syndicate of the University of Cambridge
The Pitt Building, Trumpington Street, Cambridge CB2 1PR
40 West 20th Street, New York, NY 10011–4211, USA
10 Stamford Road, Oakleigh, Melbourne 3166, Australia

© Cambridge University Press 1995

First published 1995

Printed in Great Britain at the University Press, Cambridge

A catalogue record for this book is available from the British Library

Library of Congress cataloguing in publication data

Knight, Frances. The nineteenth-century Church and
English society / Frances Knight.
p.   cm.
Includes bibliographical references and index.
ISBN 0 521 45335 6 (hardback)
1. Church of England – History – 19th century.
2. Anglican Communion – England – History – 19th century.
3. England – Church history – 19th century.
4. Church and State – England.
5. Christianity and culture – History.
I. Title.
BX5055.2.K55   1995
283′.42′09034 – dc20   95–7838 CIP

ISBN 0 521 45335 6 hardback

CE

To Clive Bright

Contents

Preface

The history of the Church of England in the nineteenth century has been largely written from the centre, from the perspective of events in Oxford and Cambridge, Lambeth and Westminster, the cathedral close and the episcopal palace. It has tended to dwell on the problems and priorities of the men who were at home in such places. The result is that historians have devoted a great proportion of their energies to a relatively small proportion of the Church. An examination of the thought of prelates, politicians and dons provides a valuable insight into the minds of those in the vanguard of shaping opinion, but it avoids the question of how (or even if) their ideas were assimilated in the country at large.

This book looks at the Church at the parish level in order to reconstruct the religious world of the nineteenth-century Anglican, and to examine the impact that the policies being formulated at the top of the ecclesiastical hierarchy had on the parishioners and clergy of England. Not all change was initiated from above; nor were the laity and parochial clergy passive in their response to it. As is demonstrated by projects to restore churches and to build schools, many plans were brought to fruition locally, with little reference to the Church's hierarchy. This study attempts to recapture something of the varied experience of church people and the clergy who ministered to them, and to consider both the national and local influences to which they were subject. It does not seek to analyse Anglicanism as a disembodied belief system, still less as a series of theological conflicts. Rather, it is a study of Anglicanism as an experience that was lived by a large number of English people.

The period from 1800 to 1870 may have been one of change and upheaval, but there remained strong continuities with the past. For most of the period laymen remained able to exercise considerable influence in their parish church, as parish clerks, churchwardens and vestrymen. To this extent it was still a Church in which the lay voice had to be taken seriously. The persistence of a supernatural under-standing of the world remained widespread during the period. There was a general belief that prayer, if offered with sufficient conviction, could change the way in which the world worked, and that death was not the end of life, but the gateway to heaven or hell. It was usual for most people, with the exception of the unchurched urban poor, to make some form of deliberate choice about religious matters – even if the choice of Anglicanism did not always result in regular church attendance.

The aims of this study are broad and ambitious. After a brief historiographical introduction, lay religion and the notion of Anglican identity are explored. Lay piety is investigated through contemporary approaches to the Bible, the Prayer Book and the concept of salvation. The study moves from the private to the public realm by analysing the role of parish churches in local communities, exploring their transition from providers of charity and poor relief to a more exclusive concern with the conduct of public worship and the occasional offices that marked social rites of passage. The focus then shifts from the laity to their clergy, explores the forces for change in clerical lives, and in particular the impact of the Ecclesiastical Commission's policies. The changing relationship between laity and clergy, and the shift in authority and control which accompanied this development is consid-ered.

This project, which began as a PhD thesis that investigated the Church of England in the South and East Midlands, is no longer simply a local study. Original research on the counties of Buckingham-shire, Bedfordshire, Cambridgeshire, Leicestershire, Lincolnshire and Nottinghamshire has been supplemented by the use of printed sources for certain other English counties. Although some reference is made to Aylesbury, Bedford, Cambridge, Lincoln, Newark and Nottingham, the book concentrates upon rural central England. This is in part an attempt to compensate for what appears to be an overly urban approach in nineteenth-century history, which ignores the fact that, until 1850, more people lived in the country than the town. The book gains internal coherence by giving particular attention to the diocese of Lincoln during the episcopate of John Kaye, from 1827 to 1853. Kaye was a 'reforming' bishop in the same tradition as his close associate C. J. Blomfield of London, yet he remains a little-known figure in the nineteenth-century Church. Like Blomfield, Kaye was a founder member of the Ecclesiastical Commission, and was zealous in putting its policies into practice. The diocese of Lincoln, therefore, provides a particularly apposite case-study of the impact of the reform movement at the grass-roots. Although this book disclaims to be a local study, its author is well aware of having considered only a fraction of the available evidence, which is scattered all over England. An exhaustive investigation of all sources could occupy a team of researchers for years, and could not be undertaken.

During the years which led up to the writing of this book, I have been assisted, supported and encouraged by many individuals and institutions. Five years as a student among the theologians at King's College, London provided a stimulating start. I owe much to Judith Champ, who introduced me to church history and supervised my initial explorations, to Bruce Kinsey, a fellow traveller at King's (and now Cambridge) and to Ian Markham, who once suggested that I write a book on lay religion. Anthony Machen gave early encouragement to my post-graduate studies, and would have been pleased to see the publication of this book. Sadly, he died in 1988.

At Cambridge my doctoral research was supervised by David Thompson, whose shrewd observations and extensive knowledge saved me from going wrong at a number of points. I have benefited from the comments of those who read the thesis that resulted – Rod Ambler, Arthur Burns, Eamon Duffy, Sheridan Gilley, Eileen Groth, John Morrill and Peter Nockles.

Research and writing were made possible by the British Academy, who awarded me a major state studentship and then a post-doctoral fellowship. I have also been financially assisted by the University of Cambridge, who elected me to a Crosse studentship in 1989/90. Selwyn College elected me to a research fellowship which ran concurrently with my British Academy fellowship. They provided a sunny room in west Cambridge with a view of apple blossom and bluebells in the springtime. It was a pleasant setting in which to work on this and other projects, and the College itself proved an appropriate environment in which to study Anglican history. I also have reason to be grateful for the generosity of the Principal and Fellows of Newnham College, Cambridge. I am indebted to my father, Edmund Knight, for helping me with the proofs of this book.

It was invaluable to have access to the collections at the Cambridge University Library, the British Library, Lambeth Palace Library, SPCK in Marylebone Road, the Bodleian Library and Pusey House,

Oxford. The staff at the Lincolnshire Archives Office were unfailingly patient and helpful, and the search room officer, Nigel Colley, made some very useful suggestions.

I have benefited from the friendship of a number of religious historians, of whom two deserve special mention in the present context. Mary Heimann has been a constant source of encouragement and good sense. She read this book in instalments as it was being written, commenting on it with insight and precision. Bill Jacob supported the research from the beginning – initially by allowing me to live at Lincoln Theological College whilst working at the Lincolnshire Archives Office. I asked to stay for seven weeks, but my visit lasted for two and a half years. He too has commented carefully on these chapters, and has helped me to develop some of my ideas. Both Mary and Bill have saved me from numerous errors, omissions and infelicities, but I take full responsibility for those which remain.

The person to whom I owe the most is my husband Clive Bright. He has always been an enthusiastic supporter of my various endeavours, and he has lived with versions of this project for almost as long as he has lived with me. Throughout it all, he has remained cheerfully tolerant of my seemingly undying interest in dead Anglicans. This book is dedicated to him, with love.

Abbreviations

ACS   Additional Curates Society
BL   British Library
Bodl   Bodleian Library
CMS   Church Missionary Society
CPAS   Church Pastoral Aid Society
CUL   Cambridge University Library
EDR   Ely Diocesan Records
ICBS   Incorporated Church Building Society
LAO   Lincolnshire Archives Office
LPL   Lambeth Palace Library
PH   Pusey House
SPCK   Society for Promoting Christian Knowledge

In the manuscript material which has been cited in the text, the original spelling and punctuation has been retained.

CHAPTER I

Interpreting the nineteenth-century Church

During the period from about 1800 to 1870 the Church of England underwent a transformation more rapid, dramatic and enduring than any which it had experienced since the Reformation. The process of change was complex and in certain respects ambiguous, but the most significant adjustment was that which took place in the relationship between Church and State. The Church moved from a uniquely privileged relationship with the State, in which it was closely bound up with the political and legal system, to being one denomination, albeit still the most powerful one and still formally and legally Established, among several in a society in which it appeared that half of those who professed any form of religious allegiance expressed a preference for a non-Anglican variety. This modification in Church–State relations was accompanied by the de-Anglicanisation of English institutions, starting at the heart of the Establishment with the admission of Protestant dissenters to Parliament on equal terms with Anglicans in 1828, and then spreading outwards to the municipal corporations, the universities and the grammar schools.

The relationship between Church and people shifted for a diverse variety of reasons, which included the drift of population to the towns, agitation from disgruntled Nonconformists, the clergy's changing perception of themselves, and the intervention of parliamentarians and Ecclesiastical Commissioners. The parish clergy moved from a *de facto* supervisory role within the boundaries of each parish (symbolised by the huge numbers who sat on the magistrates' bench) to a more limited and strictly ecclesiastical role directed towards a discrete clientele, with the rest of the population regarded as either abandoned to Nonconformity, or in the case of the 'unchurched masses', perceived as the legitimate targets for missionary activity. The attitude to the poor itself underwent a significant re-definition. At the beginning of the century attempts to church the unchurched were centred on the provision of additional free seats, and were channelled through organisations like the Incorporated Church Building Society, as well as through local endeavours. It was a remnant of the idea that a seat should be available in his parish church for every subject of the realm. Later, when this was perceived as no longer possible or even appropriate, there began a clerically-orchestrated campaign to sift and distinguish between the degrees of commitment of those who showed some interest in the Church. This resulted in a narrowing of the definition of who was and who was not an Anglican.[1]

The Church of England responded to the upheavals of the nine-teenth century by trying to make itself more effective. One way in which it did this was through the policies pursued by the Ecclesiastical Commission, a Church–State endeavour that made a significant impact on the pattern of clerical life. Another response came in the form of a spiritual revival, which manifested itself in various shades of Evangelical, Orthodox and Tractarian churchmanship. This spiritual revival had two major though largely unintended effects. The first was to drive a firmer wedge between the 'spiritual elite' in the Church (of whatever theological complexion) and the supposedly ungodly world outside. The second was to bring church people into new conflicts with one another, typified by the rise of party hostility and internecine feuding which characterised the period. For Evangelical, Orthodox and Anglo-Catholic protagonists, an even greater enemy was to emerge from within the bosom of the Church. In a highly symbolic episode following the controversy over *Essays and Reviews*, a work of liberal Anglican theology published in 1860, representatives of all three parties united to turn their collective fire on the liberals of the Broad Church.

Although the Church in the nineteenth century can be justly described as in a state of profound and lasting transition, in other important ways it remained distinctly the same institution as in the

---

[1] The term 'Anglican' in this study has been adopted for the sake of convenience and clarity as a simple description of adherence to the Church of England. It should be remembered, however, that it was a slippery term in the nineteenth century, and it was not widely used by lay church people to describe themselves (they preferred the term 'churchman'). The word gained controversial 'High Church' connotations, which caused it to fall from favour in Evangelical usage, whilst the Tractarians themselves used it pejoratively to describe 'high and dry' orthodoxy. See Peter Nockles, *The Oxford Movement in Context: Anglican High Churchmanship 1760–1857* (Cambridge: Cambridge University Press, 1994) pp. 39–41; J. Robert Wright, 'Anglicanism, *Ecclesia Anglicana*, and Anglican: An essay on terminology' in Stephen Sykes and John Booty (eds.), *The Study of Anglicanism* (London: SPCK, 1988) pp. 424–9 and Paul Avis, 'What is "Anglicanism"?' in the same volume, pp. 405–24.

past. The adoption of the terminology of the 'long eighteenth century', which interprets the period as lasting from the Toleration Act (1689) until the 1830s, continues to be popular with scholars.[2] The thesis could be adapted and pushed further to suggest that in some respects the Church of England remained little changed until the 1860s. It continued to command considerable support from lay people, who remained willing to donate large amounts of their money, and in some cases their time and skill, to maintaining and extending its fabric. These people continued to live with a view of the world that was recognisably Christian, their spirituality shaped by a high view of the Bible and the Book of Common Prayer, and by a profound sense of the changes and chances of the present world, which caused them to dwell much on the importance of preparation for a holy death.

In the attitudes and circumstances of the clergy there may also be discerned clear continuities with the preceding period. The vast majority continued to be graduates of Oxford or Cambridge, which meant that they shared the common culture and aspirations of the genteel classes, even if they sometimes lacked the financial resources (from their clerical incomes at least) to match them. Indeed, amongst the lower clergy, the curates and the holders of small benefices, there remained a degree of poverty that continued to cause hardship, despite the endeavours of the Queen Anne's Bounty and the various pieces of legislation which aimed to regulate curates' stipends. The necessity continued of mitigating financial hardship by recourse to pluralism of one sort or another, though the legislation passed in 1838 and 1850 gradually phased it out. But the important word is gradually. As existing interests were always respected, the effects of the legislation, significant though they were, were not fully felt until 1870. If pluralism and non-residence remained relatively common, however, it should not be assumed that they necessarily led to poor standards of attention to

---

[2] For a recent and comprehensive account of the Church of England in the eighteenth century see John Walsh and Stephen Taylor, 'Introduction: the Church and Anglicanism in the "long" eighteenth century' in John Walsh, Colin Haydon and Stephen Taylor (eds.), *The Church of England c. 1689–c. 1833: From Toleration to Tractarianism* (Cambridge: Cambridge University Press, 1993) pp. 1–64. The other essays in this volume provide an invaluable synthesis of recent research on the period. Other important works which emphasise the centrality of Anglicanism in the 'long' eighteenth century are J. C. D. Clark, *English Society 1688–1832* (Cambridge: Cambridge University Press, 1985); Robert Hole, *Pulpits, Politics and Public Order in England 1760–1832* (Cambridge: Cambridge University Press, 1989); James E. Bradley, *Religion, Revolution and English Radicalism: Nonconformity in Eighteenth-Century Politics and Society* (Cambridge: Cambridge University Press, 1990); and A. M. C. Waterman, *Revolution, Economics and Religion: Christian Political Economy, 1798–1833* (Cambridge: Cambridge University Press, 1991).

duty. As in the eighteenth century, many of the rural clergy lived but a short distance from their parishes, and were quite as effective as they would have been if they had been technically resident. Indeed, they were perhaps less likely to subside into idleness if they had more rather than fewer souls in their care. The ideal of a fully-resident clergy, which was a cherished ambition of 'reformers' like Bishops Blomfield and Kaye, remained difficult to put into practice. It was clumsy attempts to make it a reality which placed new and largely unconsidered financial burdens on the whole ecclesiastical structure. Amongst the higher clergy – the bishops, archdeacons, rural deans and incumbents of the prominent parishes – there may be observed the same general spirit of conscientiousness and caution, and the desire to promote unity and avoid controversy, which was a feature of the eighteenth-century Church. Until the 1860s the churchmanship of those in authority in the Church of England was often reminiscent of the High Church Orthodoxy that was firmly rooted in the previous century, and which made senior churchmen distrustful of Evangelicals on the one hand and Tractarians on the other.[3]

It will be argued in this book that the period from about 1800 to about 1870 was a complicated time in which the Church of England was simultaneously in a state both of transition and of continuity with the past. The purpose of this study is to investigate the ways in which some of these transitions and continuities were expressed at the grass-roots of Anglicanism, as the Church was forced to redefine itself as a denomination. In the past twenty years a growing number of articles and pamphlets have investigated aspects of local religion, and a number of full-scale studies have been completed, though few have found their way into print. The pioneer in the field was James Obelkevich's *Religion and Rural Society: South Lindsey 1825–1875* (1976), a social history of religion in a relatively small part of Lincolnshire which, drawing on Marx and Feuerbach, aimed to do justice to the broad spectrum of religious phenomena from magic and superstition to the activities of the Anglicans. Albion M. Urdank's *Religion and Society in a Cotswold Vale: Nailsworth, Gloucestershire 1780–1865* (1990) provided an

---

[3]   See the writings of Peter Nockles for an account of the Orthodox. For example, 'Continuity and change in Anglican High churchmanship in Britain 1792–1850' (University of Oxford DPhil., 1982); 'The Oxford Movement: historical background 1780–1833' in Geoffrey Rowell (ed.), *Tradition Renewed: The Oxford Movement Conference Papers* (London: Darton, Longman & Todd, 1986) pp. 24–50; 'Church parties in the pre-Tractarian Church of England 1750–1833: the "Orthodox" – some problems of definition and identity' in Walsh, Haydon and Taylor, *The Church of England* pp. 334–59; and *The Oxford Movement in Context.*

immensely detailed socio-economic history of a centre of Evangelical Nonconformity, which also highlighted the Church of England in a state of weakness. Staithes, another community in which the Church was weak, was the subject of David Clark's *Between Pulpit and Pew: Folk Religion in a North Yorkshire Fishing Village* (1982). At the time of writing a version of Mark Smith's 1987 Oxford DPhil. thesis 'Religion in industrial society: the case of Oldham and Saddleworth 1780–1865' is due to be published by Oxford University Press. This will provide a valuable urban foil to these rural studies.

Amongst the articles and pamphlets that provide local studies of Anglicanism, the best of which are extremely illuminating and suggestive, there has been a tendency (often the result of pressure on space) for the material to be presented in purely parochial terms, with little sense of contextual significance, or for it to be shaped by what appears to be a predetermined interpretative framework. That is to say the authors concentrate on parishes in which the theological complexion is already regarded as clear.[4] The effect, perhaps an unintentional one, is to simplify the understanding of the underlying religious geography of nineteenth-century Anglicanism, and also to focus on an overtly clerical conception of the past, in which the religious life of a community is seen as having been reshaped by the arrival of one or two clergy whose role is interpreted as having been fundamentally different from that of their predecessors. A consequence of this has been to produce an impression of conflicting ecclesiastical ideologies – Tractarian on the one hand and Evangelical on the other – battling for the souls of Anglican parishioners. Amidst the sound and fury created by the conflicting ideologies, there has been a tendency for other approaches to be overshadowed. The question of the way in which the reform movement made an impact on parish life, insofar as it has been studied at all, has tended to be conceived in narrowly liturgical and ecclesiological terms, 'parish life' being understood as a shorthand for the way in which services were conducted in parish churches. As a result

---

[4] See, for example, the earlier work of Nigel Yates, 'Leeds and the Oxford Movement: a study of "High Church" activity in the rural deaneries of Allerton, Armley, Headingley and Whitkirk in the diocese of Ripon 1836–1934', *Thoresby Society Publications* 55: 121 (Leeds, 1975); *The Oxford Movement and Parish Life: St Saviour's, Leeds, 1839–1929*, Borthwick Papers 48 (York: Borthwick Institute of Historical Research, 1975); also, Peter G. Cobb, *The Oxford Movement in Nineteenth Century Bristol* (Bristol: Bristol Branch of the Historical Association, 1988); E.P. Hennock, 'The Anglo-Catholics and church extension in Victorian Brighton' in M. J. Kitch (ed.), *Studies in Sussex Church History* (London: Leopard's Head Press, 1981).

something is known about how the externals of worship changed, but very little about the underlying texture of religious belief.

The brief sketch of some of the central themes in Anglican historiography that follows helps to place the present study in context. It is intended to give substance to the claim that Anglicanism at the grass-roots has been neglected, whilst providing an introduction to some of the larger questions that will be discussed as the study proceeds. Four contrasting approaches will be considered, each of which has made a distinctive contribution to an understanding of the period – although they should not be seen as in any sense exhaustive. The first and most widespread is the analysis in terms of party ideologies, the significance of which in local studies has already been touched upon. It is an approach that completely dominated the subject until the 1960s, and which still persists in places. The second is an analysis in terms of institutional revival, the third of clerical revival, and the last a view which sets the subject in terms of the Anglican struggle with Nonconformity.

Although Peter Nockles has pointed out that the first historians of Tractarianism were its hostile detractors rather than its hagiographers,[5] the conventions which have shaped the study of nineteenth-century Anglican history have been determined to a large extent by the influence of High Church historians in the Tractarian mould. By the early years of the twentieth century Anglo-Catholicism, albeit in a watered down form, had emerged as the predominant culture within Anglicanism, and this contributed to maintaining its historiographical ascendancy. The emergence of a victorious Anglo-Catholicism from the ferment of Victorian Anglicanism (at least until Anglo-Catholicism's decline after the Second World War), seems to have led to a tendency to see it as having miraculously revived the Church in the 1830s and 1840s. Pre-eminent among the early generation of Anglo-Catholic historians was R. W. Church, whose book *The Oxford Movement: Twelve Years, 1833–1845* first appeared in 1891, and, having assumed the status of a classic, was reprinted with an introduction by Geoffrey Best as recently as 1970. Best described the book as 'reliable, accurate and fair on almost all matters of fact and most of opinion',[6] which is itself evidence of the continuing influence of the underlying thesis.

---

[5]   Nockles, *Oxford Movement in Context* pp. 1–2. For a comprehensive discussion of Tractarian historiography see pp. 1–24.

[6]   R. W. Church, *The Oxford Movement: Twelve Years 1833–1845*, ed. G. F. A. Best (Chicago: Classics of British Historical Literature Edition, 1970), p. xvii.

It was R. W. Church's contention that in 1833 the Church and clerical life had sunk into worldliness and torpor, though not, as sometimes portrayed by its more hostile detractors, into vice and depravity. From the outset he was concerned with matters of party affiliation, an obsession which has continued. He divided the clergy of the early 1830s into three categories: the Orthodox churchmen whom he parodied as high and dry 'teachers of mere morality at their best, allies and servants of the world at their worst'; the Evangelicals, characterised as having succumbed to superficiality and now on very easy terms with the world; and finally the independent and liberal thinkers, who were at home with neither of the other parties, and who criticised both.[7] This jumble of theological opinions was in itself regarded as unedifying, and in a world turned upside down by the Reform Bill and the effects of Benthamite utilitarianism, R. W. Church described John Keble delivering his Assize sermon on 14 July 1833. The sermon was redolent with accusations of national apostasy, and with warnings of the dangers of the Church being despoiled by the State and trampled on by the people. Taking their cue from Newman himself, who had remarked in the *Apologia Pro Vita Sua* (1864) that he had 'ever considered and kept the day as the start of the religious movement of 1833',[8] the Tractarian historians adopted 1833 as the year when modern church history began.

Inspired by the memory of their first leaders, the early Tractarian historians set out to give an account of the way in which, galvanised by Keble's Assize sermon, a small band of Oxford dons had attempted to inject some fight into a Church in danger from a Whig government bent on stripping it of its temporal and spiritual authority. J. H. Overton put it thus: 'The national feeling, long pent-up, depressed, despondent, had at length obtained freedom to pour forth; and the effect was amazing. The Church suddenly came to life.'[9] Repackaged for popular consumption by the faithful, the mass-circulation histories written by Overton, Church, C. P. S. Clarke, S. L. Ollard and others sometimes subsided into ripping narratives in celebration of their heroes. The reader is repeatedly reminded of the saintliness of Keble, the scholarly austerity of Edward Bouverie Pusey, the boyish flamboyance of Richard Hurrell Froude, all set against the central motif of the

---

[7] Ibid., pp. 16–18.
[8] J. H. Newman, *Apologia Pro Vita Sua*, ed. Maisie Ward, Spiritual Masters Edition (London: Sheed & Ward, 1984) p. 23.
[9] J. H. Overton, *The English Church in the Nineteenth Century (1800–1833)* (London, 1894) p. 14.

personal crisis of John Henry Newman. The filtering of the events through the eyes of a handful of Oxford men had the effect of beguiling the reader into a sense of intimacy and participation as the plot unfolded, as in this extract from Ollard's history:

Froude stretched out his long length on Newman's sofa, and broke in upon one of Palmer's judicious harangues about bishops and archbishops and such like with, 'I don't see why we should disguise from ourselves that our object is to dictate to the clergy of this country, and I for one do not want any one else to get on the box.'[10]

The disarming frankness conveyed here, and the distinctive atmosphere of late night discussions in dons' rooms, is invoked in a way never quite equalled by historians outside the Anglo-Catholic tradition, whose heroes tend to be depicted as operating more in the public than in the private domain, against a less finely embroidered backcloth. The publication of the *Letters and Diaries of John Henry Newman*, (1978–81), which provide an almost day by day account of the development of his thought, and the progress of the Oxford Movement (welcome though this is) has only increased this sense of the magnification of the importance of individual Tractarians, and the reader's feeling of being a privileged witness to the gradually unravelling story.[11] Whilst it is appropriate for those who wish to study the Movement as intellectual history to focus more or less exclusively on key individuals, it is certainly a less fruitful approach for those who are interested in its social, spiritual, organisational or political aspects. Despite the plethora of publications, there are still aspects of the Oxford Movement that remain unexplored.

Tractarian historians made an early attempt to write the history of the nineteenth-century Church, but by the beginning of the twentieth century Evangelicals were also offering their distinctive interpretation, though they never produced histories in the same quantity as the Anglo-Catholics. The most influential book was G. R. Balleine's *A History of the Evangelical Party in the Church of England*, which first appeared in 1908 and went through five editions, the last of which was published in 1951. Balleine clearly intended to educate and inspire his fellow Evangelicals by providing a compelling account of the development of the party, and the book was laced with what are sometimes rather

10   S. L. Ollard, *A Short History of the Oxford Movement* (first edition 1915; reprinted London: Faith Press, 1963), p. 45.
11   I. Ker and T. Gornall, (eds.), *The Letters and Diaries of John Henry Newman*, 5 vols., (Oxford: Clarendon Press, 1978–81).

fanciful descriptions of the degenerate condition of the non-Evangelical clergy, the dilapidated state of their church buildings and their total neglect of worship. (One of Balleine's more eccentric claims was that there were no evening services of any kind whatever before the Evangelical revival.)[12] The High Church Orthodoxy that predated Tractarianism was almost completely ignored in this study, except in one reference to a hostile pamphlet written by Thomas Sikes.[13] Balleine dealt with the Tractarians by on the one hand emphasising the significance of Newman's Evangelical roots, and on the other the disloyalty to the Church of England of those who converted to Rome. But Balleine's intention was to publicise Evangelicalism rather than Tractarianism, and his book contained none of the innuendo or manufactured outrage of Walter Walsh's mass-circulation horror story, *The Secret History of the Oxford Movement* (1897).

As recently as 1988, Balleine's mantle was self-consciously assumed by Kenneth Hylson-Smith in his *Evangelicals in the Church of England 1734–1984.* Hylson-Smith described Balleine's book as 'excellent', and claimed that his own work was a replacement and updating of it.[14] Certainly his approach to the subject was similar to that adopted by Balleine eighty years earlier; they both began with Wesley, and focused thereafter on eminent Evangelical personalities, including William Grimshaw, William Romaine, John Newton, the Venns, Henry Ryder, Charles Simeon, William Wilberforce, Edward Bickersteth, Francis Close, the Sumners and J. C. Ryle. Both writers regarded the abolition of slavery in 1833 as the great moment of Evangelical triumph, after which they admitted that the movement suffered internal fragmentation, and began to turn its attention to less ambitious, more parochial concerns, and to attempting to defend Protestant Christianity from the incursions of an aberrant Anglo-Catholicism. The approach gives credence to a point made by John Kent, that the intention of historians in the tradition of Balleine and Hylson-Smith (including L. G. Elliott-Binns, J. S. Reynolds, J. C. Pollock and Michael Hennell) was to bring Evangelicalism into the foreground of the Victorian picture, to emphasise its theological loyalty to Luther and Calvin, to show its positive contribution to social questions, and to work out for Evangelicalism a

---

[12] G. R. Balleine, *A History of the Evangelical Party in the Church of England* (first edition, 1908; reprinted London: Church Book Room Press, 1951) p. 191.

[13] Ibid., p. 43.

[14] Kenneth Hylson-Smith, *Evangelicals in the Church of England 1734–1984* (Edinburgh: T & T Clark, 1988) p. viii.

pedigree as distinguished as that of Anglo-Catholicism, with the Wesleys, the Venns, Simeon and Ryle held in the same sort of regard as Newman, Keble, Pusey and Gore.[15] In recent years the study of Evangelicalism has become considerably more sophisticated. It has been subject to some new and much needed scrutiny from a variety of standpoints, including David Bebbington's *Evangelicalism in Modern Britain: A History from the 1730s to the 1980s* (1989), Boyd Hilton's *The Age of Atonement: The Influence of Evangelicalism on Social and Economic Thought: 1785–1865* (1988) and John Wolffe's *The Protestant Crusade in Great Britain 1829–1860* (1991).

The older, general histories of the Church, published in the 1960s and 1970s, continue to exert a considerable influence on Anglican historiography. They too pay considerable attention to party themes, and the portrait that emerges is of a Church dominated by senior clergy and politicians. This approach may be detected in one of the most readable and therefore most widely read works on the period, Owen Chadwick's two-volume study *The Victorian Church* (1966 and 1970), and in Edward Norman's *Church and Society in England 1770–1970* (1976). The thesis is also clearly stated in M. A. Crowther's *The Church Embattled: Religious Controversy in Mid-Victorian England* (1970) and in the collection of essays edited by Anthony Symondson, *The Victorian Crisis of Faith* (1970).

It is only since the late 1950s that historians with a less explicit interest in party questions have turned their attention to the Church of England. Not surprisingly, they have been less easily persuaded by the scenario of a grand spiritual battle between the forces of Tractarianism on the one hand and Evangelicalism on the other, and they have begun to investigate the other influences which were shaping the Church at this period. A number of scholars explored what may be termed the Church's 'institutional' revival. Prominent among the most significant contributions were Olive Brose's *Church and Parliament: The Reshaping of the Church of England 1828–1860* (1959), Geoffrey Best's *Temporal Pillars: Queen Anne's Bounty, the Ecclesiastical Commissioners, and the Church of England* (1964) and K. A. Thompson's *Bureaucracy and Church Reform: The Organizational Response of the Church of England to Social Change 1800–1965* (1970). The thread uniting these three books was their stress that the reform which the Church underwent from the 1830s onwards was part of a wider, utilitarian, government-sponsored movement to

[15] John Kent, *The Unacceptable Face: The Modern Church in the Eyes of the Historian* (London: SCM Press, 1987) pp. 85–6.

increase the efficiency of institutions. Geoffrey Best made the important point that church reforms were nearly all designed to enhance the parish, and that they ought to be seen alongside the efforts to improve the poor laws, and with the 'select vestry' movement for the streamlining of parochial government.[16] He suggested that the clergy, many of whom were also magistrates, knew just how difficult, yet essential, the task of maintaining law and order was, and that because of this they were aware of the desirability of making the parish an effective unit of government.[17] It was often admitted quite candidly that the Church's main function was social control; though this was not to imply that it did not also have the function of saving souls. As Best put it:

All Evangelicals, obviously, and presumably most high churchmen, would no doubt have agreed that saving souls was in some ways a higher function. But even if they allowed a qualitative distinction of this kind, they would still have seen social control as a principal function of their established church, for these reasons: first, because a state without an established religion was almost – for some, absolutely – unimaginable, on common social and political grounds; second, because it was generally assumed that a nation of Christians was collectively lacking in religious seriousness if it did not have an established church, and would be punished by God accordingly; and third, because in the minds of virtually all the upper, and, one supposes many of the middling and lower orders who were religious at all, the way to salvation lay through political good conduct.[18]

This sense of the closeness of the co-operation between Church and State was emphasised by Olive Brose, who suggested that church reform was seen as a necessary prerequisite to the Church's performing its national function. She noted that the most influential plans for church reform, those of Henley, Berens and Burton, assumed that reform would be a joint enterprise between Church and State.[19] This indeed was how it turned out: the Ecclesiastical Commission was founded in 1835 to produce reports for improving the state of the Church, and they soon became enshrined in Acts of Parliament. Its initial membership consisted of seven politicians and five bishops, and its early meetings were chaired by the prime minister Sir Robert Peel,

[16] G. F. A. Best, *Temporal Pillars: Queen Anne's Bounty, the Ecclesiastical Commissioners, and the Church of England* (Cambridge: Cambridge University Press, 1964) p. 145.
[17] Ibid., pp. 138, 145.
[18] Ibid., p. 152.
[19] Olive Brose, *Church and Parliament: The Reshaping of the Church of England 1828–1860* (Stanford: Stanford University Press, and London: Oxford University Press, 1959) p. 20.

(himself a loyal churchman) in his own drawing-room. Politicians as well as churchmen had begun to realise that the Church needed to be saved from itself, as well as from its enemies, and it became the essence of Peel's policy to make the Church the instrument of its own regeneration.[20] The significance of the Ecclesiastical Commission was central to the thesis of Kenneth Thompson, and he too regarded the methods implicit in reform by Commission as emphasising the Church's usefulness to society, especially in maintaining social control and stability.[21] Unlike Brose, however, he saw the creation of the Commission as a sign that the Church was increasingly receiving delegated powers from the State for its own agencies and officers.[22] Certainly, under the Established Church Act of 1836, Parliament became virtually redundant to the Commission's day to day operations, as Orders in Council, with the full legal force of statutes, were prescribed as the legislative method of the Commissioners, and these were merely laid before Parliament each January.[23] It was a sign that a parliament that had ceased to be exclusively Anglican was taking less interest in Anglican affairs, and that encouraging it to do otherwise could be dangerous for the interests of the Church.

Whereas both Anglo-Catholic and Evangelical historians invested 1833, the year of Keble's Assize sermon and the abolition of slavery, with particular significance, the dates adopted by the historians of 'institutional' Anglicanism was rather different. Best regarded an awareness on the part of the Establishment of the need for reform and change as dating from the end of the American War of Independence; prompted in part by the growth of political liberalism and radicalism, rational Dissent and Methodism, and an increasing fear about the breakdown of law and order.[24] Brose saw the repeal of the Test and Corporation Acts in 1828, Roman Catholic Emancipation in 1829, and the Reform Act of 1832 (which together initiated a fundamental change in the relationship between Church and State) as the key events in causing churchmen to rethink what it meant to be the Establishment, whilst giving the Church's opponents the opportunity to call into question the whole idea of an Established Church. For the government, the changes of 1828–32 meant the continued existence of a contra-

20   Norman Gash, *Sir Robert Peel* (London: Longmans, 1972) p. 103.
21   K. A. Thompson, *Bureaucracy and Church Reform: The Organizational Response of the Church of England to Social Change 1800–1965* (Oxford: Clarendon Press, 1970) p. 3.
22   Ibid., p. 5.
23   Best, *Temporal Pillars* p. 307.
24   Ibid., p. 137.

dictory situation – a national Church set in a pluralist society.[25] Thompson, meanwhile, adopted 1836 as his symbolic point of departure. This was the year in which tithes were reformed, thus ending a long standing source of irritation between clergy and tithe-payers. It was also the year in which the Registrar-General's Office was established, which gave people the opportunity of being married and having births and deaths recorded at a registry office or chapel, rather than in their parish church.[26]

When they considered what bearing churchmanship had on an individual's approach to church reform, the institutional historians agreed that it was the Tractarians who were most hostile. This position was most fully worked out in Thompson's study. His underlying thesis was that in the 1830s the Church was faced with a choice between emulating the utilitarian methods of reform favoured in wider society and symbolised by the setting up of the Ecclesiastical Commission, or adopting the transcendental framework of the Oxford Movement.[27] It may be that in presenting a stark polarity Thompson was setting up a false dichotomy, ignoring as he did the broader range of strategies for change that were available to the Church. The institutional historians were correct to stress the antipathy between the Oxford Movement and the Ecclesiastical Commission, but in doing so they may have given too much weight to the extent to which either body could claim to understand or speak for the generality of Anglicans, whether clerical or lay.

The third historiographical approach to be considered here is that which focused on changes in the structure and self-understanding of the clerical profession as a means of explaining some of the developments in the nineteenth-century Church. C. K. Francis Brown provided the first history of the nineteenth-century clergy in 1953,[28] and interest in the subject flourished again between the mid-seventies and the mid-eighties, the most recent contributions being Alan Haig's *The Victorian Clergy* (1984) and Rosemary O'Day's revisionist essay 'The clerical renaissance in Victorian England and Wales' (1988).[29] Haig's perspective was to consider how the Church was experienced as a

25 Brose, *Church and Parliament* p. 14.
26 Thompson, *Bureacracy and Church Reform* p. 1.
27 Ibid., p. 2ff.
28 C. K. Francis Brown, *A History of the English Clergy, 1800–1900* (London, 1953).
29 Rosemary O'Day, 'The clerical renaissance in Victorian England and Wales' in Gerald Parsons (ed.), *Religion in Victorian Britain: Traditions* (Manchester: Manchester University Press, 1988) pp. 185–212.

career by those who entered it, and he paid particular attention to the mechanics of clerical training and ordination, and to how the clergy fared subsequently, considering separately the fortunes of the beneficed and the unbeneficed. O'Day argued that the Victorian period did not witness the emergence of a new-style clerical profession based on secular models, but the revival of the occupational professionalism of the early modern period. An earlier contribution from a different perspective was Brian Heeney's *A Different Kind of Gentleman: Parish Clergy as Professional Men in Early and Mid-Victorian England* (1976), in which he studied the handbooks of pastoral theology written by a relatively small but theologically diverse group of clergymen for the instruction of younger colleagues. These he delineated as constituting a distinctively professional literature, and reflecting a shift in the understanding of the clergyman from being a 'professional' because of his high social status, to being so because he had adequate theological training and pastoral skills.[30] Another contributor was Anthony Russell, initially in an Oxford D.Phil thesis,[31] and subsequently in *The Clerical Profession* (1980). Russell, like Haig and Heeney, was concerned with the process by which the clergy acquired certain occupational characteristics. The contention of all three authors was that during the nineteenth century the clerical profession was revolutionised. This was in part caused by the rise of party sympathies; in part by the fact that new careers began to emerge at this period, in some cases taking over what had been traditionally clerical functions, and forcing the clergy to retreat into a more specifically ecclesiastical role – in Russell's words, to become 'the technologists of the sanctuary'; and in part by the sheer number of young men entering it – it remained the largest profession in Victorian England, dominated by the young. Haig suggested that by the middle of the century over half of the clergy were under forty-five years old, and only a fifth were over fifty-five, a situation unique in the history of the Church of England. This state of affairs gave credibility to the language of revival, and substance to Bishop Selwyn's famous remark of 1854, that on his return from thirteen years in New Zealand he detected 'a great and visible change' in the Church. The important point is that in detecting shifts in clerical attitudes, it is more

---

[30] Brian Heeney, *A Different Kind of Gentleman: Parish Clergy as Professional Men in Early and Mid-Victorian England* (Connecticut: Archon Books, 1976) pp. 4–7.

[31] A. J. Russell, 'A sociological analysis of a clergyman's role: with special reference to its development in the early nineteenth century', (unpublished DPhil. thesis, University of Oxford, 1970).

appropriate to see them as resulting from an overall takeover by a new body, rather than from a change of heart in the existing body.[32]

Although the number of ordinations increased rapidly until the 1880s, it did not keep pace with the overall growth in population, which doubled between 1800 and 1860. That this was known to be the case had the effect of galvanising Victorian Anglicans into even greater efforts, thus stimulating the twin phenomena that Gerald Parsons identified as interwoven throughout Victorian religion, the paradoxes of revival and decline, crisis and opportunity.[33] Haig argued that the appeal for a body of clergy expanding in proportion to the whole population seemed plausible as well as desirable until the mid-1890s, by which point it was clear that ordinations were falling sharply and would never keep pace with the expansion of population.[34] For most of the nineteenth century, though, the situation was one of more and more clergy being channelled into a static ecclesiastical structure that lacked the natural means of expansion.

To a considerable extent, however, the nineteenth-century Church failed to conform to the norms that governed the other professions, as O'Day has argued, and as Haig, Heeney and Russell also readily admitted.[35] By the end of the century the clergy had not gained control of the institutional Church, and a great deal of power remained in the hands of Parliament, lay patrons and bishops (these are themes which will be explored in chapter five). Secondly, the clergy lacked a national pay structure and career pattern, and had little sense of promotion being based on merit, where status and connections remained important in gaining preferment. Yet paradoxically at a time when other professions were moving to an all-graduate entry, the Church was for the first time ordaining large numbers of non-graduates, and thereby potentially diluting its intellectual resources. Most seriously, perhaps, the supernatural framework that had underpinned society's under-standing of what the clergy were for was being seriously brought into question. To Freethinkers (and of course also to Nonconformists, Roman Catholics and Jews) it was not clear what claim the clergy had to be offering professional services at all. The secular professions, by contrast, were rising to prominence on account of their unquestioned

---

[32] Alan Haig, *The Victorian Clergy* (London and Sydney: Croom Helm, 1984) pp. 2–4.
[33] Gerald Parsons (ed.), *Religion in Victorian Britain: Traditions* (Manchester: Manchester University Press, 1988) vol. 1, p. 214.
[34] Haig, *Victorian Clergy* pp. 4–5.
[35] Heeney, *Different Kind of Gentleman* pp. 7–8; Haig, *Victorian Clergy* pp. 15–18; Anthony Russell, *The Clerical Profession* (London: SPCK, 1980) pp. 239–48.

practical utility. Whereas they were moving towards enjoying state-protected or state-enforced monopolies, bolstered by powerful ruling bodies like the Law Society, the British Medical Association and the Institute of Chartered Accountants, the clerical profession found itself increasingly vulnerable, and locked into a competitive relationship with Roman Catholic priests and Nonconformist ministers. Though it is useful to regard a metamorphosis as having taken place amongst the ranks of the nineteenth-century clergy, clearly the professionalisation model is not wholly valid.

In addition to this body of literature on the transformation of the clergy is another – almost its second cousin – that examines the transformation of the episcopate. This literature conventionally regards Samuel Wilberforce as having revived the pastoral office of bishop, first at Oxford between 1845 and 1869, and then to a lesser extent at Winchester from 1869 to 1873. Certainly Wilberforce was an active diocesan, but his fame rests very largely on the fact that his many deeds were so lovingly recorded: by his son Reginald, who with A. R. Ashwell produced a three-volume *Life* in the 1880s, by J. W. Burgon, who featured Wilberforce in his *Lives of Twelve Good Men* (1888), by G. W. Daniell, G. W. E. Russell and J. C. Hardwick, all of whom produced biographies between 1891 and 1933, and by Sabine Baring-Gould in *The Church Revival* (1914). Wilberforce's bishoprics have also received attention from a host of modern scholars, including R. K. Pugh, who edited his letter-books (1970), C. K. Francis Brown in his *History of the English Clergy, 1800–1900* (1953), Standish Meacham in *Lord Bishop: The Life of Samuel Wilberforce 1805–1873* (1970), Desmond Bowen in *The Idea of the Victorian Church: A Study of the Church of England 1833–1889* (1968) and David Newsome in *The Parting of Friends* (1966). The existence of very large deposits of Wilberforce papers in the Bodleian Library and elsewhere has been a significant factor in stimulating scholarly interest. Nevertheless it is clear that by 1845, when Wilberforce was elevated to the see of Oxford, the diocesan revival was already well established in certain places, and that Wilberforce followed rather than led. John Kaye had been reviving the far more unwieldy diocese of Lincoln since 1827[36] whilst Thomas Burgess had brought significant reforms to the diocese of St David's from as early as 1803.[37] But there is a danger in seeking out proto-Wilberforces, as Arthur Burns warned in his thesis on

---

[36] Frances Knight, 'Bishop, clergy and people: John Kaye and the diocese of Lincoln 1827–1853' (unpublished PhD thesis, University of Cambridge, 1990).
[37] J. S. Harford, *A Life of Thomas Burgess D.D.* (London, 1840).

diocesan revival from 1825 to 1865 (1990).[38] Burns rightly suggested that to see diocesan reform purely in terms of episcopal initiatives was highly misleading. He provided a timely reminder of the importance of paying attention to forces for change emerging from the grass roots and from the middle, rather than from the top of the Church.

The three historiographical traditions sketched out so far have concentrated entirely on Anglicanism, a reflection of the tendency for most Anglican historiography to marginalise the importance of Nonconformity. This is despite the fact that much of the excitement in politics in the nineteenth century was generated by persistent Nonconformist campaigns for disestablishment, a long-running battle to remove restrictions on Dissenters' civil rights, and violent rows over the control of schools.[39] The fourth interpretation, expounded most explicitly in Alan Gilbert's *Religion and Society in Industrial England: Church, Chapel and Social Change 1740–1914* (1976), did however take Nonconformity seriously, regarding the determining factor in the religious history of the period as being the creation and gradual resolution of a conflict between the established Church and Protestant Nonconformity, as the Church was forced to shift from a monopolistic to a voluntaristic position, from the only officially recognised religious institution in England to a competing denomination.

Gilbert argued that 'Church' and 'Chapel' occupied two distinct worlds, and that to choose one's affiliation meant to opt for one of two very different religious and social value systems.[40] The application of this theory will be discussed in chapter two. According to Gilbert, the attractions of the Evangelical Nonconformist way of life were considerable, and not to be lightly dismissed. In purely religious terms it offered a truly popular version of Christianity, geared to achieving the widest possible support in a society where commitment was nothing if not voluntary.[41] Unlike the Anglicanism with which it was in competition, it placed a strong emphasis on conversion, on itinerancy and local preaching, and on the activities of lay people. But to be a Nonconformist also linked the adherent to a wider nexus of social and political concerns. In the 1840s the Anti-State Church Association attracted support from the same range of people as the Anti-Corn Law League,

[38] R. A. Burns, 'The diocesan revival in the Church of England *c.* 1825–1865' (unpublished DPhil. thesis, University of Oxford, 1990) p. 2.

[39] Kent, *Unacceptable Face* p. 81.

[40] A. D. Gilbert, *Religion and Society in Industrial England: Church, Chapel and Social Change 1740–1914* (London: Longman, 1976) p. 69.

[41] Ibid., p. 53.

though of course it was much smaller. In the second half of the century, renamed as the Liberation Society, it shared members with the Reform Movement, the Ballot Society and the Peace Society. In addition to articles on disestablishment and the need to redress dissenting disabilities, journals like *The Nonconformist* and *The Liberator* published pieces on electoral reform, reform of the educational system and the armed services and on the curtailment of the privileges of the landed interest.[42] Thus in addition to its specifically religious concerns, Nonconformity became a cry of protest at a multitude of injustices; an act of rebellion against a decaying social structure, with an appeal to those whom Gilbert described as the socially deviant, and who were perceived by Anglicans (particularly clergy) as socially wilful.[43]

For Gilbert, Nonconformist agitation was part of a much wider process of bringing reforming political pressure to bear for the general reduction of privilege. The relationship between the Churches and the political establishment was explored in more depth by G. I. T. Machin in *Politics and the Churches in Great Britain 1832 to 1868* (1977). Like Gilbert, Machin emphasised the alliance between Dissent and democracy, but he failed to subscribe to Gilbert's theory linking Dissenters and deviance. 'Order was as important as liberty to Nonconformists – a fact which helps to explain the social and political influence they attained in the nineteenth century.'[44] The rapid expansion of Nonconformity caused the Establishment to look at itself and become aware of its extreme fragility. Machin argued that successive governments were convinced of the urgency of reforming the Church as a means of re-asserting the Establishment's influence, and to bolster it against the demands of Dissenters and voluntaryists. At the same time it became increasingly crucial for governments not to be seen to be alienating Nonconformist and Roman Catholic voters by exhibiting undue favouritism to the Church of England. Clearly this is a thesis which offers much to support the view that the most significant shift experienced by the Church of England was the movement from State Church to denomination.

With the possible exception of the early Anglo-Catholic and Evangelical historians, proponents of the approaches outlined above have been generally willing to acknowledge the interaction of other influ-

---

[42] Ibid., p. 164.
[43] Ibid., p. 76.
[44] G. I. T. Machin, *Politics and the Churches in Great Britain 1832 to 1868* (Oxford: Clarendon Press, 1977) pp. 14–15.

ences, and have not presented their theses as if they were self-contained explanations. Machin, for example, argued that the rapid expansion of Nonconformity led to the Church being (for the most part) willing to co-operate in government-sponsored institutional reform along the lines described by Brose, Best and Thompson. It was this reform, regarded as overdue by one section of the Church, which was to be met with outright hostility by another, and Pusey's remark that the Ecclesiastical Commission would set up the Prime Minister as a Protestant Pope, illustrated the level of party feeling involved.[45] Again it could be argued with Haig that there was a close link between the clergyman's loss of his once unquestioned role in traditional society, and the conflict with Nonconformity.[46] The clergyman's subsequent redefinition of himself in more strictly ecclesiastical terms was also likely to be stimulated by new definitions of churchmanship that stemmed from Evangelicalism and Tractarianism.

The present study naturally draws on the insights offered by these and other historians, but it also attempts to break away from existing historiography. In particular, there is a deliberate avoidance of an interpretation based on the rise of party, although when evidence concerning churchmanship has emerged, it has not been ignored. As has been argued above, the subject has been so dominated by 'party' explanations in the past, that it would seem timely to consider what the effects might be of clearing away such presuppositions. More importantly, this approach arises from the conviction that labels of churchmanship do not always offer much assistance in the quest to uncover the concerns of lay members of the Church of England. In the period up until 1870 Anglicans generally understood themselves to be Protestants, and they sometimes defined themselves further according to whether they were sympathetic or hostile to Protestant Nonconformity. The party conflicts that undoubtedly raged at a higher level in the Church generally passed them by. In researching this study, party considerations emerged as important for understanding archdeacons, but they were of less significance for many of the lower clergy. I have argued elsewhere that the parochial clergy were often indifferent to such matters; for example, with the exception of a relatively few urban areas, the Tractarian parish priest was rare indeed in the period to

---

[45] See Machin, *Politics and the Churches* p. 85, and Desmond Bowen, *The Idea of the Victorian Church: A Study of the Church of England 1833–1889* (Montreal: McGill University Press, 1968) p. 21.

[46] Haig, *Victorian Clergy* pp. 16–17.

1860.[47] This book looks at the Church from the bottom rather than the top. In some ways, it is a modest response to David Hempton's observation that 'working-class Anglicanism in particular has been strikingly under-researched'.[48] The task is to consider what Anglicanism meant for ordinary Anglicans – as a supernatural belief system and as a social and cultural phenomenon – in the parishes of nineteenth-century England.

---

[47] Frances Knight, 'The influence of the Oxford Movement in the parish *c.* 1833–1860: a reassessment' in Geoffrey Rowell and Paul Vaiss (eds.), *From Oxford to the People* (Fowler Wright, 1995).

[48] David Hempton, 'Popular religion 1800–1986' in Terence Thomas (ed.), *The British: Their Religious Beliefs and Practices 1800–1986* (London and New York: Routledge, 1988) p. 193.

CHAPTER 2

Lay religion

It is customary for people to attend the church at those times when a Sermon is preached and the Methodist Meeting house at other times.

The curate of Stretham, Cambridgeshire, in 1825[1]

To a large extent lay people remain the forgotten participants in the Anglican history of the modern period. This omission is now even more apparent when it is contrasted with the growth of interest in lay religion among medievalists and early modernists.[2] Several reasons may account for the neglect. One is the common assumption that the onset of industrialisation led to the final collapse, in the popular imagination, of the Christian world-view, and that from the middle decades of the century Christianity became a solely middle-class preoccupation.[3] The publication of Horace Mann's Report on the Religious Census of 1851 did much to propagate this notion among contemporaries, by drawing their attention to the extent to which the working classes stayed away from church. Yet such interpretations tend

---

[1] CUL EDR C1/6, 1825.

[2] Earlier important contributions came from Keith Thomas, *Religion and the Decline of Magic: Studies in Popular Beliefs in Sixteenth- and Seventeenth-century England* (London: Weidenfeld & Nicolson, 1971); Claire Cross, *Church and People 1450–1660: The Triumph of the Laity in the English Church* (London: Fontana, 1976); Patrick Collinson, *The Religion of Protestants: The Church in English Society 1559–1625* (Oxford: Clarendon Press, 1982), chapter 5; and C. J. Somerville, *Popular Religion in Restoration England* (Gainesville, 1977). More recent work includes Eamon Duffy, *The Stripping of the Altars: Traditional Religion in England 1400–1580* (New Haven and London: Yale University Press, 1992); Judith D. Maltby, 'Approaches to the study of religious conformity in late Elizabethan and early Stuart England' (University of Cambridge PhD thesis, 1991); Donald Spaeth, 'Parsons and parishioners: lay–clerical conflict and popular piety in Wiltshire villages, 1660–1740' (Brown University PhD thesis, 1985); and Susan J. Wright (ed.), *Parish, Church and People: Local Studies in Lay Religion* (London, 1988).

[3] K. S. Inglis, *Churches and the Working Classes in Victorian England* (London: Routledge & Kegan Paul, 1963) p. 322ff; Peter Laslett, *The World We Have Lost – Further Explored* (London: Methuen, 1983) pp. 71–2; John Kent, 'Feelings and festivals: an interpretation of some working-class religious attitudes' in H. J. Dyos and Michael Wolff (eds.), *The Victorian City: Images and Realities*, 2 vols. (London and Boston: Routledge & Kegan Paul, 1973) pp. 855–71.

21

to overlook the tenacity of aspects of Anglicanism (and also the extent to which varieties of Nonconformity and Roman Catholicism had taken root in the urban environment). They tend to equate religiosity rather narrowly with Sunday attendance, and they ignore the experience of the majority of Britons, for whom life in a rural community remained the norm until the second half of the century.[4] Whilst the growth of the urban world was clearly of great significance for those whose lives were changed, historians who make too complete an equation between nineteenth-century Britain and the industrial town may find themselves gazing at just a part of the canvas.[5]

Lay Anglicans can seem difficult to pinpoint, and this has been another cause of their neglect. They may appear more elusive and less committed than lay Nonconformists or Roman Catholics. By contrast, lay Nonconformists are more visible because of the greater emphasis on lay ministry and lay preaching, and because of the absence, within certain strands at least, of a clear distinction between lay and ordained. The smaller numbers involved, and their more articulate self-consciousness, increase their accessibility to the historian. The same is true of lay Roman Catholics, who could be perceived as a separate and largely unassimilated community within British society, standing against an incoming tide of secularisation by holding fast to a package of distinctive beliefs and devotions. To be a lay Nonconformist or Roman Catholic is to be seen as being spiritually, and usually also financially and practically, committed to the Church. To be a lay Anglican is to be perceived as in a more ambiguous position, linked with a broader nexus of non-religious attachments that result from membership of a religious establishment. Against such a background it is all too easy to attribute lay allegiance to a mixture of class or social factors, and to minimise the significance of any religious motivation. For these reasons, perhaps, traditional church historians have tended to remain silent about lay people, preferring to interpret the Church in strictly institutional and clerical terms.

There is indeed a real difficulty in getting at the evidence. In this chapter, use has been made of popular religious literature aimed chiefly at the working classes. This was clearly of significance in shaping

[4]   Geoffrey Best, *Mid-Victorian Britain 1851–1875* (London: Weidenfeld & Nicolson, 1971) p. 6. The 1851 Census revealed that urban dwellers were in the majority for the first time.

[5]   For a useful corrective, see David M. Thompson, 'The Churches and Society in Nineteenth-century England: A Rural Perspective' in G. J. Cuming and Derek Baker (eds.), *Popular Belief and Practice*, Studies in Church History 8 (Cambridge: Cambridge University Press, 1972) pp. 267–76.

and reinforcing religious views, but it can only provide a part of the picture. Glimpses of lay life in the nineteenth-century Church tend to be fleeting, and often mediated through clerical eyes. Where evidence survives, it is naturally more likely to concern the externals of religion – church attendance, for example – rather than the interior world of the believer. Any sort of systematic understanding of the latter is unattainable; all that can be done is to strike a few matches in an otherwise dark landscape, and to peer briefly at what is illuminated.

Recent research has suggested that, far from being reviled and discredited, the eighteenth-century Church enjoyed a good measure of popular support.[6] There was a continuity between lay commitment in the eighteenth century that extended into the next, and though declining in relative terms, the nineteenth-century Church continued to be able to attract high levels of interest. The results of the Religious Census of 1851 can be interpreted positively as well as negatively. They revealed that on 30 March 1851 approximately one quarter of the entire population attended worship in an Anglican church.[7] The figure was not as high as it would have been a hundred years earlier, but on any objective assessment it remains impressive. No other institution could command the support of one in four of the people.

Most of the hundreds of thousands of pounds needed for building, extending, and refurbishing Anglican churches and schools, as well as for supporting Anglican charities and missions, came out of lay pockets. This points to commitment of a most tangible kind. Clearly Nonconformists and Roman Catholics did not have a monopoly on readiness to make material sacrifices to maintain their religion. The rapid expansion and movement of population brought challenges to which Anglican lay people strove to respond. It can be argued that the comprehensive social and spiritual networks that were in place in many larger parishes by the end of the period were a measure of their

---

[6]   See for example Viviane Barrie-Curien, 'London clergy in the eighteenth century' in John Walsh, Colin Haydon and Stephen Taylor (eds.), *The Church of England c.1689 – c.1833: From Toleration to Tractarianism* (Cambridge: Cambridge University Press, 1993) pp. 96–9 and Mark Smith, 'The reception of Richard Podmore: Anglicanism in Saddleworth 1700–1830' in the same volume, p. 114; W. M. Jacob, 'Church and Borough: King's Lynn, 1700–1750' in W. M. Jacob and Nigel Yates (eds.), *Crown and Mitre: Religion and Society in Northern Europe since the Reformation* (Woodbridge: Boydell Press, 1993) pp. 63–80; and Jan Albers, 'Seeds of contention: society, politics and the Church of England in Lancashire, 1689–1790' (Yale University PhD thesis, 1988).

[7]   Owen Chadwick, *The Victorian Church*, 3rd edn, 2 vols. (London: A. & C. Black, 1971), part I, vol I, pp. 363–9. Whilst there are clear problems with using the census data, there seems sufficient evidence to show that this conclusion is not invalidated.

success. Furthermore, in the period up to 1870 there was little effective challenge to a popular world-view that was recognisably Christian. Most people continued to believe that their prayers, if uttered with sufficient conviction, could change the way in which the world worked, that all their deeds were being recorded in a great book that would be opened on the last day, and that their dead children were sleeping in the arms of Jesus. When it came to making choices between belief systems, the decision was normally still between Anglicanism or Nonconformity or Roman Catholicism, rather than between Christianity and unbelief. For some Protestant Christians, however, the concept of a rigid denominational allegiance, adhered to throughout life, remained alien for much of the century.

THE PROBLEM OF IDENTITY: ANGLICAN OR METHODIST?

According to the classical theory of Anglicanism, the Church of England was coextensive with the nation, and therefore every citizen was automatically a member of the Church. By the beginning of the nineteenth century rising numbers of Nonconformists and Roman Catholics meant that this theory had ceased to have much practical credibility; but the Church was only just beginning its transition from national to denominational status, and so it would have been premature for the idea to be dispensed with entirely. As far as some lay people were concerned, Anglican identity remained an ambiguous concept for much of the period. Sometimes Anglican Evangelicalism blended with accessible forms of Nonconformity, with the result that many who regarded themselves primarily as church people had some experience of chapel activities, and many who regarded themselves as Nonconformists – and particularly Wesleyan Methodists – continued to maintain some contact with their parish church. Indeed, an Evangelical Anglican or a Wesleyan Methodist might well have been seen as lacking in religious seriousness if he or she did not take advantage of the spiritual opportunities provided by both communities. As the Wesleyans began to adopt a distinct identity as a separate denomination, and as the Anglicans became deposed from their central position in national life, both began to try to draw a sharper demarcation around their own supporters, and the pattern of dual identity became less common. Thus the pinpointing of certain individuals as Anglicans does not become straightforward until towards the end of the nineteenth century. The Church never compiled official membership statistics in the way that the Nonconformists did; to have done so would in any case have been misleading, for there was no accepted definition of membership. A member of the Church could be variously defined as a person who had been baptised, or as a person who was a communicant or who attended services regularly. He (or more often she) could be defined more precisely as someone who went exclusively to Anglican services, and shunned the other denominations. Different definitions were favoured at different points in the century. In the search for Anglican identity it is impossible to ignore the complexity of nineteenth-century religious practice.

As the theory that linked Anglican identity to national identity became finally redundant in the period from 1800 to 1830, a new emphasis began to be placed on the significance of Anglican baptism. Before the implementation of the Civil Registration Act, in 1837, the only legal method of recording a birth was in a parish register, and an Anglican baptism certificate functioned very much as a birth certificate has done subsequently, conveying definitive information about a person's age, parentage and the place of their birth. Possession of a certificate was necessary for legal rather than religious reasons. This state of affairs constituted a major grievance for Baptists, Independents, Quakers and Presbyterians, who were set apart from the Church of England by custom and theology. In contrast, however, Methodists, and Wesleyans in particular, continued to look to the parish church as the place where baptism and other rites of passage should be observed, and to use it as a means of registering a continuing sense of loyalty. The exact relationship between Wesleyans and Anglicans varied according to local circumstances,[8] and it seems to be too simple to suggest, as Robert Currie has, that Methodism did best where the Church of England was weak.[9]

Local evidence seems to suggest that both groups were at their most open to mutual influence in the period up to 1870. The attitude of a Dissenter in East Dereham in Norfolk, the father of twins, who had had his children baptised at the parish font in 1862, seems to have been

[8]   See for example K. D. M. Snell, *Church and Chapel in the North Midlands: Religious Observance in the Nineteenth Century* (Leicester: Leicester University Press, 1991) for detailed discussions of the different relationships in Leicestershire, Lincolnshire, Nottinghamshire, Derbyshire and Rutland, and B. I. Coleman, 'Southern England in the Census of Religious Worship, 1851', *Southern History*, 5 (1983) for a discussion of the counties of Surrey, Kent, Sussex, Hampshire, Berkshire, Wiltshire, Dorset, Devon, Cornwall and Somerset.

[9]   Robert Currie, 'A micro-theory of Methodist growth', *Proceedings of the Wesley Historical Society*, 36 (October 1967) p. 68.

typical. 'Oh,' said the man, when questioned by the vicar, 'I ollus say *begin and end* with the Church whatever you do between-whiles.'[10] In many rural areas Anglican church and Methodist chapel existed almost in parallel, although the extent of their overlapping support is difficult to gauge. The vicar of Lockington, Leicestershire, said in 1872 that all were baptised, married and buried in the parish church, even though there was a Methodist chapel available.[11] In the Cornish mining town of St Agnes, a stronghold of Methodism, the first wedding to take place in a Wesleyan chapel was not until 1852, and throughout Cornwall, despite the superiority of Methodism in the county, Methodists expressed a preference for being married in the parish church, as they 'belonged to do'.[12] It remained usual for Cornish Methodists to be buried in Anglican churchyards.[13] On occasions when children had been baptised by Nonconformist ministers, it was not unknown for Anglican clergy to receive requests to re-baptise them, as happened to Hector Nelson in the parish of Pinchbeck, Lincolnshire, in 1850. 'I have been requested to Baptise children who have been "named" at meeting houses of dissenters. It is remarkable as being entirely a suggestion of the Parents' own mind – a disbelief in the validity of such Baptism'.[14] At Staithes in North Yorkshire Nonconformists seem to have preferred to have their children baptised in the parish church as late as the 1930s. David Clark remarks that although Anglicanism had always remained remote from village life in Staithes, the attitude seems to have been that rites of passage were more effectively validated by the Established Church.[15]

Methodist support for the Establishment was not restricted to baptism, marriage and burial. The large numbers being confirmed in the period up until 1860 make it probable that many who were not Anglicans in an exclusive sense were presenting themselves, although some Wesleyans claimed to disapprove of confirmation.[16] By the

---

[10] Herbert B. J. Armstrong, *Armstrong's Norfolk Diary: Further Passages from the Diary of The Reverend Benjamin John Armstrong Vicar of East Dereham 1850–88* (London: Hodder & Stoughton, 1963) p. 96.

[11] David M. Thompson, 'Baptism, Church and Society in Britain since 1800' (University of Cambridge Hulsean Lectures, 1983–4) p. 50.

[12] Thomas Shaw, *A History of Cornish Methodism* (Truro: Bradford Barton, 1967) p. 31.

[13] Ibid., p. 44.

[14] LAO CorB5/4/38/2 H. Nelson to John Kaye, 24 October 1850.

[15] David Clark, *Between Pulpit and Pew: Folk Religion in a North Yorkshire Fishing Village* (Cambridge: Cambridge University Press, 1982) p. 118.

[16] James Obelkevich, *Religion and Rural Society: South Lindsey 1825–1875* (Oxford: Clarendon Press, 1976) p. 134.

middle of the century the clergy were under increasing pressure to demonstrate their ministerial effectiveness by sending the largest possible number of youngsters to the confirmation, and some may have dispensed tickets to the candidates rather indiscriminately; alternatively, they may have seen it as perfectly reasonable for youngsters with fairly tenuous Anglican connections to wish to be confirmed. A confirmation ticket was withheld from one candidate because she would not promise never to attend a meeting house service. Two days before the confirmation the clergyman changed his mind and issued a ticket, though he was still uncertain whether he was right to do so.[17] In 1839 George Wilkins, the archdeacon of Nottingham, wrote to his bishop asking advice on what to do with candidates presenting themselves for confirmation who also attended Dissenting places of worship.[18] It seems unlikely that confirmation could be withheld from those who had been baptised as Anglicans, which at that date the majority would have been, if they could give an adequate rendition of the catechism, the creed, the Lord's prayer and the ten commandments. The Prayer Book stated explicitly that the baptised should be brought to the bishop for confirmation as soon as they had mastered these rudiments of religious knowledge, and the Prayer Book continued to be used by Wesleyans until 1883.[19]

Among Methodists, the feeling that Anglican rites of passage possessed a greater authenticity was accompanied by a continuing belief in the value of Anglican Sunday worship. The personal legacy of John Wesley was largely responsible. It is well known that he considered that he lived and died in the Church of England, and that he attended Anglican worship in whichever parish he happened to be, and expected his followers to do the same. There is plenty of evidence that in the early days of the movement Methodist attendance at church was a usual Sunday morning occurrence, and that this continued well into the nineteenth century. Care was taken to ensure that Methodist services did not coincide with Anglican ones, and Methodists were urged to think of themselves as also, though presumably not primarily, Anglicans, and to partake of the Anglican sacrament. On 5 February 1804 Richard Robarts, a Cornish local preacher, made a typical entry in his diary: 'Sunday. A good day in general: I found profit at Church

[17] Peter J. Jagger, *Clouded Witness: Initiation in the Church of England in the Mid-Victorian Period, 1850–1875* (Allison Park, Pennsylvania, 1982) p. 167, citing *The English Churchman* of 8 May 1851.
[18] LAO CorB5/8/22 G. Wilkins to John Kaye, 29 July 1839.
[19] James Munson, *The Nonconformists: In Search of a Lost Culture* (London: SPCK, 1991) pp. 4–5.

and Sacrament. In the evening, according to my plan, I preached for the first time at home, Trispian'.[20] William O'Bryan, the leader of the Bible Christians, the body which seceded from Wesleyanism in 1815, informed a Devonshire rector that he was a member of the Church of England, and that he wished his hearers to attend the parish churches.[21] From an early date, however, Methodists were aware of the tensions to which theological differences could give rise, if the Arminianism taught by Wesley came into conflict with the Calvinism espoused by some Anglicans. After attending Wesley's conference in Bristol in 1781, James Chubb, a Methodist from St Germans wrote: 'A question put wether the Methodists should hear a Clergiman speak which spoke against the pardoning love of God and knowing our sins forgiven. Mr Fletcher said he would stay in Church while the Prayers were Reading, and then take his hat and walk out of Church. All agreed . . .'[22]

The Religious Census of 1851 reveals that some Methodists were still continuing to worship in Anglican churches, and that some Anglicans were going to the chapels. The rector of Swaby, Lincolnshire, commented in his census return that

What is all but universal, in this part of Lincolnshire at least, [is] the attendance of members both at church and the (Wesleyan) chapels. In most churches, the practice has been to have the one service in the church alternately morning and afternoon and the service (or preaching as it is at the chapels) is regulated accordingly, so that but few attend the church or chapel exclusively. Therefore no accurate estimate can be made of the relative numbers of attendants at each.[23]

This tendency was confirmed by the vicar of Elsham, Lincolnshire: 'The congregations vary very much in this parish owing to there being many Dissenters, who at times come to church.'[24] It was corroborated also from the Wesleyan side; the chapel steward at Kelstern wrote: 'No service in church hours, the congregation attends the church also.'[25] The incumbent of St Mary Magdalene's in the city of Lincoln summed up the tendency when he answered the enquiry about average attendance by writing, 'Very uncertain. They go from church to

[20] Shaw, *Cornish Methodism* p. 32.
[21] Ibid., p. 33.
[22] Ibid.
[23] R. W. Ambler, *Lincolnshire Returns of the Census of Religious Worship 1851* (Lincoln: Lincolnshire Record Society, 72, 1979) p. 172.
[24] Ibid., p. 236.
[25] Ibid., p. 189.

church, from chapel to church, and from church to chapel.'[26] This would seem to indicate that even apparently committed Anglicans might lack a sense of belonging to the church of the parish in which they resided, and in a city like Lincoln, with fourteen Anglican places of worship in 1851, they had plenty of opportunity to move from church to church. In doing this they may have been satisfying a need for variety that might otherwise have been met by turning to Methodism.

In the neighbouring county of Nottinghamshire, the Anglican clergy at Treswell, Morton and Kirton noted in their census returns that on 30 March their congregations had been diminished because a proportion of their parishioners had gone instead to Wesleyan love feasts or other gatherings.[27] In this case, when faced with a choice between a love feast and Anglican evening prayer, people opted for the love feast. Furthermore, the clergy seem to have accepted this as inevitable. Nevertheless by 1851 this level of toleration on the part of the clergy may have been restricted to the more rural areas. There is no evidence of it in Nottingham itself, a city where Anglicans were outnumbered by Nonconformist worshippers, and as a result had adopted an embattled mentality, seeing themselves as a faithful remnant fighting against a tide of infidelity. Joshua Brooks, vicar of St Mary's, the principal Anglican church, was so distrustful of Dissenters that he insisted on forwarding his census returns direct to the registrar general, 'in order to prevent any improper use being made of them by the officers appointed to receive them, the majority of whom in Nottingham are Dissenters'.[28] In this urban area denominational boundaries had hardened, and people had ceased to flit between church and chapel.

This evidence may be considered in the light of Alan Gilbert's theory of urban religion – that a decision for church or chapel represented a choice between two very different social and religious belief systems. Gilbert's theory may well explain the workings of the religious culture of more highly politicised urban areas, where Nonconformity was more frequently harnessed to political radicalism, and where Baptists and Congregationalists might outnumber Methodists. It may also shed light on counties like Hampshire and Sussex, where in 1851 Independency was stronger than Wesleyan Methodism, and

---

[26] Ibid., p. 109.
[27] Michael Watts, (ed.), *Religion in Victorian Nottinghamshire: The Religious Census of 1851*, 2 vols. (Nottingham: University of Nottingham, 1988) pp. 36, 202, 221.
[28] Ibid., p. 183.

where the census returns make no reference to Anglicans and Non-conformists attending each other's services.[29] It does not, however, seem possible to transpose Gilbert's theory into those rural areas where Methodism was the chief rival to the Church of England – or where relations with an older body of Dissenters were good. In these parts of the countryside there existed the people described by David Hempton as a 'band of denominational gypsies of no fixed abode',[30] the group that moved freely between church and chapel. A glimpse may be caught of such a community at Stretham, in the example cited at the beginning of the chapter; the curate complained that in the parish and the whole neighbourhood there was 'a lamentable indifference as to what particular party in religion a man belong so that he profess Xtianity'.[31] Another such group existed at Melton Mowbray, Leicestershire, in 1839. The parishioners there were 'highly offended' when Mr La Trobe, the parish lecturer, was given notice to leave by the new vicar, on account of his supposedly Evangelical opinions. The anxious archdeacon reported: 'The Church-People talk of building a new Church, and the Dissenters, who went to hear him, are gone back to their Chapels: The Independent-Chapel, which was by no means full, has now only 2 pews unoccupied.'[32]

Henry Pelling has argued that the tendency of members of the working classes to attend both church and chapel, which he documents from visitation returns, was a sign of their lack of commitment and indifference in religious matters.[33] Yet widespread working class indifference hardly seems an adequate explanation for the extraordinary extent and variety of religious activity in nineteenth century Britain. Nonconformity, and Primitive Methodism in particular, gave a voice to the religious conscience of the manual worker, in a way that the more clerically-dominated Anglican and Roman Catholic Churches did not. Yet Roman Catholicism became a predominantly working class Church at this period, and the Anglicans too commanded the allegiance of a significant proportion of the poor. Where religious indifference existed, it was more likely to result in absence

[29] John A. Vickers (ed.), *The Religious Census of Sussex 1851* (Sussex Record Society, 75, Lewes, 1989); John A. Vickers (ed.), *The Religious Census of Hampshire 1851* (Hampshire Record Series, 12, Winchester, 1993).
[30] David Hempton, *Methodism and Politics in British Society 1750–1984* (London: Hutchinson, 1984) p. 12.
[31] CUL EDR C1/6, 1825.
[32] LAO CorB5/5/17/4 T. K. Bonney to J. Kaye, 25 November 1839.
[33] Henry Pelling, *Popular Politics and Society in Late Victorian Britain* (London: Macmillan, 1968) pp. 19–25.

from all forms of organised religious activity, rather than, as Pelling supposed, participation in the activities of more than one denomination.

The question arises of what, beyond loyalty to Wesley or the desire to escape from the familiarity of Anglicanism, led some people to maintain a double allegiance. There has been a tendency for historians to assume that people who attended chapel to any extent were Dissenters or 'church Methodists'. A significant proportion, however, may have regarded themselves primarily as Anglicans, and as only occasional 'hearers' at the chapel, and were perhaps perceived by the Methodists as among the uncommitted and unconverted. Double allegiance, rather than implying indifference, in fact seems to indicate an underlying seriousness about religious matters. 'What must I do to be saved?' was the question that was formulated and reformulated, and that echoed throughout the century. What was meant within Anglicanism by 'being saved' will be explored later; it is worth noting that it was the last time in British history that the search for salvation was a pressing concern for a large proportion of the population. When people went to both church and chapel, it was because both were available. In many places almost everybody now had an alternative to the established church within a convenient distance of their doorstep.[34] In the confusion of an increasingly plural religious culture it was not unnatural for those concerned about their souls to take advantage of the variety of religious opportunities available, particularly if the offered paths to salvation appeared intriguingly different. A cautionary note about the dangers of pew-hopping was sounded in a long poem printed on the bottom of the Grantham Wesleyan Methodist circuit plan for 1832, but it fell short of condemning the practice outright. It concluded:

> Art thou then curious, and fond of choice?
> Eager to hear some stranger's tuneful voice?
> And art thou led by novelty to roam
> To other meetings distant from thy home?
> But ask thy conscience, 'Is this conduct wise?'
> New things may feast thy fancy – please thy eyes,
> And tickle itching ears; – but truth's refulgent ray
> Beams without novelty, nor knows decay,

---

[34] But this was not universal. In Sussex in 1851, of the 267 smaller rural parishes (i.e. with a population below 2,000) 65 per cent still had no other place of worship beside the parish church, and in the west of the county this figure rose to 76 per cent of the rural parishes. In such places, to be a Christian meant to be an Anglican. Vickers, *Sussex* p. xvii.

> And truth should be the object of research,
> Where'er thou goest, to chapel or to church.[35]

It was not just Anglicans who were concerned about the effects of 'novelty' in religion.

Alan Gilbert concluded that Anglicanism became little more than a 'cultural expression of national identity ... an obvious if merely nominal concomitant of being English'.[36] Besides failing to acknowledge that it was in the process of being exported all over the world, this does not seem to do justice to the varied motives in lay religion. There remained something about the Church of England that the mushrooming meeting-houses could not rival. In the minds of Methodists, the Church was associated with citizenship and loyalty to the Crown and Englishness – and it gave a reassuring sense of being legal – 'by law established' – which lingered even after full civil rights had been granted to Dissenters. It had a clear appeal to the temperamentally conservative. The Newark father who as late as 1851 angrily demanded baptism as his child's legal right, and claimed that if the curate refused it, his child would be subject to 'certain civil disabilities' when mature, was clearly articulating this sense of the need for legal security.[37] Yet Anglican baptism also conveyed a spiritual meaning, as it did to the parents of infants in Whaplode, Lincolnshire, who protested that if they were forbidden to bring their children to be baptised at the vicarage three days after birth, and the children should die prematurely, they would be committed to the earth 'like dogs', without Christian burial.[38] These parents were displaying a concern for the eternal welfare of their offspring that was a predominant element in the lay religion of the period. The Church of England's links with the political and social order, strong though they remained, did not preclude it from also being capable of conveying religious meaning to a broad spectrum of society.

In the second half of the nineteenth century, the pattern of double allegiance to Methodism and Anglicanism began to come under new pressure, as the worlds of church and chapel became more sharply delineated. There were reasons for this development from both the

[35] Grantham Wesleyan Methodist Plan, November 1831– April 1832. Cited by Barry J. Biggs in 'Saints of the soil: early Methodism in agricultural areas', *Proceedings of the Wesley Historical Society*, 48:6 (October 1992) p. 190.

[36] A. D. Gilbert, *Religion and Society in Industrial England: Church, Chapel and Social Change 1740–1914* (London: Longman, 1976) p. 207.

[37] LAO CorB5/8/34 R. J. Hodgkinson to John Kaye, September 1851.

[38] LAO CorB5/4/54/1 T. Tunstall Smith to Kaye, 17 January 1845.

Methodist and the Anglican sides. Methodists increasingly found that the full range of their religious needs could be met within Methodism. In addition, it appears that members of most denominations were less inclined to spend as many hours at church as they had at the beginning of the century, and this led to their developing a loyalty to a single place of worship. The parish church at St Just in Cornwall had contained many Methodists in the 1860s, but a marginal note in the burial register in 1889 described Betsy Bottrall as the last one who regularly attended communion services there.[39] One apparent explanation for this Wesleyan departure is to interpret it as a sign that the pan-Protestant Evangelical consensus had run out of steam, and that after the rise of Ritualism it became harder to perceive the Church of England as a Protestant body.[40] But at ground level the reality may prove to have been more complex. Though Tractarian and Methodist leaders had been locked in mutual hostility for years, as evidenced by Pusey's pamphlet war with Thomas Jackson in 1841, little of this acrimony seems to have filtered through to the parishes. When Ritualism began to have an impact on Anglican parochial worship, Nonconformist hostility was not universal. For example, many Cornish Methodists supported the revival of the bishopric at Truro in the 1870s, despite the distinctively Anglo-Catholic tone of the venture.[41] For many Wesleyans, the Anglo-Catholic emphasis on sacramental worship was not in the least alien to their theological understanding.[42]

On the Anglican side, pressure to conform exclusively to the Establishment continued to come from landlords with strong Anglican principles, and from the clergy. The clergy spent a great deal of time agonising about how best to deal with their Methodist parishioners, particularly when they had received friendly overtures from them, and were thus unable to dismiss them as politically-motivated trouble-makers. A case in point was that involving the incumbent of Everton, Nottinghamshire, who in 1839 had received a request to preach and celebrate the sacraments for the centenary of the Wesleyans in his parish. The Methodist who approached him chose to appeal to their common Protestant heritage, suggesting that it was 'the desire of the

---

[39] Shaw, *Cornish Methodism* p. 122.

[40] Rupert E. Davies, *Methodism* (London: Epworth Press, 1963) pp. 125–6; David M. Thompson, *Nonconformity in the Nineteenth Century* (London: Routledge, 1972) pp. 8–9.

[41] Shaw, *Cornish Methodism* p. 125. See also P. S. Morrish, 'History, Celticism and propaganda in the formation of the diocese of Truro', *Southern History*, 5 (1983) pp. 238–66, especially pp. 257, 260.

[42] Trevor Dearing, *Wesleyan and Tractarian Worship* (London: Epworth/SPCK, 1966) pp. 7–15.

Methodist leaders to unite with the Church to make a stand against the threatened encroachments of Romanism'. When asked to give a ruling on the legitimacy of the request, the Bishop of Lincoln responded by suggesting that any service held to mark the occasion should be advertised without reference to the Methodists, or to their centenary; although it would be permissible to preach a sermon 'on Brotherly Love, or on the necessity of co-operation against the encroachments of Romanism'.[43] It was perhaps offhand treatment of this sort that caused Methodists to question the value of maintaining their links with the Church of England. It began to seem more appropriate to invite a Methodist preacher to celebrate a Methodist centenary, and not to allow a bishop to determine how the service should be conducted.

The increasing numbers of Anglican clergy who were residing in their parishes for the first time, often the result of being compelled to do so by the Pluralities Acts of 1838 and 1850,[44] were another factor that led to cross-denominational movement becoming markedly less common in the second half of the century. From the perspective of lay Anglicans, perhaps the most obvious sign that the Church was changing was the disappearance of the band of transitory, sometimes non-resident curates – which had been so familiar a part of the ecclesiastical landscape in the first half of the century – and the arrival of the permanent, resident incumbent. Although this was generally assumed to be a desirable development – both by church reformers at the time, and by church historians subsequently – the benefits for the laity were much dependent upon the character of the clergyman who arrived. Given an attentive clergyman, parishioners could expect a higher standard of pastoral care, and also the reassurance that the revenues which the incumbent derived from their parish would be used in their parish, whether as charitable donations, or in the form of support for local trade. Unfortunately, however, the state of pastoral relations after the arrival of the resident parson has been little documented from the perspective of lay Anglicans. What is clear, however, is that his arrival coincided with a hardening of denominational divisions. The newly resident incumbent set the tone of the worship and ethos of Anglicanism within his parish, where previously it had been less sharply defined. He was also able to provide more services, and could time them to coincide with chapel worship, thus

[43] LAO CorB5/8/28/13 R. Evans to John Kaye, 10 October 1839; Kaye to Evans, 12 October 1839.
[44] See chapter 4 for a full discussion of the impact of the Pluralities Acts.

forcing his religiously-inclined parishioners to make a choice. Faced with the need to carve out and defend his territory, and feeling under threat from the proliferation of Nonconformist chapels, he was likely to be less tolerant of Dissent than his non-resident predecessors, and to be perceived as hostile and undesirable by the Nonconformists themselves. Church identity and chapel identity were no longer easily compatible, and people began to choose one or the other, or neither. As co-operation gave way to hostility, religious life in the countryside began to fragment along denominational fault lines in the way that it had done a few decades earlier in the towns.

By the 1870s the clergy were beginning not merely to make a sharper distinction between Anglicans and Nonconformists, but also between those parishioners who had some sort of general affiliation to Anglicanism, perhaps extending no further than participation in Anglican rites of passage, those who were nominally communicants and those who attended the sacrament on a regular basis. Visitation articles began to make distinct enquiries about all three groups. The visitation returns for the archdeaconry of Bedford in 1873 reveal that out of an estimated population of 138,000 people, 46,447 were seen as being 'church people' rather than 'chapel people' or 'nowhere people', but only 7,235 were perceived as communicants, and only 3,878 were seen as regular communicants who could normally be expected to be present when the sacrament was celebrated.[45] As precise figures, these underestimate the actual situation, for not all incumbents provided the information requested on the visitation form. Nevertheless, a general trend of a very low level of participation in eucharistic worship seems incontrovertible. This is particularly interesting in view of the fact that Bedfordshire was not a notably irreligious county, registering the highest index of attendance of any county in the Census of 1851.[46] On the basis of the figures available it appears that a mere 3 per cent of the entire population of the county were regular communicants, 5 per cent were occasional communicants and 37 per cent were nominally Anglican. Of those who were perceived by the clergy as nominally Anglican, only 8 per cent were regular communicants. Obelkevich's examination of the visitation returns in South Lindsey in the same year reveals a similar picture. Of the entire population, 12 per cent were communicants in parishes of under 100 people, but only 2 per cent in

[45] CUL EDR C3/40 Archdeaconry of Bedford visitation returns, 1873.
[46] K. S. Inglis, 'Patterns of religious worship in 1851' *Journal of Ecclesiastical History* II (1960) pp. 74–86.

parishes with a population of more than 600. In parishes with a population of between 400 and 499, the figure was 3 per cent.[47] If statistics such as these had been available to contemporary clergymen, they might have paused to consider the wisdom of trying to transform their parishes into eucharistic communities, which, as will be shown, was becoming the predominant trend. By the 1870s participation in the Eucharist had become the clergy's index to measure the commitment of Anglicans; it was a definition that permitted none of the flexibility of the past. The majority who for whatever reason chose not to participate, were to some degree left unchurched.

THE CONSTRUCTION OF ANGLICAN PIETY: THE BIBLE AND THE PRAYER BOOK

In 1850 Edward Monro, a Tractarian clergyman, complained about the spiritual condition of the poor:

Ask nearly any poor man if he says his prayers daily, and he will probably answer that he does so in the evening after he is in bed; which amounts to this, that he never prays nor makes any recognition of God, His providence or His moral government by an act of worship in the morning, and only does so at night in a careless and irreverent manner after he has gone to rest: that he never kneels to perform this act of worship, or if he does it is in most cases an act performed once only in the day.

The forms used are equally deficient; with the exception of the Lord's Prayer, no other is generally in use but an address to the holy Evangelists to bless their rest, and this with the Creed said as, and mistaken for a prayer, sums up the usual amount of devotion of many a poor man among us ... If any other form is added to these it usually consists of some words remembered from childhood, and will be found with few exceptions to contain the mention of the names of persons long since past away from the Church militant. Consequently, half of the devotions of our English poor consist of prayers to the saints, or intercessions for the dead.[48]

What it was that continued to impel a cottager to say prayers on a regular basis, even if in bed rather than on his knees, remains beyond the reach of historical judgement. The private world of the individual believer is unfathomable by the historian, unless the believer leaves behind some form of written testimony. Yet the weight of the literary and documentary evidence suggests that private prayer in the home remained a commonplace in nineteenth-century Britain, even if it fell

[47] Obelkevich, *Religion and Rural Society* p. 139.
[48] Edward Monro, *Parochial Work* (Oxford and London, 1850) pp. 18–19.

short of the ideal espoused by the Tractarian clergy. There is a temptation to dub lay Anglicans as 'church-goers'; as if church-going were the only religious activity in which they engaged. Church-going was important, and will be examined in the next chapter. The less public aspects of religious life and thought will be considered here; in particular, the construction of Anglican piety and beliefs about salvation.

Much that could be defined as Anglican piety took place in the domestic setting, as had always been the case. In addition to the well-documented existence of private and family prayers, the vast circulation of tracts, sermons and devotional works points to a considerable amount of religious reading by the fireside. Even the poorest homes would normally possess a Bible, or at least a New Testament, and very often also a Book of Common Prayer. Bibles and Prayer Books were owned even by those who seldom made an appearance in the pew. In 1839 the perpetual curate of Christ Church, Newark, undertook a survey of the households in his district. A total population of 3,578 lived in 556 houses in six streets. He judged that only 385 adults attended Anglican worship at Christ Church or at St Mary's, the parish church, but he counted a total of 503 Books of Common Prayer in circulation, and 518 Bibles and fifteen New Testaments.[49] It seems implausible that all these prayer books had been dumped on unwilling householders by parish visitors. Rather, it suggests that some attempt at religious reading was being made even by the urban poor, and even if reading proved beyond them, the presence of the Bible and the Prayer Book in the home was seen as having a distinct value.

Biblical stories and pictures remained crucial as a way in which a first exploration of faith could be made. Anglican piety was communicated through visual media to a greater extent than has been realised. John Rashdall, an Evangelical curate in Exeter in the 1830s, recorded in his diary detailed accounts of his dealings with many parishioners, among them a woman who claimed that she had murdered the child which had been born to her after she had been seduced by her employer:

Going by a print-shop she saw a print of 'Nathan sent to David' – a print I also was led to stop and look at – she did not know the story – but as she

[49] LAO CorB5/8/22/32. The perpetual curate was Robert Simpson. His statistics reveal the cosmopolitan state of the religious life in this part of Newark. In addition to Anglicans, there were (in descending order) Methodists, Independents, Kilhamites, Baptists, 'Ranters', Roman Catholics and Stephensonians. Only six people claimed to be of no religion. There were nineteen beer shops in the six streets.

looked at ye *manner* of David as expressed in the picture & ye *reproving manner* of Nathan – she said to herself 'That man must have done some great sin': she saw beneath the reference to 2 Samuel – and she went home, & borrowed of a pious friend a Bible, she havg. only a Testament – and was agitated beyond expression when she read ye story. Then she felt she must confess her own dreadful sin to me – be the consequence what it might – when her agitation was observed – she could only say 'I have seen a picture – and I am reading about the story'.[50]

The practice of Bible reading in the home was regarded as an obligation on the Protestant Christian, and was not of course confined to Anglicans. Editions of the Bible intended for domestic use proliferated, and ranged from the plainest and simplest printed on the cheapest paper, or printed in parts at intervals,[51] to the heavily annotated and lavishly illustrated. Those in the last category contained far more than the bones of the text; Thomas Bankes, editor of *The Christian's New and Complete Family Bible*, which first appeared in 1790, claimed that the whole work – which included an index, 350 engravings, a concordance and notes 'historical, chronological, biographical, geographical, theological, moral, systematical, practical, admonitory, divine and explanatory' – offered the reader 'a complete body of Christian Divinity, explained and illustrated in such a manner as to guide the reader through the paths of happiness in this world, and lead him to the Mansions of eternal Bliss in that which is to come'. Even *The Cottage Bible*, which appeared between 1825 and 1827, edited by Thomas Williams and dedicated to Thomas Burgess, Bishop of Salisbury, ran to three large volumes, with the exposition longer than the text itself. Cheap, legible Bibles were made possible by advances in printing. The British and Foreign Bible Society, founded in 1804, used the new methods for the mass production of Bibles, and the Oxford press became the biggest producer in the world, rising from an average of about 127,000 Bibles and prayer books in 1780–90, to well over a million a year in 1860. As paper became still cheaper in the sixties, prices fell. The British and Foreign Bible Society was able to sell a Bible at sixpence in 1864, and a New Testament for a penny in 1884.[52] Daily reading in the family circle was an expectation and often also a reality among the middle classes. The Evangelical Edward Bickersteth

[50]   Bodl MS Eng. Misc. e. 352 9 June 1836.
[51]   William Alexander's *The Holy Bible . . . Principally Designed to Facilitate the Audible and Social Reading of the Sacred Scriptures*, 3 vols. (London, 1828) was printed in twenty parts at quarterly intervals in three different paper qualities, at four shillings, five shillings or six shillings for each part.
[52]   Chadwick, *The Victorian Church*, part II, p. 56.

prefaced his edition of 1861 by explaining that the New Testament had been set out so that the whole of it, with the commentary, could be read through in the course of a year in households where twenty or thirty minutes at most were assigned to daily family prayers.[53]

Even the most humble domestic Bibles tended to include a few illustrations. The use of pictures may have served to reinforce the sense of the literal historicity of the text, particularly if they were arranged four to a page to narrate the sequence of a single story, when they could produce the effect of a strip cartoon, as occurred in the Thomas Bankes' edition of 1790. The Books of Genesis and Exodus, and the Gospels, contained the favourite subjects for illustrators, and there was a tendency for them to dwell on violent as well as theologically significant themes: Cain and Abel, the Flood, Abraham and Isaac; the Massacre of the Innocents, the Woman taken in Adultery, the Crucifixion. Engravings of well-known art works were sometimes reproduced, as were small woodcuts illustrating Eastern customs – a headdress, a weapon, a coin. John Cassell's *Illustrated Family Bible* (1859), with more than a thousand illustrations, sold 300,000 copies a week at a penny a time.[54] The emphasis was on instructing and broadening the understanding of readers who were never likely to visit the Middle East. The provision of extensive footnotes and questions to be used at the end of family reading served the same purpose. 'How old was Noah when he entered the ark? How long was the rain upon the earth?' *Cobbin's Domestic Bible*, published in 1844, provided hundreds of similar questions on every portion of Scripture. Maps, and the dates and places of events were supplied. Difficult expressions were sometimes altered or 'improved'. A general air of optimism may be discerned in these editions; editors were aware of the considerable historical and cultural gulf that existed between their readers and the people and places in the Bible, but they believed that the Scriptures could be made fully comprehensible if sufficient footnotes were supplied. A phonetic edition was published in 1850, aimed at the barely literate; paragraph Bibles appeared at about the same time, as arrangement in paragraphs was seen as easier than verses: 'Much obscurity is removed from the sacred text, and the common and dangerous error of quoting isolated passages of scripture without regard to their context, a practice which the division into verses has had a tendency to

---

[53] R. Jamieson and E. H. Bickersteth (eds.), *The Holy Bible with Devotional and Practical Commentary*, 2 vols. (London, 1861).

[54] Chadwick, *The Victorian Church*, part II, p. 56.

foster, is rendered almost impossible' claimed Robert Blackader in the preface to his paragraph edition of 1868. It reflected the beginning of an awareness of the value of contextual interpretation.

It has already been suggested that merely possessing a Bible was a mark of respectability among the poor, and further evidence can be seen in the popular customs of not throwing away old Bibles, for fear of unleashing some form of misfortune or divine displeasure, and in the practice of using them to record family births, deaths and marriages. The impulse to maintain a family register inside a family Bible was perhaps more than just a wish to keep family records. It was also an attempt to knit together the realm of the eternal and transcendent with the concerns of the family, at a period when the importance of the family was being magnified as never before. Registers were usually bound into the front, or between the Old and New Testaments. They were often decorated with borders depicting the cycle of life from birth to death and sometimes going as far as bodily resurrection – the *Imperial Family Bible* (1840) portrayed husband and wife ascending simultaneously heavenward in their burial clothes; the implication was that the family unit would survive death and continue eternally in heaven. With what was perhaps an unconscious appropriation of the imagery of the Book of Revelation, the compiling of a family register ensured that the name of every member of the family was written in the Book of Life. Thus the Bible became an icon in the Victorian veneration of the family, despite the interesting predilection of biblical illustrators to depict scenes of crisis in family life. 'In Thee all the Families of the world shall be blest' declared a legend on the frontispiece of *Beeton's Illuminated Family Bible* of 1861. The 'nations of the world', the phrase used in the usual rendering of the quotation, had been overshadowed by the family.

Beyond the immediate family circle, cottage meetings extended the influence of Anglican piety in the domestic realm, although they were seldom exclusively a lay preserve. The clergy were aware of the need to provide something for their more devout parishioners which approximated to the informality and intimacy of the Methodist class meeting, but were determined that they, rather than lay people, should exercise control. In the week-night cottage meeting, or evening lecture, which typically consisted of Bible readings, a short address and extempore prayer, the rigid social hierarchy that prevailed when the community assembled in the parish church could (theoretically at least) be temporarily suspended, and worship need not be subject to the constraints of the Book of Common Prayer. It was also hoped to attract those who might feel ashamed to attend the parish church on Sunday because of the state of their clothes.[55] The use of cottages and other unlicensed premises, and the frequent absence of the Prayer Book, tended to provoke episcopal censure, and as a result cottage meetings were usually seen as a hallmark of Evangelicalism. The Evangelical baronet Sir Harry Verney, who was squire and patron at Steeple Claydon, Buckinghamshire, and also an active member of the Bible Society, the Church Missionary Society and (later) the Evangelical Alliance, described the cottage meetings that the curate held in his parish in 1832: 'I have attended [the curate's] lecture several times – it is conducted with simplicity and piety – his exposition is plain and practical and adapted to the capacity of his hearers who are almost all labourers and their families, and his prayer is short and has reference to the portion of Scripture which he has been reading.'[56] Though most cottage meetings and evening lectures were conducted by clergy with Evangelical leanings, there were sometimes exceptions. In another part of Buckinghamshire, Stoke Poges, there is evidence that an energetic High Church rector, Lord Sidney Godolphin Osborne, was willing to adopt the usages of Evangelicalism in an attempt to combat both Dissent and Evangelical Anglicanism. He explained his strategy to Bishop Kaye in 1836:

The Dissenters (Wesleyans) in my parish having almost given up their Chapel I was rather afraid that the zeal of some part of my Congregation would have led them into preaching themselves, not in opposition to but in connection with the Church: – as I am not fond of amateur preaching I thought it right to take the only steps I could in the matter – my Carpenter has done up some old cottages into a very real sort of chapel for me. I am to rent it, and I intend giving a weekly Service in it. The interior is a real cottage and I have avoided everything *conventiclish* in the fittings. It will hold from 40 to 50 – my neighbour at the hospital assists me in it, so that I hope to put a finishing blow to dissent and to do good in a part of my parish distant from the Church. I shall use *the Liturgy*. My object in writing to your Lordship is to ask whether I ought to licence it, and the method and expense of so doing. I shall be glad to do so, as it will secure me against the offers of lay aid. My intention is to dignify it with the name of 'Church Lecture Room' and to use it probably for a Sunday Schoolroom also.[57]

[55] The week night lecture was the earliest mission strategy adopted at Trinity church, Nottingham, which opened in 1841. LAO Cor B5/8A/16 T. Hart Davies to J. Kaye, 4 March 1842.

[56] LAO CorB5/3/26 H. Verney to J. Kaye, 16 July 1832.

[57] LAO CorB5/3/12/4 S. Godolphin Osborne to J. Kaye, 11 October 1836.

This was about as far as one could get from the spirit of a Methodist cottage meeting, of which Godolphin Osborne was anxious to appropriate the outward trappings.

Later on, a more usual High Church response to the need to provide a devotional focus for the pious was the founding of a communicants' guild, which stemmed naturally from the new definition of church members as communicants. The idea was promoted by E. H. Browne, bishop of Ely from 1864 to 1873, who made enquiries about the existence of communicants' guilds and communicants' classes in his visitation articles. In the parish of Knotting, Bedfordshire, a guild was established in 1872 that met quarterly and had twenty-four members. In response to the visitation articles of 1873, the incumbent of Knotting wrote: 'I am thankful to find an increasing number of communicants, especially among the rising generation. I attribute this partly to the establishment of a Parochial Guild for communicants or intending communicants, and of having celebrations mostly at an early hour.'[58] Communicants' guilds aimed to identify the Anglican spiritual elite in the parish, and to mould them into a self-conscious eucharistic community. The effect was to strengthen the allegiance of those who were already committed to Anglicanism, rather than to bring in those who were on the periphery. The guilds drew their inspiration more from Continental Roman Catholicism than from the Methodist class meeting. They were far removed from the informality of the cottage meeting of fifty years before, and were an institutional more than a domestic form of piety. Jeremy Morris has suggested that in Croydon, where communicants' guilds began to appear from the late 1870s, they became the precursor of the church councils that began to be formed in the 1900s.[59]

In the construction of Anglican piety, whether public or private, it was adherence to the Book of Common Prayer that set Anglicans apart from other Christians. When the Wesleyans used the Prayer Book as laid down, or Wesley's abbreviated version, they were demonstrating the value they attached to their Anglican roots, but they did not use it to provide the cornerstone of Wesleyan worship, which was dominated by the centrality of the Sunday preaching service.[60] Anglicanism was, more than any other denomination, a tradition of a book, a single

[58]   CUL EDR C3/25, 1873.
[59]   Jeremy Morris, *Religion and Urban Change: Croydon 1840–1914* (Woodbridge: Boydell Press, 1992) pp. 66–7.
[60]   Biggs, 'Saints of the soil' pp. 186, 189.

book, the Book of Common Prayer.[61] It provided a structured liturgical framework, and its melodic Cranmerian prose was seen as the natural medium of communication with God. Prolonged and repeated exposure to its language and imagery patterned religious experience and expression, so that even in their private devotions, Anglicans readily adopted its distinctive style.[62] Cranmer had intended his liturgy to be spoken aloud, even when used in private, and the regular cadences and parallelism were meant to work on the ear. Its inner rhythms played a major part in shaping four centuries of Anglican piety, as well as providing what was really the only tangible connecting thread between communities that by the end of the nineteenth century were spread all over the world.

The Prayer Book was the most accessible theological resource for Anglicans. Children were required to memorise the service, and many or all of the psalms and collects. Attendance at morning or evening service fixed certain concepts and metaphors in the imagination. Examples can be found in the general confession, used at both services: 'Almighty and most merciful Father, we have erred and strayed from thy ways like lost sheep ... We have left undone those things which we ought to have done; And we have done those things which we ought not to have done; And there is no health in us ... ' And in the terse narrative of the Apostles' creed:

I believe in God the Father Almighty, Maker of Heaven and earth: And in Jesus Christ his only Son our Lord; Who was conceived by the Holy Ghost, Born of the Virgin Mary, Suffered under Pontius Pilate, Was crucified, dead and buried: He descended into hell: The third day he rose again from the dead: He ascended into heaven, and sitteth on the right hand of God the Father Almighty; From thence he shall come to judge the quick and the dead ...

The imagery in the prayer of humble access in the communion service was equally arresting: 'We are not worthy so much as to gather up the crumbs under thy Table ...' The tone was penitential, but not exactly unworldly. God, the maker of every good thing, had promised that

---

[61] James F. White, *Protestant Worship: Traditions in Transition* (Louisville, Kentucky: Westminster/John Knox Press, 1989) p. 95.

[62] An example is seen in a handwritten prayer that is pasted into the front of an 1832 edition of the Prayer Book which belonged to Beatrix Wherry, now in the Cambridge University Library. 'Sanctify unto me, O Lord, I beseech Thee, the words which I have heard this day, that the truths of thy blessed Gospel may sink deep into my heart, that I may observe them through the whole course of my life, and receive the full comfort of them in my dying hour, through the merits and mediations of my Saviour and my God.' The emphasis on hearing the words is typically Cranmerian. See White, *Protestant Worship* p. 97.

when two or three were gathered together in his name he would grant their requests. The manner suggested intimacy without over-familiarity, and the tone was life-affirming; God desired not the death of a sinner, but that he may turn from his wickedness and live. The repeated use of the first person plural reinforced the sense of a community of believers, and to some extent mitigated against the stark individualism of the question, 'What must I do to be saved?' The Prayer Book helped to expand and consolidate knowledge of the Bible, and allowed the stories to remain familiar. Sunday morning matins with sermon followed by the litany and sometimes ante-communion as well, and afternoon evensong with either a sermon or public catechising, and often incorporating baptisms and churchings, provided a rich dose of Scripture: a chapter from both Testaments, an epistle and gospel lection plus psalmody and canticles.[63]

The liturgy had always been important as a means to generate uniformity and bind Anglicans together. This remained the case in the nineteenth century, despite renewed strain. Compulsory use of the Prayer Book provided a security against the excesses of the theologically illiterate, and could to some extent rein in those prone to Evangelical extemporaneity on the one hand or to Ritualism on the other, though it was not of course always successful. The desire to maintain a distinctive and uncontroversial Anglican identity was the reason for bishops trying to insist on the use of the Prayer Book at cottage meetings.[64] The Society for Promoting Christian Knowledge, the moderately High-Church publishing and missionary organisation, produced hundreds of tracts during the nineteenth century, which aimed to convert their readers explicitly to Anglicanism, and to steer them away from other forms of Christianity. When the SPCK tract writers tried to distil the essence of Anglicanism to make it simple and popular, they alighted upon the Book of Common Prayer as a cornerstone of their evangelistic strategy. One tract writer put these words into the mouth of a rector's wife, as she instructed two housebound women on the importance of using the Prayer Book at home:

[63] White, *Protestant Worship* p. 99.

[64] An example of Bishop Kaye trying to insist upon the use of the Prayer Book in these circumstances can be seen at Trinity church, Nottingham in 1842 (LAO CorB5/8A/16 J. Kaye to T. Hart Davies, 7 March 1842. In this case it appears that his strictures went unheeded, for nearly two years later the Archdeacon of Nottingham complained that Davies' curates had been holding services and lectures in rooms in the evenings, 'conducted after the manner of dissenters' worship ... Thus Mr Davis' [*sic*] curate has attracted a congregation of Calvinistic Methodists, who resort on Sundays to the Zion meeting house.' (LAO Cor B5/8A/16 G. Wilkins to J. Kaye, 5 December 1843.

'All over the land are churches – and, thank God! there are more and more every year – and in all there is this grand and beautiful form of prayer ... hands and hearts are lifted up; while, with one mind and one mouth we glorify God.'[65] By this date (about 1860) the liturgy had become a vehicle for bolstering a certainty and a uniformity that in reality were already passing away.

As the adoption of family prayers in the home became more popular, collections of material deemed suitable for family devotions were published. This raised a question for compilers who did not wish their collections to appear sectarian. The favoured solution continued to follow the eighteenth-century usage[66] of lifting prayers straight out of the Prayer Book, removing those (such as the prayer of absolution) that were reserved for priests and giving greater prominence to the collects to make shorter, more manageable offices. Sometimes other prayers were added, to be used in circumstances for which Cranmer had made no provision, such as before and after receiving communion, a further reflection of the changing priorities of the period.[67]

Although the impact of the Prayer Book was primarily aural, prayer books, like Bibles, developed an increasingly visual appeal during the first half of the nineteenth century.[68] Improvements in printing techniques and paper quality were partly responsible, but prayer books also succumbed to the changing religious and artistic conventions of the age, with the simple biblical woodcuts that adorned editions at the beginning of the century gradually replaced by more ornate illustrations, elaborate page borders, red ink and gothic typefaces. The fashion for highly decorated prayer books seems to have raged from the 1830s to the 1860s, and to have developed in two distinct directions. The first direction pointed to a celebration of the Englishness of the Church and its liturgy. A fine example of this genre was the pictorial edition produced by Henry Stebbing in 1838. Bound in heavy leather, it boasted over seven hundred woodcuts 'compiled from the vast storehouse of devout antiquity'. They included Lambeth Palace, the

[65] *How to Use the Prayer Book at Home* (SPCK tract no. 1741, n.d., but probably 1860s).
[66] John Walsh and Stephen Taylor, 'The Church and Anglicanism in the "long" eighteenth century' in Walsh, Haydon and Taylor, *The Church of England* p. 25.
[67] J. Wenham, *Private and Family Prayers* (London, 1855). See also W. E. Gladstone's *Manual of Prayers from the Liturgy Arranged for Family Use* (second edition, London, 1845) for another example of this genre.
[68] The observations in this section are based on an examination of the extensive collection of prayer books in the Cambridge University Library.

interiors and exteriors of most of the cathedrals and a number of romantic ruined abbeys. Hundreds of illuminated capital letters were decorated, predominantly with maidens, their long hair flowing and clothed in loose white shifts, bending in attitudes of prayer amid vine leaves, fern fronds and wisteria blossom. This was a prayer book that only the wealthy could aspire to own, more an object of art than an aid to devotion. It marked a high point in the English decorated prayer book style. The second phase was a rage for medievalism, an example of which can be seen in the Bickers and Bush edition of 1863, which adopted the long 's' throughout, incorporated biblical texts in Gothic script and bordered each page with medieval-style woodcuts. The pages containing the psalms were decorated with a *danse macabre*; a grinning, skeletal grim reaper carries off people from every walk of life. This was a clear example of the attempts of Anglo-Catholic Gothic revivalists to obscure the Protestant and Reformed elements within the English liturgy. Even inexpensive, mass-circulation prayer books were often illustrated – with biblical scenes at the beginning of the period, and with biblical scenes and borders towards the end. Depictions of baptism, matrimony and burial were also popular. In the 1860s, however, illustrations began to appear less often, and prayer books began to assume what was to become their twentieth-century uniform style, set in ruby type and more or less pocket-sized. Perhaps this too was a sign that even the physical appearance of the Prayer Book was being appropriated in the quest for Anglican uniformity.

THE ESSENCE OF ANGLICAN BELIEF: SALVATION AND THE LAST THINGS

The frontispiece of Thomas Bankes' *The Christian's New and Complete Family Bible* (1790) contained an illustration (reproduced as the frontispiece to this book) depicting what would later come to be known as salvation history. Some of the symbolism in the illustration was complicated, and a rubric was thought necessary to explain it to the viewer:

Religion [depicted as a female figure holding a large cross] attended by the twelve Apostles descending in a cloud with a glory to crown the Children of Adam [depicted as a representative cross-section of humanity]. Angels adoring the Supreme Being [depicted as shafts of light breaking through cloud]. Moses, attended by Aaron and the Patriarchs trampling on Idolatry [depicted as a dismembered torso]. St John pointing to the village of

Bethlehem and Mount Calvary, the first as the Place of our Saviour's Nativity and the last that of his Crucifixion. [The star and the stable were superimposed as adjacent to Calvary]. In the front, Cain turning his face from Religion and Death grasping our first Parents as a Punishment for the Transgressions.

This was a visual representation of the Christian story, which in 1790 was evidently considered sufficiently orthodox to merit reproduction at the front of a family Bible. The picture is intriguing, not least because it appears to offer salvation through a female agent, 'Religion', rather than through Jesus Christ. Indeed, what little New Testament imagery exists is obscured by the jostling of Old Testament figures with the children of Adam in the foreground. It is, of course, important to interpret a picture in the context in which it was created. At a period when classicism predominated, Christian symbolism was reworked in classical terms, just as it was later to be subject to the influences of the Gothic revival. By 1870 it would have been unthinkable for a devout Anglican to meditate upon 'Religion descending in a cloud'; the religious imagery of the later period derived from the Pre-Raphaelites and the Gothic revivalists. Holman Hunt's *Light of the World* (1853) was the icon of the period. The image of Christ knocking at the door of the human heart suggested a new closeness between Christ and the believer, and a readiness on the saviour's part to enter the human realm as a guest rather than as a judge. The picture touched something profound in the popular religious imagination, and it was copied and recopied until it hung in virtually every home in Britain.[69]

Christian iconography, like Christian theology, was in a state of transformation. The devotional literature aimed at the poor both reflected and helped to create the popular understanding of theology. Anxiety about salvation predominated; the question 'What must I do to be saved?' continued to haunt people. For most Christians, 'being saved' was a shorthand for 'being saved from hell and eternal damnation', understood in individual and literal terms. Thus the spirituality of this period was predominantly shaped by an emphasis upon the so-called four last things: death, judgement, heaven and hell. The understanding of both heaven and hell was in the process of a significant shift,[70] which made itself felt also at the level of popular devotional

---

[69] Jeremy Maas, *Holman Hunt and the Light of the World* (London and Berkeley: Scolar Press, 1984) p. 73.

[70] See Geoffrey Rowell, *Hell and the Victorians: A Study of the Nineteenth-century Theological Controversies Concerning Eternal Punishment and the Future Life* (Oxford: Clarendon Press, 1974); also Hugh McLeod, *Class and Religion in the Late Victorian City* (London: Croom Helm, 1974) pp. 223–31.

literature. Hell as a literal reality had a greater prominence in the
period roughly between 1800 and 1850 than it had earlier or later, and
a greater attention was given to heaven from the 1860s.

It was widely believed that at the moment of death the eternal
destiny of the individual soul was fixed forever, and the choice was
between heaven and hell. A Tractarian production of 1845 entitled *A
Week's Meditation on the Four Last Things*, stated the position clearly: 'If
when death comes you are in a state of grace, oh what joy, what
inconceivable happiness! henceforth you can never be lost. But if you
are out of God's favour, you can never be in God's favour again to all
eternity.'[71] In the cheap literature, the fate of the individual soul after
death was believed to depend on a person's deeds whilst on earth, and,
to a varying degree, on whether the person had accepted the atoning
sacrifice of Jesus Christ before or at the moment of death. This
amounted to a composite doctrine of salvation by works and salvation
by faith, and the relation between faith and works was often left
undefined. Evangelicals were likely to emphasise the absolute necessity
of faith in the atoning blood of Christ; the SPCK Tract Committee, on
the other hand, whilst continuing to give significance to the blood of
Christ, was willing to authorise a rather more this-worldly approach to
salvation, as illustrated in their tract entitled *Do you Want a Good Place? A
Question for Farm Servants with Hints for Enjoying a Holiday Week*, which
offers one of the simplest accounts of the doctrine of the work of Christ:

Nay, would you not shrink from letting even your fellow-creatures know how
much money goes in your holiday week? But remember, though you might
not like to keep account of it, God does. He has a book in which everything is
written, and which will be brought forth on the judgement day, when you will
be judged by what is written in it concerning you ... Whatever your sins may
have been, if you really repent of them, and wish to have them blotted out of
God's book, go and tell Jesus, and his blood will remove every trace of
them.[72]

The tract continued to fuse the doctrines of faith and works, making it
clear that the man who would be saved was the one who spent his
holiday week tidying up the garden, making the cottage more comfortable and buying his mother a new gown ('you can get a neat one for 3s
6d'). The author recommended that after charity donations, most of

---

[71] 'W. F. W', *Prayers for the Dead, for the Use of Members of the Church of England, and Meditations on the
Four Last Things* (London, 1845) p. 114.

[72] *Do you Want a Good Place? A Question for Farm Servants with Hints for Enjoying a Holiday Week* (SPCK
tract no. 1105, n.d.).

the year's wages should be laid aside in a savings bank against a rainy day. 'Your brothers and neighbours, seeing how happy and respectable you were, would be constrained to say, "We will go with you, for God is with you of a truth".' This was SPCK in its fulsome late nineteenth-century mood, appearing to advocate salvation as much through prudent budgeting as through the merits of Christ.

To understand popular Anglican attitudes to salvation in the earlier part of the period, it is perhaps necessary to look to the death-bed rather than the church. Death was inevitable, but its moment uncertain, and this stark reality was considered the natural starting point for faith. The author of *A Week's Meditations on the Four Last Things* dwelt in graphic detail on the stages of decomposition of a corpse:

At the moment of death ... still bathed in perspiration ... after a few days when an offensive smell begins ... in its grave it turns yellow, then black, then it is covered in white mould – a putrid liquid flows, from which crowds of worms are bred. The worms first devour the flesh, then one another. The skeleton becomes dust. Soon it will happen to you.[73]

There were parallels to this style of writing in late medieval England,[74] and the Christian tradition's continuing obsession with death marks a forceful continuity with the past. It began to lose its power only when advances in public health began to make the possibility of sudden death less likely. But the ritual surrounding the deathbed in Protestant Britain departed in significant respects from its medieval precursors. It was no longer 'a cult of the living in the service of the dead', in which vast amounts of human and material resources were put to work to intercede for the souls of the departed and ease their path through purgatory.[75] Rather, it had become a strictly individual affair; a personal trauma in which family and friends could offer only limited assistance. The compiler of *Prayers for the Dead, for the Use of Members of the Church of England* (1845) commended prayer for the departed as a primitive and pious practice, and prescribed prayers for use at the death-bed, but he stopped short of implying that it could alter the soul's post-mortem state.[76]

Religious literature abounded with death-bed scenes, as did much

---

[73] 'W. F. W.' *Meditations*, pp. 108–9.
[74] Duffy, *Stripping of the Altars* pp. 306–8.
[75] Ibid., pp. 301–2.
[76] 'W. F. W.' *Prayers for the Dead* p. v and *passim*. The question of prayers for the dead was a vexed one for the Tractarians. See Rowell, *Hell and the Victorians* pp. 99–108.

prose fiction, poetry and biography.[77] Papers such as *The Friendly Visitor*
and *The Soul's Welfare*, cheap and Evangelical, specialised in recounting
pious deaths, and warning against the dangers facing the unrepentant
if they were caught by death unawares. Some of the accounts were
intended as factual, others were clearly fictional. The tone was stark
and emotionally charged. The dying person's speech was recorded,
with few preliminaries or embellishments. These examples are representative of a genre, which was repeated time and time again:

After having been raised up in bed, [Mrs E.] said 'I shall soon be raised from
earth to heaven, to glory and immortality. I shall live in the presence of my
Saviour Jesus forever; forever, forever. I *know* I shall, for I have trusted in His
righteousness and depended alone on the merits of his blood, for the remission
of my sins and acceptance with God. Oh! take me, blessed Saviour, to live
with Thee: thou art my all in all! Thou art the lamb of God, the strength of
my life!'[78]

'I shall soon sleep in Jesus', said Mary, with a soundness of voice and a
calmness of manner which surprised the physician. 'Blessed by my Saviour, I
shall soon be permitted to see Him in his glory ... My friends tell me that I
may recover from this illness; but I desire, O Lord, to depart and to be with
thee; disappoint me not, thou portion of my soul.'[79]

A little boy, on his death-bed, was urging his father to repentance, and fearing
he had made no impression, said: 'Father, I am going to heaven; what shall I
tell Jesus is the reason why you won't love him?' The father burst into tears;
but before he could give the answer, his dear Sunday school boy had fallen
asleep in Jesus.[80]

A fever pitch of eschatological excitement was reached in the 1840s
and 1850s, and public demand for material of this sort, as well as the
more sophisticated versions offered by poets and novelists, appeared to
be insatiable. As well as making an appeal to morbid and mawkish
instincts, it seems that in promoting the cult of the death-bed the
devotional writers were also providing a form of words for the believer
to assimilate, even if unconsciously, to prepare him for the moment
when his own words would break down or appear inadequate. In the
crisis of death, Evangelical doctrines were pared down to the essentials:
an articulated belief in the saving merits of the blood of Christ, and a

---

[77] M. Wheeler, *Death and the Future Life in Victorian Literature and Theology* (Cambridge: Cambridge
University Press, 1990) p. 25.
[78] *The Friendly Visitor*, January 1847.
[79] *The Soul's Welfare* (1850), vol. I, p. 82.
[80] Ibid., p. 12.

certainty of salvation, leading to confidence in the prospect of eternal life. Protestants had only one chance to die well, and as their soul passed from one world to the next there was no sense of the support of the whole company of heaven, an idea forcefully conveyed in the Catholic Newman's *The Dream of Gerontius* (1865). The possibility of being too befuddled to remember what Christianity was about in the crucial final hours or moments made it all the more important for the appropriate responses to have been absorbed fully beforehand, and for pious relatives or clergy to be present to provide a prompt if necessary. However frail the dying person became, he or she would at least hope to be able to make a slight squeeze of the hand in response to the question, 'Do you accept Jesus Christ as your Lord and Saviour?' The death-bed literature was also a consolation to the bereaved, and helped them to cope with acute emotional distress. Their pain could be eased if they believed that death was not the end of life, but simply an antechamber to heaven; and that the beloved person now dying would soon be reunited with other relatives, and would continue family life in a perfected form.

It is intriguing to speculate about the extent to which the death-bed scenes so abundantly described in popular religious literature, approximated to the reality of death as experienced by ordinary people. John Rashdall, the Evangelical curate, recorded in his diary detailed accounts of the sick-beds at which he ministered. In the Autumn of 1835 he attended a young man with consumption in Dawlish, Devon:

26 October. Prayed and talked with him but he was too weak to bear catechising & his mother seemed to think it enough to assure me that he was an obedient son, & a strict churchman. This last they are very anxious to convince you of, thinking it will be in your eyes the greatest virtue. And I fear the clergy have given too much encouragement to the idea.

21 November. Visited my poor dying youth. His mother does everything she can to lead him into false security, & she seems utterly ignorant that my advice to him is quite difft. from hers – altho' she hears it all & seems very grateful ... he is much weaker than when I saw him a week previously. He told me that he could not feel his own utter sinfulness – & necessity of a Saviour – that he saw the necessity of knowing and feeling it, & wished that he could. I talked to him & explained how the fact of the Son of God being crucified for him both proved his own sinfulness & also the exceeding love of God to him. And he seemed to feel. I prayed with him and he groaned and sighed deeply, as if in mental conflict. Upon the whole I am led to hope much – if he be spared a short time ... O what a privilege to be the bearer of the glad tidings or the

means and the instrument used by God for the glorious work of saving souls –
O that this could be the *one sole object* of my life!

23 November. He was more able to talk, and I see that he has not yet been able
to apprehend his own sinfulness & need of a Saviour: tho' he acknowledges
the doctrine; & is evidently labouring under a desire to feel its practical
influence upon the soul. I kept him to the contemplation of a crucified
Saviour, as being the strongest proof of our utter depravity in the sight of
God; & of the exceeding love of God, who when we were yet sinners died for
us ... His mother's dark views must be doing him much harm ... What a
work it is to be engaged in; making inhabitants for heaven; & exalting the
glory of Christ.[81]

Rashdall left Dawlish on 30 November 1835 and returned to Exeter. A
few weeks later he was called to another death-bed:

25 December. Last night at 11 o'clock was sent for to a young man supposed to
be in the agonies of death. I found him in a dreadful state of agitation arising
from a sudden fear of approaching death.
'Speak to me (said he) say something to me. I am dying – O God – I am dying
– O God – O God –'
I spoke to him of Christ.
'No, no, I know nothing about him. I have never thought about him – I can't
look up to him – O no – I am dying – O God – O God –'
I prayed with him – he was thankful and wished to see me again. & so I left
him with no hope – but commended him to the prayers of his relations, &
promising him my own and the prayers of the congregation on the morrow.
I was not able to see him again till 8 on Sunday evening – he was much
weakened, but in no pain, tho' evidently fast approaching his end. I heard he
had been praying all night & to my astonishment I found him calm, & Having
a strong hope of mercy.
I asked him how he was. He said he had prayed – his hope was in Xt, [Christ]
the cross of Xt – the blood of Xt. He then seemed a little delirious – spoke of
light – & glory – & heaven – & Xt.
'I see them – I see them'
Then relapsed again – but in answer to my question – & by putting my ear
close to his mouth I heard him say –
'My pardon, I've got my pardon.'
I prayed with him – he afterwards said 'talk to me – talk to me! I hope I shall
be better tomorrow. Come & see me again – he grasped my hand and held it
for some time in his own clammy grasp.
I then left him and called on him on Monday 28 Dec. & he had been in a high
delirium all the night – at first in much prayer – then carried into all kinds of
extravagances & since has remained in the same state.
His is indeed a case for hope – but hope with much trembling – who shall

---

[81] Bodl Eng. Misc. e. 352, entries for the dates stated.

limit the grace of God? but we must take care not to buoy up the living with false hopes of the efficacy of a death bed repentance.[82]

Discourse at the death-bed could obviously be more complicated than the one-dimensional accounts provided for the edification of the pious would suggest. People who had not been noted for particularly pious lives could be moved to a death-bed repentance, and, as in the case of the second example cited above, have a sufficient grasp of the Christian vocabulary to make it seem plausible. Rashdall's accounts of his visits to ailing females approximate more closely to the models provided in the cheap tracts. The women are portrayed as showing greater resignation and placidity. Catherine, a consumptive maidservant in Cheltenham in 1836, could almost have modelled herself on the fictional Mary, cited above.

She is exhibiting a lovely instance of the power of divine grace on an untutored mind. In her own simple language expressing the experience of one deep in the faith. I hardly know how to wish her to live – her wish being to die: and the prospect of life being rather gloomy ... [but] it is delightful to feel that a saint of God is yet to be amongst us.[83]

Concerning a Miss Luke, also consumptive, Rashdall wrote:

The greater her sufferings, the greater she finds her spiritual consolations. The prayers of ministers by her bed-side leave her in a state of peace – which is rapture ... I do not omit visiting her once each day – I comfort her – and she feeds my soul. She said that long before her illness it was her desire, if she could be of any spiritual use to her family – *to be their sacrifice*. Her desire has been given to her.[84]

The Eucharist was seen as a rite for the dying rather than for the living, which was a further example of the importance attributed to Christian dying above Christian living. The clergy were always swift to complain that their church-going parishioners would not come to the Eucharist. The reason for their absence was not, on the whole, indifference to the sacrament, but a fear of its power, and more particularly a fear of incurring eternal damnation through unworthy reception. This was the legacy of Paul's injunction in I Corinthians 11.29: 'For he that eateth and drinketh unworthily, eateth and drinketh damnation to himself, not discerning the Lord's body.' Just as some of the early Christians postponed baptism until they were on the point of death for fear of

82 Ibid., 25 Dec 1835.
83 Ibid., 11 Feb 1836.
84 Ibid., 24 Oct 1836.

being stained by post-baptismal sin, so a large proportion of nineteenth-century Anglicans postponed receiving the Eucharist, either
until they were close to death, or indefinitely. The Tractarian Edward
Monro had this to say about the custom:

It will be found in nearly every part of England, that the prevailing impression
is, that there is no necessity laid on them to receive communion, that it is a
duty which may be dispensed with safely till death; that it is rather an act
intended for the saintly character, than the means necessary for forming it;
that the possibility for sinning after communicating is sufficient reason for
abstaining, and that the existence of any daily temptation, such as the
blasphemous conversation of fellow workmen, or the cares of a surrounding
family, are direct hindrances to reception.[85]

The deep-rooted nature of fears about the Eucharist go a long way
to explaining why it was that the re-modelling of the parish as a
eucharistic community would have the effect of discouraging church
membership amongst those on the fringe of participation. Like the cult
of the death-bed, anxieties concerning the Eucharist point to the
continuing strength of the fear of hell, a fear that seems to have
become particularly acute under Evangelical influence in the period
between 1800 and 1840. Some of this anxiety was planted in people's
minds by the clergy, and cannot therefore be dismissed as a product of
the popular imagination. The author of *The Clergyman's Assistant in the
Discharge of Parochial Duties Especially those of a Private Nature* (1805)
provided an outline homily which he proposed that clergy use to
instruct the newly confirmed about the Lord's supper. In it he warned
that God would regard the service of the unworthy as an abomination,
and that the Christian should not presume on God's mercy, or expect
the assistance of his grace, whilst continuing to lead a sinful life.[86]
Further evidence can be seen in the revisions made to William Vickers'
mass-circulation tract *The Companion to the Altar*, which was widely
available between about 1730 and about 1830. This tract, about
twenty-two pages in length, is of particular significance because it was
very often bound into the Prayer Book, which had the effect of giving it
a quasi-official status. Indeed, many readers may have assumed that it
was as much a part of the officially sanctioned Prayer Book as the
catechism and the Thirty-nine Articles. The purpose of the tract was to
encourage ordinary people to attend Holy Communion as frequently

[85] Monro, *Parochial Work* p. 20.
[86] J. Robinson, *The Clergyman's Assistant in the Discharge of Parochial Duties Especially those of a Private
Nature* (London, 1805) pp. 31–40.

as possible, and to allay their fears about unworthy reception, which were seen as the inevitable consequence of Paul's remarks in I Corinthians II. The first, non-Evangelical, version of *The Companion*, which was bound into prayer books until the 1790s, adopted a comparatively liberal and reassuring tone about participation in the Eucharist. The offending piece of Pauline theology was dealt with by asserting that no English community could be as wicked or disorderly as the Corinthians, and therefore Paul's words could not literally apply. Even the fate of the unruly Corinthians was softened:

This word *damnation* does not signify *eternal condemnation*, but on the contrary some temporal punishment or judgment (as you have it in the margin of your Bible) such as sickness or death, with which the city of Corinth was afflicted for their great abuse and profanation of this solemn institution ... the damnation here threatened, hath no relation to us, unless it could be proved, that any of us were ever guilty of the same wickedness as these Corinthians; which I believe no man ever was.[87]

The author continued to develop the thought a few pages later: 'God will never cast any man into eternal flames for striving to do his duty as well as he can ... If we were not sinners we would have no need of the sacrament ... they that are whole have no need of a physician, only those that are sick.'[88] The importance of some preparation before receiving the sacrament was emphasised, and suggestions were made, but it was stressed that the preparation should not be so onerous as to deter anyone from participation.

Any person may come (if it should be required) at an hour's warning, as safely as he may come to church and say his prayers, or hear a sermon. The dueness of preparation doth not so much depend upon our setting aside so many extraordinary days for the forcing ourselves into a religious posture of mind, as upon the plain natural frame and disposition of our souls, as they constantly stand inclined to virtue and goodness through the general course of our lives.[89]

Sometime between 1800 and 1820 the *Companion to the Altar* underwent an Evangelical revision that resulted in a significant shift in its theology, and which reflected increasing levels of anxiety about the dangers of post-communion sin. The later version, though still encouraging regular lay participation in and preparation for the Eu-

[87] William Vickers, *Companion to the Altar* (first version, London: continuously reissued during the eighteenth century).

[88] Ibid.

[89] Ibid.

charist, made it clear that the sacrament was not appointed for the remission of past sins, and was

only a commemoration of that all sufficient sacrifice which was once offered for an eternal expiation ... Pardon is the purchase of the blood of Christ; and is granted unto men by the mercy of God, not as a consequence of our eating and drinking the sacrament, but upon the condition of a true and unfeigned repentance, which only can prepare those who have sinned for a safe and worthy receiving of it.[90]

The author issued strong and repeated warnings against unworthy reception:

It is not safe, yea it is dangerous for such to approach as are yet in their sins ... the cup will be a cup of trembling; and the consequences of eating, sickness, and death to such ... The only true penitent that is worthy and welcome to communicate, is he that hath ceased from sin, that he should no longer live the rest of his time in the flesh, to the lust of men; or it is he that is now firmly resolved upon an eternal adieu to all sin, and hath effectually left it. He that continues under the power of evil habits, that still delights in former excesses, and has not as yet either left or determined to leave his sins, is a wicked and unprepared man. He is not only unfit for the Lord's Supper, but also for all religious worship: he is unfit for the religious assembly of saints, who meet for the worship of a God, who is of purer eyes than to behold evil, and cannot look on iniquity. And he is to be excluded from their company and friendship.[91]

Despite their divergent theological understandings of the sacrament, an interesting social parallel may be discerned between early nineteenth century Evangelical and later Tractarian views of the Eucharist. Both parties wanted to appropriate it as the badge of their own people, and to raise the stakes by making participation into the test of doctrinal orthodoxy. For the Evangelical, 'the sacrament is to separate the sinner and the saint, the impenitent and the pious'.[92] For the Tractarian, it became the reward of the most devout and the fully instructed. In March 1851, for example, 158 parishioners were confirmed in the Tractarian parish of Wantage, but the vicar, W. J. Butler, permitted only between forty and fifty to become communicants. The non-communicants were selected for a further course of instruction, and were only finally permitted to receive communion if Butler could discern evidence of a suitable disposition, an interest in religion and

---

[90] William Vickers (attrib.), *Companion to the Altar* (second version, London: regularly reissued between *c.*1820–*c.*1830).
[91] Ibid.
[92] Ibid.

regular church attendance.[93] Both Evangelical and Tractarian views were a notable departure from eighteenth- and twentieth-century understandings of the sacrament as a means of grace available to members of the Church, and as a ratification of the baptismal covenant.

Many early nineteenth-century Anglicans surely escaped into Wesleyan Methodism, with its explicitly Arminian theology and doctrine of sanctification, in order to avoid the ordeal of either making an adequate preparation for the quarterly communion service or absenting themselves from it altogether. A further cause of their departure was the terrifying Athanasian creed, which was directed to be said on feast days in place of the Apostles' creed. 'Whosoever will be saved: before all things it is necessary that he hold the Catholic Faith / Which Faith except everyone do keep whole and undefiled: without doubt he shall perish everlastingly ... And they that have done evil into everlasting fire.' By the end of the period unease about the Athanasian creed had become sufficiently widespread for inquiries to be made about it by anxious bishops in visitation articles. The fact that the Athanasian creed was being perceived by bishops as a 'problem' for the laity points to an underlying shift in Anglican attitudes. Belief in the medieval imagery of hell, with its fire and torture and burning, was finally on the wane, but the doctrine itself had not disappeared; instead it was being re-mythologised as eternal separation from God and from loved ones, drawing on the language of loss and regret. The shift was popularised explicitly by the American evangelists Dwight L. Moody and Ira D. Sankey, who carried out highly successful missionary tours in Britain in the 1860s and seventies.[94]

As the hell-fire waned, a more optimistic strand within the religious consciousness began to assert itself. Its roots can be traced to the 1830s, but it did not become sufficiently prominent to be seen as a general shift in thought until the 1860s. This strand emphasised heaven as the eternal home of Christians, and was largely silent about the difficult

---

[93] G. W. Herring, 'Tractarianism to Ritualism: a study of some aspects of Tractarianism outside Oxford, from the time of Newman's conversion in 1845 until the first ritual commission in 1867' (unpublished D.Phil thesis, University of Oxford, 1984) p. 131.

[94] Gerald Parsons, 'Emotion and piety: Revivalism and Ritualism in Victorian Christianity' in G. Parsons (ed.), *Religion in Victorian Britain: Traditions*, vol. 1 pp. 219–23. See also James R. Moore (ed.), *Religion in Victorian Britain* (Manchester: Manchester University Press, 1988), vol. III, *Sources*, pp. 274–80, for a contemporary, eye-witness account of a Moody and Sankey mission in London.

questions concerning judgement and hell. Much of it was assimilated into Anglican circles from Protestant sources. The body of literature it produced aimed to describe the joys in store, and to arouse the interest of Christians in their eternal destiny. A favoured image was that of the person who was about to depart for life in a foreign land; such a person would surely wish to know about the new country and its customs. In the same way, a Christian should wish to know as much as possible about heaven, to which he would soon depart. An early example of the genre was Robert Weaver's *Heaven: A Manual for the Heirs of Heaven; Designed for the Satisfaction of the Inquisitive, as well as for Assistance to the Devout. Also, on Angels and their Ministry* (1837). Weaver was a Congregational minister, but the work was explicitly non-sectarian. Many of Weaver's central ideas, for example that heaven was the Christian's home, and that in it the Christian would dwell in one large family, alongside members of his earthly family, with God as his father and Jesus as his elder brother, were taken up by Thomas Branks, a Scottish Presbyterian minister, who published *Heaven our Home* in 1861, a book said to have been read by Queen Victoria and Prince Albert in the last six months of Albert's life.[95] Branks' heaven was highly imaginative and not even biblical in its imagery. Rather, it marked the virtual divinisation of the Victorian family as the most perfect of all human institutions. The significance of this idea is illustrated by Walter E. Houghton, who argues that the Victorians increasingly saw family and home as the source of virtues and emotions that could not be found elsewhere, least of all in business and society, and that as institutional religion waned, the living church more and more became the 'temple of the hearth'.[96] Branks stated his understanding in the preface to *Heaven our Home*:

The mechanism of our moral nature – God's own workmanship – fits us for a *social heaven*. We are *social beings*. A heaven from which *saint-friendship*, and *social intercourse* among those who are in glory, are excluded, *is* not and *cannot* be a suitable abode for us, who have received from God's own plastic hand those *social affections* which we are to possess forever. A *social heaven* is accordingly the leading idea which I have endeavoured to embody and illustrate in the following treatise . . .[97]

Although initially it was highly popular, Branks' approach became self-parodying. Michael Wheeler has commented that the heavens created

95 Wheeler, *Death and the Future Life* p. 128.
96 Walter E. Houghton, *The Victorian Frame of Mind 1830–1870* (New Haven and London: Yale University Press, 1957) pp. 341–8.
97 Anon. [Thomas Branks], *Heaven our Home* (Edinburgh, 1861).

by the authors in this genre were more like a middle-class suburb in the sky than the City of God.[98] Popular attempts to describe heaven literally were doomed from the outset. If the author dwelt on the pleasures in store, the impression was bacchanalian; if he dwelt on perfected beauty and eternal worship, the impression was monotonous. Nor were the attempts to cast the Victorian family into eternity unproblematic, despite the appeal of this approach. Branks was obliged to devote paragraphs to soothing the anxieties of remarried husbands about possibly cool heavenly meetings between their former wives.[99] Jesus' instruction that there is no marriage in heaven (Luke 20.35), though sometimes cited, was infrequently taken to heart. The comic ludicrousness into which much of the heaven literature swiftly degenerated left Christian eschatology as a whole vulnerable to secularist attack. George Austin Holyoake's pamphlet, *Heaven and Hell: Where Situated?* appeared in 1873, at the end of the last major revival of popular interest in the subject, and took aim at a number of sitting ducks.[100]

Towards the end of the period the all-pervasive emphasis on the four last things began to show signs of breaking down. For the first time greater attention was given to Christian living than to Christian dying. A more optimistic tone crept into the SPCK tracts. The tracts, which took the form of simple stories concerning ordinary people with a firmly-pointed moral message, developed a greater this-worldliness. Children who fell ill recovered, couples who fell out were reconciled, people who had thought life to be hopeless suddenly found meaning, sceptics became persuaded of the truth by their Anglican friends. In fact, in a random sample of tracts in circulation in the last thirty years of the nineteenth century, nobody died at all. The new emphasis – implicit if not explicit – on leading a good life caused SPCK to begin to propagate Christian virtues, such as not losing one's temper and not wasting time, rather than Christian doctrines. The author of *Diamond Minutes,* a tract about a poor woman who could not manage both her family and her farm, declared that every golden hour was set with sixty diamond minutes. 'It's a kind of dishonesty to waste our time, just as it would be to waste money. And, as everything gets so sadly wrong if people are behind with money payments, so it must be with our time ...'[101] From the Evangelical side, the *Friendly Visitor* began in the 1860s to move away

[98] Wheeler, *Death and the Future Life* p. 121.
[99] Branks, *Heaven our Home* p. 127.
[100] Wheeler, *Death and the Future Life* p. 129.
[101] *Diamond Minutes* (SPCK tract no. 1950).

from the death-bed scenes which had previously been its great staple, in order to concentrate upon morally-improving stories concerning Christians whose virtues brought them happiness in their earthly lives. Anglicanism began to be portrayed as a means to living well. A favourite theme was the value of church-going, and the importance of maintaining the practice when moving from the country to the town. But a spirituality based on Sunday attendance and saving money would have been rather impoverished. Though the fires of hell were at last being brought under control, it would be misleading to conclude that Anglicans ceased to have any interest in heaven or hell. Heaven was being transformed into the almost universal destination, and certainly the destination of all who 'believed in Jesus'. 'Believing in Jesus' was itself becoming a more attractive proposition, as Jesus underwent a metamorphosis from being simultaneously the stern judge of humanity and the victim in the transaction of substitutionary atonement, to a friendly big brother, waiting to welcome the faithful to his family in heaven. In the back of a prayer book that belonged to Beatrix Wherry is a pencil sketch of the back of a man's head (was he the occupant of the pew in front of hers?) and two handwritten prayers, which both dwell on the familiar heavenly themes. The second one reads:

> Near is our dying bed
> and near Eternity
> Lord, when we wake as from the dead
> Take us to dwell with Thee.
> Southport, 9.8.1874.[102]

It was confirmation of the centrality of eschatological concerns, and it conveyed a sense of certainty about a future life.

---

[102] This prayer book, originally published in 1832 with annotations by Elizabeth Cust, is now in the Cambridge University Library.

CHAPTER 3

Church and community

PROVIDING CHURCHES

Is this a time to plant and build,
Add house to house, and field to field,
When round our walls the battle lowers,
When mines are sprung beneath our towers,
And watchful foes are stealing round
To search and spoil the holy ground?[1]

Keble's verses from *The Christian Year,* the book that became the period's most popular work of Anglican poetry, express a sense of anxiety about the displacement of the Church from its central role, and its vulnerability in a new and hostile environment. In the face of this anxiety, the Anglican response fused elements of yearning for the past with an appreciation of the need to be practical. The apparently tranquil English village, with its ancient church built in a local style, became invested with a new, somewhat nostalgic, significance. It was hardly surprising that Victorian Anglicans should have alighted upon the medieval parish church, and the orderly, God-fearing society with which they associated it, as a most potent emblem of the world they were losing. The high evaluation of all things medieval – a feature of the Gothic revival – was partly responsible. The ancient building was, furthermore, a powerful monument to the pre-industrial age, seemingly at one with the natural landscape, and pointing also to the integrity of local building styles and materials. In Cornwall the churches were built from tough, weather-resistant granite; in Cheshire they might be timber-framed; in Norfolk and Suffolk they were flinty, thatched buildings or elegant 'wool' churches; in the Cotswolds, parts of Lincolnshire, Leicestershire and the West Country, they were con-

---

[1] John Keble, *The Christian Year* (1828) – a stanza from his verses for the Eleventh Sunday after Trinity.

structed in delicately-carved oolitic limestone.[2] Ancient churches stood for regional variety and against bland architectural conformity, which was a by-product of the mass-building of an industrialising nation. They made an emphatic statement about the integrity of the past in a landscape at risk from being scarred by industrial debris.

The significance of the ancient parish churches went deeper still. From their towers and spires, the surrounding inhabitants could pick up a variety of subtle messages. One was stability in a changing world; indeed the very principle of pew allocation implied order and hierarchy. Another was to remind a community of its history; of the values, craftsmanship and generosity of the parish's forebears, of an age when there were no Dissenters, and when everybody seemed to agree about religion. If it was a little far-fetched to suppose that the remains of the medieval craftsmen who had constructed the building were preserved in the graveyard, there was no doubt that it was the resting place for the community's more recent ancestors. Eventual burial alongside family and neighbours was regarded as a normal and natural expectation. Unlike the Nonconformist chapel, the parish church belonged to the whole of the community. Theoretically at least, all could call upon the ministrations of the parson, a consideration that impinged upon Methodists in their decision to mark the important events of their lives in the church rather than the chapel, and which in previous generations had impinged also upon Baptists, Congregationalists and Presbyterians.[3] As it was invariably the oldest building in the parish, the church witnessed to the continuity of the invocation of God, as well as to the piety of previous generations.

Anglican literature of all sorts abounded with engravings of stylised ancient parish churches. The Church Pastoral Aid Society, an Evangelical body set up for 'the maintenance of Curates and Lay-agents in populous districts', and which did most of its work in cities and large towns, had on the front page of its monthly journal *Church and People* a sketch of a medieval church in a tiny village. As K. S. Inglis has pointed out, the unspoken aim was to reproduce in an urban environment the relationship between church and society that was thought to have existed in an earlier and happier England.[4] The rage for Gothic revival

---

[2] Derry Brabbs, *English Country Churches* (London: Weidenfeld & Nicolson, 1985) pp. 41–67.

[3] Jonathan Barry, 'The parish in civic life: Bristol and its churches 1640–1750' in S. J. Wright (ed.), *Parish, Church and People: Local Studies in Lay Religion 1350–1750* (London: Hutchinson, 1988) p. 158.

[4] K. S. Inglis, *Churches and the Working Classes in Victorian England* (London: Routledge & Kegan Paul, 1963) p. 24.

architecture in towns and cities, with its attempt to give a medieval appearance not merely to churches, but to the symbols of a modern economy such as banks, hotels and railway stations, pointed in a similar direction.

The Anglican middle classes observed the expansion of population and responded by building and enlarging churches. This was the practical aspect of their response. Between 1831 and 1851 2,029 churches were opened, of which 849 were in the new centres of population, Cheshire, Lancashire, Middlesex, Surrey and the West Riding of Yorkshire.[5] Many thousands more were enlarged or re-pewed. It was an extraordinary example of middle class philanthropy. If they were nostalgic for the medieval village church, the middle classes were utilitarian about the function of the church in the industrial town. The motives of early-Victorian Anglicans in this respect were not narrowly religious. They made an explicit link between church-going and the disciplined behaviour that they wished to instil in the lower orders. If there were more churches with free seats, they reasoned, working people would fill them and learn to be moral. Amongst the many benefits this would bring, would be (to take one example) fewer illegitimate births. If there were fewer illegitimate births, there would be less poverty and misery, and illegitimacy itself would have a greater stigma attached to it, resulting in less fornication. This logic persisted into the 1870s, as illustrated by the incumbent of St Mary's, Bedford, who commented on the satisfactory state of his parish and noted that 'the birth of an illegitimate child in the parish is an event of rare occurrence'.[6]

The middle classes observed that in many towns the Anglican churches were full, or that there were insufficient free seats for all who wished to attend. Not unnaturally, perhaps, they were inclined to attribute the rapid expansion of Nonconformist chapels to the lack of space in Anglican churches, rather than to any intrinsic merits in Nonconformity. William Fry, the curate of Markfield in Leicestershire, reflected this view in 1825:

Markfield is almost proverbial for dissent and is a kind of nursery for the supplying of the adjacent Hamlets with preachers. There are two dissenting Meetings in it one is called *the Methodist* and the other *the Primitive* (alias

[5] John Kent, 'Feelings and festivals: an interpretation of some working-class religious attitudes' in H. J. Dyos and Michael Wolff (eds.), *The Victorian City: Images and Realities*, 2 vols. (London and Boston: Routledge & Kegan Paul, 1973) p. 856.

[6] CUL EDR C3/25, 1873.

Ranting) Methodist meeting ... the parish church will scarcely seat 1/5 of the population of 950. Those who cannot get sitting or standing room in the church stand in the church porch.[7]

The incumbent of Ruddington in Nottinghamshire had made a similar observation in 1819:

There is a disposition in the parishioners to go to church. It has been uniformly manifested during the 17 years that I have had the living, and I found a large congregation when I first came. The Methodists have a meeting house in the village, and many have been induced to go to it only because there was no room for them in the church.[8]

In the early decades of the nineteenth century the demand for new or enlarged churches was not the result of the neglect of church buildings by earlier generations, nor did it stem from the desire to attract the unchurched. Rather, it was due to the lack of space for existing worshippers. In the archdeaconry of Derby in the mid-1820s, only between 14 and 15 per cent of the seats were available to the poor.[9]

Until the end of the first quarter of the century, the provision of churches was regarded as not simply the duty of the philanthropic middle classes; it was also a government responsibility. The Chancellor of the Exchequer allocated funds and entered into discussions with churchmen and politicians about how the money should be spent. The Church Building Act of 1818 set aside one million pounds to build churches in new centres of population, and set up the Church Building Commission to administer what was a huge sum of money. A further half a million pounds was allocated by the government in 1824, the last occasion on which such a grant was made. The Society for Promoting the Building and Enlargement of Churches and Chapels – which became the Incorporated Church Building Society in 1828 – was established in 1818, in order to co-ordinate donations from members of the public and give assistance to parishes that did not qualify for help from the parliamentary grant. After little more than a year since its establishment, in February 1819, the Society had banked £53,738.17.0 in donations and £547.4.0 in annual subscriptions. It had received 110 applications for help, of which forty-two

[7]   LPL ICBS 691, W. Fry to W. J. Rodber, 23 August 1825.
[8]   LPL ICBS 157, W. B. Cocker to W. J. Rodber, 5 June 1819.
[9]   M. R. Austin (ed.), *The Church in Derbyshire in 1823–4: the Parochial Visitation of the Rev Samuel Butler, Archdeacon of Derby in the Diocese of Lichfield and Coventry*, Derbyshire Archaelogical Society, 5 (1974) p. 4.

had been considered, and thirty-five grants had been made.[10] 'In the space of one year', the secretary wrote in the Society's first minute book, 'the Society has contributed in an essential manner to promote the social peace and political welfare of our Country, and the temporal and eternal interests of so many of our fellow creatures.'[11] Yet all it had done was contribute to the enlargement of a few dozen churches. The secretary's comment reveals the breadth of the agenda which church building was expected to be able to address.

The ICBS was not able to sustain its initial level of income, and showed the first signs of financial crisis by the end of the 1820s, which coincided with a shift in the responsibility for church building from the government to Anglicans themselves. Analysis of the ICBS's files in the sequence 1 to 850 (a total of 758 surviving files) reveals the extent of the decline. In particular, a comparison of the first fifty successful applications and the last fifty successful applications in the sequence, which covers the period 1818 to 1828, shows that in the first fifty the Society granted a total of £15,725 or an average of £314 per grant; in the last fifty it could only muster £8,064, or an average of £161 per grant.[12] The minute books begin to refer to the low state of the Society's funds in the autumn of 1827,[13] and from then on the pages are peppered with references to its depleted finances. In May 1828 the committee was obliged to turn down an application to enlarge the parish church in the rapidly expanding Yorkshire town of Keighley, because of 'the present exhausted state of the Society's funds'.[14] Keighley, with a population of over 10,000, and only thirty-six free seats in the parish church, was just the sort of place that needed urgent attention from the Anglicans; there were six Nonconformist chapels. As the rector noted gloomily, 'the poor must become dissenters or nothing'.[15] It was not until 1849 that the ICBS was in a position to give a grant of £400 towards an enlargement of Keighley church by the architect Robert Chantrell, which provided 589 free seats.

The financial fortunes of the ICBS rallied somewhat in 1838 when, like the National Society and the Society for the Propagation of the Gospel, it began to be aided by triennial royal letters for collections in

10 LPL ICBS minute book, vol 1, fo. 100.
11 Ibid., fo. 116.
12 In 1990 the Leverhulme Trust provided funding for a five-year project to computerise and index the records of the ICBS. There are 10,000 files in all.
13 LPL ICBS minute book, vol. 3, fo. 229.
14 LPL ICBS 818, W. J. Rodber to T. Drury, 14 May 1828.
15 Ibid., T. Drury to W. J. Rodber, 22 March 1828.

parish churches. They had raised £258,000 by 1853, when Palmerston put a stop to the royal letters on the grounds that they made too close a link between Church and Crown.[16] By 1868 the ICBS had spent £599,785 in 4,210 grants, of which 1,197 went towards new churches, 697 towards rebuilding and 2,316 towards enlarging churches or increasing their seating. It had helped to provide an additional 1,092,000 sittings, of which 850,000 were free. Most of the money was spent in rural or suburban areas, because of the rule that required grants to be matched by local contributions, a factor that underlines the continuing role of local philanthropy in the provision of churches.[17]

The campaign to provide church sittings for all illustrates the extent to which middle-class Anglicans had difficulty in coming to terms with the disappearance of the Anglican hegemony. They hesitated to challenge the assumption that the Church should be the spiritual provider for all, and they were unable to tolerate the notion of apparently subversive competition. In 1839 Bishop Blomfield began his project of building ten new churches in London's Bethnal Green.[18] In the same year Bishop Kaye was contemplating a scheme to provide church accommodation for two-thirds of the inhabitants of Nottingham, a rapidly expanding city with a population well in excess of 50,000. Taking existing accommodation into account, this would have entailed the creation of 30,000 new sittings.[19] Such a scheme could never be realised, and by the middle of the century Anglicans were beginning to lose confidence in such measures. By 1851 there were seven Anglican churches in the city of Nottingham, yet the Religious Census of that year suggested that only 31 per cent of the church-going citizens of Nottingham attended Anglican worship, as against 62 per cent who attended Nonconformist chapels.[20]

Plans to 'restore' (a word that often implied an accompanying change in liturgical practice) or to enlarge churches did not always meet with the approval of the representatives of the local community, even if they were partly funded by local donations. Building plans were a source of contention in struggles between clergy and vestry, as at St

---

[16] B. I. Coleman, 'Anglican church extension and related movements *c.*1800–1860 with special reference to London' (unpublished Ph.D thesis, University of Cambridge, 1968). See appendix on ICBS.

[17] Ibid.

[18] Owen Chadwick, *The Victorian Church*, 3rd edn (London: A & C Black, 1966) pp. 331–2.

[19] LAO CorB5/8A/16, Kaye to J. H. Browne 6 December 1839.

[20] Richard Dennis, *English Industrial Cities in the Nineteenth Century: A Social Geography* (Cambridge: Cambridge University Press, 1984) pp. 30–1.

Nicholas', Leicester, where the vicar Richard Davies finally abandoned his attempts to rebuild the church in 1830, a project that he had been attempting for the previous eight years. He claimed that the select vestry was dominated by five individuals, the first 'a very large dealer in wool – a Whig and a Saint', the second 'a thorough Methodist – wily, smooth, plausible', the third a 'Roman Catholic of very great influence', the fourth a churchwarden, a 'stern and bitter demagogue' married to a Catholic and the fifth, also a churchwarden, 'well meaning, but no match for his confreres'.[21] Davies' description evokes the rather menacing character that church management could sometimes assume. At the heart of the dispute was the churchwardens' indignation at being deprived of their authority over the free sittings; pew allocation was an important part of their role, and it was not one that they were usually willing to concede.

An equally acrimonious dispute between vicar and vestry broke out at Stow in Lincolnshire in the late 1840s, when the vicar made plans for an extensive restoration and wished to fund it from the church rate. Local disquiet was expressed that the work was motivated by ecclesiological rather than functional considerations. The vestrymen noted in their minute book that 'a class of men calling themselves Archaeologists have resolved to fasten upon the Church of Stowe and the Parish funds, that they may use *both* for the display of their skill in the science of Antiquities'.[22] In the end the restoration was funded by private subscription rather than rate, and the vestry itself, perhaps sensing that it had lost a significant battle, became a less influential body, and seems to have ceased intervening in church concerns.[23] When church rate lapsed the clergy were able to gain more control over the building, and to determine the nature of any alterations that were made to it. Church restorations, which were invariably promoted by clergy and architects, marked an important phase in the shift in local ecclesiastical authority from laymen to clergy.

PAROCHIAL RESPONSIBILITY REDEFINED: THE POOR AND THE RATEPAYER

The parochial system had proved one of the most enduring elements in English Christianity, emerging more or less unscathed even from the

---

[21] LPL ICBS 418, R. Davies to W. J. Rodber, 16 February 1827.

[22] Stow vestry book, 23 October 1848. Cited in Mark Spurrell (ed.), *Stow Church Restored 1846–1866* (Lincoln: Lincolnshire Record Society, 1984) p. 28.

[23] Ibid., p. xxi.

upheavals of the Reformation.[24] The eighteenth-century mind understood that the stability of society was underwritten by the stability of
the parish. As the social order became visibly less stable in the wake of
the agrarian and industrial revolutions, the Napoleonic wars and the
Peterloo massacre, legislators and reformers turned instinctively to the
parish as the place where a remedy should be sought. A Church that
functioned more efficiently within the local community, with a more
active clergy taking a greater interest in local affairs, and providing
schooling and material relief as well as pastoral support and religious
instruction, would make the countryside altogether more safe and
secure. The parish system provided a unique combination. It ensured
the secular jurisdiction necessary for the administration of local government and poor relief, and the ecclesiastical jurisdiction necessary to
provide churches, worship and the ceremonies that marked the
significant moments in life.

It should be no surprise that the parliamentarian Thomas Gilbert,
one of the leading reformers of his age, promoted bills for both church
reform (1777 and 1781) and poor law reform (1776 and 1782).[25] Bishops
and senior clergy were closely involved in the remaking of the poor law
from an early date.[26] The plight of the poor had long been a cause for
Christian concern, and the Church had always been the primary
provider of charity, though Soloway and Waterman argue that by the
early nineteenth century the senior churchmen who interested themselves in poor relief were chiefly motivated by the doctrines of the
political economists, doctrines that tended to make life less pleasant for
the poor themselves. At the local level, however, there is evidence of
clergy taking pains to ensure that relief was administered in the best
interests of the beneficiaries.[27] Under the old poor law, relief had been
organised on a parish-by-parish basis. It came from two sources,
charitable endowments and poor rates, was controlled by justices of the
peace, who were often local clergy, and was supervised by churchwardens and overseers of the poor. Both churchwardens and overseers
were elected by the parish at the Easter vestry. The much-hated Poor

[24] For a useful survey of the parish over the centuries, see D. M. Palliser, 'Introduction: the
parish in perspective' in Wright (ed.), *Parish, Church and People* pp. 5–28.

[25] John Kent, *The Unacceptable Face: The Modern Church in the Eyes of the Historian* (London: SCM
Press, 1987) p. 140.

[26] R. A. Soloway, *Prelates and People: Ecclesiastical Social Thought in England 1783–1852* (London:
Routledge & Kegan Paul, 1969) especially pp. 85–192.

[27] Arthur Warne, *Church and Society in Eighteenth Century Devon* (Newton Abbot: David & Charles,
1969) pp. 148–65; Diana McClatchey, *Oxfordshire Clergy 1777–1869: A Study of the Established
Church and the Role of its Clergy in Local Society* (Oxford: Clarendon Press, 1960) pp. 123–34.

Law Amendment Act of 1834 began to unravel the link between parish and poor relief. It set up a non-parochial administrative unit, the poor law union, under the direction of elected guardians, and by 1838 only 1,000 parishes remained outside the poor law unions.[28] The secular and ecclesiastical functions of the parish were being prised apart. Furthermore, the doctrines of political economy were becoming widely assimilated among the clergy. As Diana McClatchey remarked, 'If we hear less about the administration of parochial charities in the mid-nineteenth century, it may be that thrift and not charity was becoming the more fashionable parochial virtue, to be invoked from the pulpit and given expression in the numerous clothing clubs, rent and shoe clubs and provident societies which were such a feature of the 1840s, 1850s, and 1860s.'[29]

As this transition in the provision of poor relief took place, the overseers of the poor ceased to record in their account books that they had met with the churchwardens, the clergyman and principal inhabitants in order to decide who would receive pay from the poor rates 'in the Parish Church after Evening Prayer'.[30] The basis of the payment of annual charitable doles was also altered, as both clergy and Charity Commissioners began to question the legal validity of charitable distributions for which no written record existed.[31] R. W. Bushaway has provided an illuminating account of events at Piddlehinton, Dorset, where the practice had been for the rector to make an annual distribution to the poor on old Christmas day of a pound of bread, a pint of ale and a large mince pie – baked, with the bread, in a purpose-built oven in the rectory. The distribution took place until 1841, when it was discontinued by the new rector, Thomas T. Carter, an old Etonian in his first incumbency, and also, it may be noted, a Tractarian. Carter disapproved because the dole went to the poor from miles around, to people not in need, to persons of bad character and to illegitimate children. He was prepared to substitute the dole with a distribution of blankets to the same value, but only to those whom he regarded as respectable, and who did not claim it as a right.[32] Carter's distinction between the deserving and undeserving poor seems to

---

[28] Warne, *Church and Society* pp. 166, 177.
[29] McClatchey, *Oxfordshire Clergy* p. 133.
[30] Warne, *Church and Society* p. 154.
[31] R. W. Bushaway, 'Rite, legitimation and community in southern England 1700–1850: the ideology of custom' in Barry Stapleton (ed.), *Conflict and Community in Southern England* (Stroud, 1992).
[32] Bushaway, 'Rite, legitimation and community' p. 128.

have reflected the new poor law of 1834, although such shifts in attitude can be traced back to at least 1818.[33] He also displayed a typically Tractarian desire to disentangle the church from a secular obligation, and to make a sharper distinction between parishioner and non-parishioner, respectable and non-respectable, Anglican and non-Anglican.

Diana McClatchey's Oxfordshire evidence points in a similar direction. At Yarnton the custodians of Alderman Fletcher's charity put their signatures to a new schedule of directions in 1855, almost certainly drafted by the vicar. It included the following conditions:

None but the Poor Inhabitants of Yarnton are to partake of his Xmas gifts etc. Poor parishioners dwelling out of the parish are not to partake of these gifts, and if anything be given to them, it is given wrongfully and redress may be sought ... Seeing that the Alderman was a sincere and single-hearted Christian and an exact observer of the Sabbath day ... we are of opinion that in distributing the Bread, Meat and Cakes a distinction should be made between those who worship in the Parish Church that he fitted up, and those who seldom or never enter it. To conclude: it is recommended that in making out the lists of the year, all persons (males, females, boys or girls) whose conduct during the past year has been wicked, should be dropped from the charity lists.[34]

McClatchey relates two similarly illuminating incidents from Wheatley. The first concerned a Dissenter who asked an Anglican clergyman for relief, and was told to go to his own minister; the second concerned a chapel-going girl who went to the vicarage to seek help for her sick father, and was told that she should go where she went on Sundays for help in the week.[35] The clergy were redefining their responsibilities as being solely to church-going Anglicans, and, in the case of Piddlehinton and Yarnton, reinterpreting the intentions of pious benefactors in accordance with their own views.

Clergy who were narrowing their definition of who was a respectable Anglican and who was not were less willing for their churches to be appropriated for non-liturgical, community use than their predecessors had been. The whole focus of a restored church, with its immovable fittings, was on worship and worship alone. Vestry meetings, at which parish business was settled, might continue to be summoned in the church, but it was likely that they would be adjourned fairly rapidly to

33 Soloway, *Prelates and People* p. 127.
34 McClatchey, *Oxfordshire Clergy* pp. 131–2.
35 Ibid., p. 133.

a public house. The ecclesiologist J. M. Neale discouraged any vestry meetings from taking place in churches.[36] Bishop Kaye, who held high views on the consecrated nature of churches, refused to sanction their use for any purpose other than divine worship, for which, as he pointed out, they had been set apart at the time of their consecration. His condemnation extended to concerts of sacred music, and to Church Missionary Society meetings. He wrote disapproving letters concerning the former to several Nottinghamshire clergy in the 1840s, expressing to one his sense of the unworthiness of sitting 'upon the seats of a Church as upon the Boxes of a Theatre'.[37]

The new understanding of the parish church as being appropriate solely for worship and the occasional offices had the effect of reducing its significance in the lives of many parishioners. This ran exactly counter to the vision of the idyllic rural church at the centre of a stable community, which figured so prominently in the Anglican imagination. In reality the church became a resort for the devout rather than a resource for the community. The narrowing of its role naturally made non-Anglicans less inclined to contribute to the upkeep of the church fabric, as they were supposed to do by means of church rate, although attitudes to rate varied from parish to parish. In some places, it became the most contentious issue in local politics from the 1820s to 1868, when it was finally made voluntary.[38] The origins of church rate were as ancient as local taxation itself, the legacy of a time when maintaining the church building was seen as being as much a public duty as repairing the highways and relieving the poor. It was levied on all occupiers of property, no distinctions being made between Anglicans and non-Anglicans. As the State gave full legal recognition to non-Anglicans, it was inevitable that the continued imposition of rate would enrage those who wished to have nothing to do with the Anglican parish church. The situation was made worse by the terms of the Church Building Act of 1818. The Act provided that when churches were built in newly-created districts, the repairs were to be paid by a church rate of the inhabitants after twenty years and that during the

[36] Graeme Drewery, 'Victorian church building and restoration in the Diocese of York, with special reference to the archdeaconry of Cleveland' (unpublished PhD thesis, University of Cambridge, 1994) p. 133.

[37] LAO CorB5/8A/6, Kaye to R. W. Almond, 30 January 1843, and CorB5/8A/2, Kaye to R. Simpson, n.d. For the C.M.S. meetings, see CorB5/3/17/11, Kaye to Lord Wriothesley Russell, 16 April 1842.

[38] See Chadwick, *The Victorian Church*, part 1, pp. 81–9; G. F. A. Best, *Temporal Pillars* (Cambridge: Cambridge University Press, 1964) pp. 192–4; E. R. Norman, *Church and Society in England 1770–1970* (Oxford: Clarendon Press, 1976) pp. 109–112.

twenty years, the inhabitants should continue to pay for the upkeep of their old parish church. In some parishes, depending on the application of local acts of parliament, a Nonconformist found himself legally compelled to pay rate to two Anglican churches, that of the district in which he lived, and that out of which the district had been carved.[39] Church rate agitation began, unsurprisingly, in the new district parishes. In the larger towns, where religious Dissent was more likely overtly to be harnessed to political radicalism, it became the most aggravated of the grievances between Dissenters and churchmen.

St Mary's, the ancient parish church of Nottingham, was the scene of one of the most bitter and protracted of the church rate disputes. Neglected by successive churchwardens, the church had become structurally unsafe by 1842, and it remained closed for months on end. It was estimated that £4,600 was needed to carry out repairs. One of the churchwardens, George Eddowes, had not asked the parish for a rate for eight of the fourteen years in which he had been in office, and declared that he did not care whether a rate was granted or not.[40] Eddowes was eventually compelled to summon a vestry meeting by the vicar of St Mary's, on pain of imprisonment. The meeting took place on 12 January 1843, and after acrimonious scenes (gleefully recorded verbatim by the radical *Nottingham Review*) the rate was rejected by a majority of 784 votes.[41] In April a Chartist leader named Sweet attempted to stand as churchwarden, with the intention of blocking all vestry meetings that proposed the setting of a rate. It is not clear whether Sweet was successful in the election, but St Mary's remained in a shambolic state, often locked, for several months.

Such scenes of hostility should, perhaps, be seen as isolated and untypical. In rural and semi-rural areas a different picture emerges. Some parishes experienced the end of the imposition of rate on the general population, favouring instead the raising of subscriptions among Anglicans themselves. Two examples are seen in Buckinghamshire. At Princes Risborough in 1845 a vestry meeting decided that repairs to the church steeple should not be paid for by a rate, but by subscription. As the incumbent explained:

Such is the state of feeling in the Parish generally, that, if an attempt were made to levy a rate for the repairs of the steeple, an angry spirit would be stirred up productive of much evil: and I have no doubt that a decided

---

[39]   Chadwick, *The Victorian Church*, part 1, p. 85.
[40]   *Nottingham Review*, 13 January 1843.
[41]   LAO CorB5/8/18, G. Wilkins to Kaye, 14 January 1843.

opposition would be made to the rate. The present proposal to repair the steeple by subscription has given great satisfaction, both to Church-people and Dissenters: and I am in great hopes that the proposed plan if successful will intend to bring some back to the Church: at all events, to diminish the bitter feeling some of the Dissenters entertain towards the establishment and lead them to think more favourably of it.[42]

Likewise at Steeple Claydon voluntary subscription was preferred to rate. This was a state of affairs of which the Archdeacon of Buckingham, Justly Hill, strongly disapproved, noting bitterly that 'Mr Jarvis [the churchwarden] is himself the chief opponent of Ch. rates, and Mr Price, the curate, I understand favoured the opposition. I told the Churchwardens that they *must* demand & levy a church-rate as was the ancient custom . . .'[43] In both these cases there is a clear sense of a local wish to conciliate Dissenters coming into conflict with the Anglican hierarchy's desire to continue imposing church rate as before. Bishop Kaye brusquely refused to subscribe towards the repairs to the steeple at Princes Risborough, on the grounds that if the parishioners had let it become dilapidated, they could not expect help in having it repaired.[44] This response implies a fairly limited understanding of the complex relations that existed between Anglicans and others at parochial level. In his visitation charge of 1834, Kaye had argued that the very principle of a church establishment was at stake in the levying of church rate, and that it was the duty of Dissenters to pay, submitting their private judgement to the will of the majority.[45] Appeals to the will of the majority were to become increasingly problematic, particularly after the verdict was delivered in 1853 in the Braintree church rate case, which found that churchwardens had no power to enforce a rate against the will of the majority.

In other places, however, church rate remained the major source of parochial funding. Where relations with the Established Church were good, people remained willing to pay. The rector of a Cambridgeshire parish, Knapwell, remarked in his visitation return for 1837, 'No one ever objects to pay his rate – the parish affairs are conducted peaceably and quietly.'[46] In a sample of fifty Cambridgeshire parishes in the same year, there were only two recorded cases of rate refusal, at Waterbeach

42 LAO CorB5/3/2/4, C. E. Gray to Kaye, 4 August 1845.
43 LAO CorB5/3/1/1, J. Hill to Kaye, 22 November 1839.
44 LAO CorB5/3/2/4, Kaye to C. E. Gray, 24 August 1845.
45 John Kaye, *Charge: Triennial Visitation, 1834*, reprinted in W. F. J. Kaye (ed.), *The Works of John Kaye* (London, 1888), vol. VIII, pp. 5–7.
46 CUL EDR C1/8, 1837.

and Gamlingay.[47] It was customary in the county at this time for the senior churchwarden, rather than the clergyman, to preside at the vestry meeting at which the rate was fixed. The sight of a respected local man, elected to the office, arguing the case for setting a rate to his neighbours may have done much to alleviate hostility. In contrast, the advice from bishops and archdeacons, who seemed fearful of this aspect of lay participation, was that the clergyman should always preside at the vestry.[48]

Even in urban areas non-Anglican parishioners could remain willing to pay rate if the church was seen to be offering some form of practical assistance to all members of the community. At Radford, in the heart of industrial Nottinghamshire, just a few miles from the strife-torn city-centre church of St Mary's, a motion to levy a church rate was passed unanimously in 1841. The popular vicar, Samuel Creswell, operated a gardens scheme, which permitted parishioners – regardless of their religious affiliation – to rent well-managed plots of land at a rent far below the market rate. The gardens scheme was clearly appreciated by parishioners, though Creswell's low rents led another landlord – who rented allotments to the poor 'at a most grinding rent' – to make an attempt to blacken his character. Five self-styled 'Protestant Dissenters' sprang to Creswell's defence, explaining the situation in a letter to the bishop.[49] Creswell's philanthropy in the form of allotments was not an isolated example at this period. At Sherington, Buckinghamshire, the rector J. C. Williams divided eleven acres of glebe land into forty-four garden allotments for labourers in 1845. In January of that year he wrote:

I shall let the men into possession in a few days, but charge them rent only from Lady Day next, [25 March] so that they will get their crops in before having to pay anything. They are very thankful, and I hope all will work out well.[50]

The following year, during the potato blight, he was able to report that all had worked out well: the tenants 'have benefited greatly' and 'sustained very trifling loss among their potatoes'. Moreover, 'the congregation, morning and afternoon, has more than doubled, many

[47] Ibid.
[48] LAO CorB5/3/1/1, Justly Hill to Kaye, 20 November 1839.
[49] LAO CorB5/8/32/1, S. Creswell to Kaye, 10 November 1840; 'Five Protestant Dissenters' to Kaye, 15 November 1841; 'Rules and Regulations for the Management of Spring Field Gardens', November 1840.
[50] LAO CorB5/3/6/4, J. C. Williams to Kaye, 20 January 1845.

of the dissenters have return'd partially, and some altogether'.[51] Once again, this provides evidence of the conciliation of Nonconformists at parish level, and of the fluid state of denominational identity.

SUNDAY CHURCH-GOING

At the beginning of his study of the churches in Lambeth from 1870 to 1930, Jeffrey Cox noted that 'Anglican parishes in particular were not designed merely to produce regular churchgoers.'[52] This was probably even more true in the period before 1870, when the Church of England was closely tied to a range of social and philanthropic activities, and when denominational allegiances had a greater flexibility. John Kent, writing in 1972, claimed that the working classes saw church-going as the most mechanical (and by implication the least attractive) side of religion.[53] Whether or not it was attractive is very difficult to gauge, but that it was to some degree mechanical seems a less controversial claim. Regular Sunday church-going was a more routine activity than attending church to mark the rites of passage, and differed also from the inward impulse that led people to study the Bible, or to private prayer, or to devotional reading.

The approaches of church-goers, the parochial clergy and the diocesan hierarchy to Sunday attendance reveal significantly different objectives. The most basic question was that of how often and at what times Sunday worship should take place. It was accepted on all sides that, unless the circumstances were exceptional, every parish church should hold at least one service on a Sunday. Bishops and archdeacons took a stern view of failures in this respect, and outright neglect of any provision for Sunday worship was rare. The evidence suggests that clergy – and clergy wives – went to considerable lengths to ensure that alternative arrangements were made in the event of unavoidable absence or sickness, and that services which had been advertised did indeed take place. Examples of total neglect of Sunday worship are more or less confined to the handful of parishes in which the clergy were wayward or dissolute.[54] But beyond the consensus of a minimum

---

51 Ibid., Williams to Kaye, 20 March 1846.
52 Jeffrey Cox, *The English Churches in a Secular Society: Lambeth, 1870–1930* (New York and Oxford: Oxford University Press, 1982) p. 7.
53 Kent, 'Feelings and festivals' p. 860.
54 In a study of the counties of Buckinghamshire, Leicestershire, Nottinghamshire and Lincolnshire between 1827–53, neglect of Sunday worship was noticed at Haddenham, Bucks (LAO CorB5/19/11); Addington, Bucks (LAO CorB5/3/3/1); Hallaton, Leics (LAO CorB5/5/1/2); Markfield, Leics (LAO CorB5/5/13) – all parishes in which the clergy had committed other offences against ecclesiastical discipline, and were known to be dubious characters.

of at least one Sunday service, opinions differed sharply. Lay people were sometimes willing to press for two services on a Sunday; after his visitation of Buckinghamshire in 1832, Archdeacon Hill reported that 430 parishioners at Marsworth had begged for two services.[55] But more often they raised objections to the holding of services at irregular hours, as in this vivid complaint from Colnbrook in Buckinghamshire, in which a number of grievances were fused together:

Colnbrook Chaple as before the Townspeople do not like the presant Minister therefore the trades people is all turn'd Decenters and If no alteration there will be no Chaple Warden there is only Five people at presant to chuse from. If there was a resident Minister at Colnbrook the Duty should be done twice a Day Mr Brown doing duty at Horton he cannot do duty at Colnbrook in proper time the Sacrament Sunday we are called at Ten O Clock in the Morning and Afternoon Service a Quarter past Three.[56]

For bishops and archdeacons, however, 'Sunday duty' increasingly came to mean double duty; the provision of two services on a Sunday. The desire for competition rather than co-operation with Nonconformity seems to have been a major reason for the Anglican hierarchy becoming adamant on the matter in the 1820s, about forty years before such views became widely assimilated by the parochial clergy. In 1825 the Ely diocesan visitation articles were redrafted in order to find out why two services were not held, if they were not. At Lincoln, Bishop Kaye began his episcopate by declaring in his primary Charge of 1828 that he would enforce double duty wherever practicable. He explained the policy to a Buckinghamshire vicar in 1830: 'The performance of a single service is an abuse: an abuse which has contributed more than any other single cause to fill the Kingdom with Dissenting places of worship.'[57]

The parochial clergy, however, were often reluctant to co-operate with episcopal directives, and even when willing, were sometimes disturbed by the results of the policy. Some incumbents took the view that no additional service should be performed without a commensurate increase in the parish's endowment, on the grounds that a specific income was allotted to a specific duty.[58] In 1830 William Thomas Eyre

[55] LAO CorB5/3/32/12, notes on Hill's parochial visitation, May 1832.
[56] LAO CorB5/3/1/3, a Bill of Presentment made by the chapel wardens at Colnbrook at the archdeacon's visitation on 10 May 1830. Another example of the lay demand for services at regular times came from Askham, Notts, (LAO CorB5/8/28/1, a memorial signed by thirty-four inhabitants to Bishop Kaye in December 1840).
[57] LAO CorB5/3/25/4, Kaye to W. T. Eyre, 6 April 1830.
[58] Ibid., Eyre to Kaye, 30 March 1830.

had been recently instituted to the Buckinghamshire living of Padbury in succession to his father, who had only ever performed single duty on account of his serving nearby Addington as curate. The younger Eyre had planned to continue this arrangement, and was perturbed by the bishop's intervention. Eyre argued, with some force, that by supplementing his stipend by £50 per annum with the Addington curacy, he would be able to increase his professional income to £150, and,

by strict economy and living in Lodgings, could have yet spared something for the poor. Should your Lordship now prohibit me from serving any curacy (as very many clergy in the neighbourhood are still obliged to do) the Parishioners must suffer from the arrangement as well as myself, in temporal point of view, for if they gain more doctrine it is impossible that I should illustrate my own faith with charitable works.[59]

The bishop proved unsympathetic to an argument derived from an eighteenth-century view of Anglican charity, and Eyre was obliged to put up with what turned out to be a long and impoverished incumbency at Padbury.

Other clergy, particularly the old and frail, protested against double duty on practical grounds. Jonathan Brigges of Thornbrough, Buckinghamshire, was aged eighty in 1830, and described himself as an 'old worn out clergyman'.[60] He explained that on arrival in the parish in 1790, he had been told that morning prayer was only held four times a year on sacrament Sundays. The usual service was evening prayer with sermon at 2 p.m. Over the years he had offered the parishioners morning prayer and evening prayer alternately, but they had always declined, saying that they could more easily attend in the afternoon.[61] In large, scattered parishes the prospect of making four journeys to and from church was a significant deterrent. The rhythms of rural life meant that any departure from the customary service times was likely to result in a decline in the numbers attending. Thomas Knowles, rector of South Somercotes, Lincolnshire, tried to explain the position to Bishop Kaye in 1829. Half past ten and half past two were the only times at which people would come; at other times they would be sleeping or tending their cattle. 'Believe me, my Lord, the mischief arising from the service being performed at inconvenient hours is

[59] Ibid.
[60] LAO CorB5/3/28/4, J. Brigges to Kaye, 27 August 1830.
[61] Ibid. Preference for afternoon services seems to have been quite widespread. See for example, R. W. Ambler, *Lincolnshire Returns of the Census of Religious Worship 1851* (Lincoln: Lincolnshire Record Society, 72, 1979) pp. xxv–xxvi.

irreparable!'[62] He probably was not exaggerating; if the clergy persisted in trying to provide services that were deemed unnecessary or inconvenient, the laity had their own methods of sabotaging them. As late as 1843 just one service was provided at Balderton, Nottinghamshire, although the population there was in excess of one thousand. The incumbent explained that he had been hoping to introduce an afternoon service, but that the parishioners (with one exception) refused to incur the expense of lighting the church in winter.[63]

For those accustomed to attend once on a Sunday, two long Anglican services within hours of each other may have been more than they could bear. A potential cause of disaffection was the level of similarity and repetition in the liturgy of the Book of Common Prayer. Those who said the words of the general confession at evening prayer in the middle of the afternoon must sometimes have wondered what sins they could possibly have committed since half past ten that morning, when they last made the confession. If so much repetition was needed at such frequent intervals, could they be sure that their sins were really forgiven? For the evangelically-inclined, the very different atmosphere of the meeting house or the chapel beckoned in the evening. A parishioner told Edward Steere, curate of Skegness, that 'we come to church in the morning to please you, Sir, and goes to chapel at night to save our souls'.[64] For the less devout, staying away from one service could become the prelude to staying away from both.

In the period after 1830 double duty became the norm throughout England,[65] and diligent clergy watched what had once been good congregations ebbing away. Double duty could have the effect of splitting – and demoralising – scattered congregations. This occurred at Cowbit, Lincolnshire, where the perpetual curate, John Steel, decided to introduce an evening service after seeing it recommended in the bishop's Charge of 1828. Soon he lamented that on some Sundays the aggregate of the two congregations scarcely exceeded the single one.[66] Steel's puzzlement at this, and his claim that Dissent was weak, suggests that for the parishioners of Cowbit, one visit to church on

[62] LAO CorB5/4/140, T. Knowles to Kaye, 20 October 1829.
[63] LAO CorB5/8A/2, F. Apthorp to Kaye, 26 September 1843.
[64] James Obelkevich, *Religion and Rural Society: South Lindsey 1825–1875* (Oxford: Clarendon Press, 1976) p. 157.
[65] Nigel Yates, *Buildings, Faith and Worship: The Liturgical Arrangement of Anglican Churches 1600–1900* (Oxford: Clarendon Press, 1991) pp. 55–65 for the most comprehensive recent survey of the pattern of services at this period.
[66] LAO CorB5/4/33/6, J. Steel to Kaye, 17 October 1829.

Sunday was perceived as quite sufficient, a consideration that does not seem to have occurred to senior Anglicans in their wholesale advocacy of the importance of going to church twice on Sunday. At St Vigor's, Fulbourn in Cambridgeshire, the vicar provided two services where previously there had been one, but complained that the parishioners 'think once a Day self-sufficient Duty to their God'.[67] Francis Massingberd, rector of South Ormsby, Driby and Calceby in Lincolnshire, introduced a second service in 1830. By June 1833 he was expressing his concern at this policy:

The result is that a very good congregation has been divided into two rather scanty ones, which, as the people themselves are little apt to reflect upon the cause, tends to convey the impression to their minds of the service being ill attended, and, by consequence, naturally promotes the evil it supposes.[68]

He had, furthermore, received a request from the parishioners to revert to a single service, morning and afternoon alternately, at Ormsby and Driby churches. This placed Massingberd in a dilemma; he was reluctant to concede to this plan, lest it should be seen as an encouragement to Dissenters. Instead, he preferred to offer at Ormsby 'morning prayers, at about nine O'clock, when the full service was in the afternoon, and evening prayers, at 4 or 5 (at least in the summer) when it was in the morning'. He intended to make the shorter prayer service 'a rendez-vous for the more religious in the parish, and ... a point with all regular communicants ... as it is with the Methodists to attend their class meetings'.[69] It was these sorts of attitudes, this almost unconscious sorting of parishioners into more religious and less religious, communicants and others, which marked Massingberd out as a distinctively nineteenth-century churchman of the new breed.

The absence of service registers for this period makes it impossible to be certain about the precise pattern of parochial worship. It is, however, tempting to suggest that one of the reasons for arguments about the frequency of Sunday worship was that relatively little could be done to alter its form. It could be shortened, but it must still be derived from the Prayer Book. Until the middle of the century, 'morning service' was understood to mean matins with a sermon followed by the litany and sometimes ante-communion as well. Later, it was divided into its constituent parts to form

[67] CUL EDR C1/4, 1807.
[68] LAO CorB5/4/84/3, F. Massingberd to Kaye, 10 June 1833.
[69] Ibid.

separate services. 'Evening service' was evensong with either sermon or public catechising, and sometimes incorporating churchings and baptism.

One of the most noticeable shifts in the structure of Sunday worship during the period was the abandonment of quarterly communion in favour of a monthly service, a trend in which the towns were far in advance of the countryside. Patterns of Sunday worship in town and countryside require separate consideration. In the city of Cambridge in 1825, five of the ten Anglican churches in use held communion services at monthly intervals, as well as at the major festivals, and one church, St Mary the Less, held them every six weeks.[70] In the city of Lincoln in 1828, three out of the eleven churches had a monthly administration of Holy Communion.[71] This pattern of monthly communion available in the towns for those who wished to partake of it had existed also in the eighteenth century.[72] In the countryside, communion services were usually restricted to Easter, Whitsun and Christmas and sometimes occurred additionally at Michaelmas as well. Investigation of fifty rural Cambridgeshire parishes and fifty rural Bedfordshire parishes suggested that it was not until the 1860s that monthly communion became more common than quarterly services. In 1865, ten parishes in the Cambridgeshire sample held a quarterly celebration of communion, ten held it six times a year, twenty-three had a monthly service and seven held it at some other frequency, of which only one parish, Over, had a weekly communion. In the Bedfordshire sample only two parishes retained a quarterly service, five had a service six times a year, thirty-one held it monthly and twelve held it at some other frequency, though none on a weekly basis. These figures contrast with those derived from the 1850 visitation returns, in which sampling fifty parishes from each county produced figures for Cambridgeshire of twenty-eight quarterly services and eight monthly services, and for Bedfordshire of nineteen quarterly services and ten monthly ones. The rest of the parishes in the sample held the service at some other frequency, or refused to disclose the information.[73] Similar evidence emerges from Obelkevich's study of South Lindsey[74] and from Edward

[70] CUL EDR C1/6, 1825.
[71] LAO CorB5/4/141/10 is a table of services in Lincoln city, compiled by Archdeacon Goddard.
[72] Yates, *Buildings, Faith, and Worship* p. 58.
[73] CUL EDR C1/12, 1865, and C1/9, 1850. Incomplete survival of the visitation returns meant that it was impossible to sample the same one hundred parishes in both years.
[74] Obelkevich, *Religion and Rural Society* p. 138.

Royle's work on York[75] of the adoption of monthly communion services as a phenomenon of the early 1860s.

The provision of additional communion services did not of course guarantee that larger numbers of communicants would attend. Communion services were not universally popular among church-goers, and, as has already been shown, many were deterred at the prospect of taking the sacrament to their own damnation. David Robinson has estimated that less than 2 per cent of the total population of the archdeaconry of Stafford were communicants in the 1830s.[76] Once again there is a contrast between town and country. In Staffordshire the lowest figures were recorded in the most populous towns and in scattered mining and manufacturing villages. The highest proportion of communicants was found in a few small villages where the inhabitants were servants or tenants of a single landowner; here the figure could exceed 25 per cent.[77] In the Cambridgeshire village of Harston there were twelve communicants amongst a population of 420 in 1807. At West Wratting the figure was thirty communicants in an estimated population of 800. At Arrington there were never more than four in 1807, although the number had risen to between eight and ten by 1825.[78] In the city of Cambridge the situation was complicated. At St Benedict's, there was a monthly communion and a full range of other services in 1807, but the numbers participating in the Eucharist were small – six to twelve on a monthly basis, eighteen to twenty-five at the three great festivals. Other churches in the centre of the town attracted greater numbers; forty at Little St Mary's and twenty to thirty out of a population of 310 at St Michael's. But the largest concentration of communicants in the county was to be found at Holy Trinity church, where the famous Evangelical Charles Simeon was vicar. Holy Trinity reported 150 in the visitation return of 1807. It is apparent that many of these individuals did not live in the parish, and were regarded by some of the Anglican clergy in the town with considerable suspicion. The curate of the neighbouring parish of All Saints remarked: 'There are also many Methodists, who attend Trinity Church only.'[79] In 1825 the rector of St Botolph's commented in a similar vein on 'Methodists or frequenters of Trinity Church ... [who] within these few last years

[75] Edward Royle, *The Victorian Church in York* (York: Borthwick Papers, 64, 1983) p. 21.
[76] David Robinson (ed.), *Visitations of the Archdeaconry of Stafford 1829–1841* (London: Staffordshire Record Society, 1980) p. xxvii.
[77] Ibid.
[78] CUL EDR C1/4, 1807; EDR C1/6, 1825.
[79] Ibid.

have multiplied considerably'. More frequent participation in the Eucharist was an Evangelical rather than a High Church innovation.[80] Even several decades later those who came to the Eucharist might still be Methodists, as at Seamer and Newton-upon-Ouse in Yorkshire, where the Methodist class leaders were still Anglican communicants in 1865.[81]

Preaching remained a central element of Sunday worship. Many thousands of printed sermons survive, but, as Françoise Deconinck-Brossard has pointed out, 'published sermons represent the tip of the iceberg', and they are more informative about what the Establishment wanted to place in the public domain than about the reality of regular preaching.[82] A service without a sermon did not satisfy the religiously inclined, as was illustrated in the previous chapter at Stretham in Cambridgeshire, where the curate provided two Sunday services but only one sermon, and where in the absence of a sermon, the church-goers were likely to visit the Methodist chapel. Indifferent perhaps to Anglicanism, the parishioners of Stretham were clearly not indifferent to the power of preaching. People had little scope for objecting to the manner in which a minister performed the service – unless he fell down drunk at the reading desk – but they had ample opportunity to object to his preaching. In 1835 T. W. Carr was nominated to a curacy at Irby-in-the-Marsh, Lincolnshire, but he was never licensed because the parishioners objected that he could not preach. When the congregation had dwindled to half a dozen, the wife of a churchwarden and the wife of a Methodist preacher set off for Lincoln to secure the services of another clergyman, a Mr Pridham.[83] Appalled by this example of lay usurpation, the bishop sent a rural dean, Joseph Walls, to investigate. Walls' report confirmed what the parishioners had already said:

The Churchwarden of Irby is the principal occupier of land in this parish and is a most respectable old man ... he had heard many clergymen but never one like Mr Carr; that Mr Carr at first preached without a book, but got on so ill, that he was requested through Mr Sutton [a neighbouring curate] to write out his Sermons, but still there was no improvement; that the congregation had dwindled away very much, sometimes five or six, sometimes a few more attended. This is the information I have received and I regret exceedingly that

---

[80] Yates, *Buildings, Faith and Worship* p. 128.

[81] Drewery, 'Victorian church building' p. 225.

[82] Françoise Deconinck-Brossard, 'Eighteenth-century sermons and the age' in W. M. Jacob and Nigel Yates (eds.), *Crown and Mitre: Religion and Society in Northern Europe Since the Reformation* (Woodbridge: Boydell Press, 1993) p. 111.

[83] LAO CorB5/19/2/4, Cholmeley to Kaye, 13 April 1835.

I am obliged to report the insufficiency of Mr Carr. They all said that he was a good young man, but that he really could not preach. The present curate, Mr Pridham, gives satisfaction to the Parish and the Church is again fully frequented.[84]

At this the bishop capitulated and granted a licence to Mr Pridham, the curate selected by some local women.

People were willing to take issue with clergy over the theological content of sermons, as well as with the method of delivery. At High Wycombe in 1844, twenty-nine parishioners complained they were obliged to quit the church in what was clearly a conflict between their own Evangelical beliefs and the hardline Calvinism, which appeared to verge on antinomianism, preached from the pulpit. The parishioners protested that sinners were not addressed as such, but as 'God's dear elect'; that the vicar believed that the gospel was exclusively for the elect; that he gave people no encouragement to amend their immoral lives; and that although sinners came to church, they had no business to be there.[85] A disheartened member of the congregation argued that the practical effects of the preacher's doctrine of election had been to split the congregation, some people being set up as the elect, others becoming exceedingly depressed, imagining themselves irretrievably lost. 'If you could my dear Sir, simply set forth the love of God instead of his election, how very acceptable it would be.'[86] Such a group of disaffected parishioners were obvious potential recruits to Wesleyan Methodism. Contentious cases, however, attracted publicity. People who were happy with the preaching they heard tended to remain silent, though there are occasional references to the sermons of Mr So-and-so being well received or giving general satisfaction. It is difficult to judge which sermons were typical, and what people thought about them. Henry Winn, parish clerk of Fulletby in Lincolnshire from 1838 to 1914, claimed to prefer sermons 'illustrating scripture history' that had 'something rich and striking in them, which is sure to take better with the generality of hearers, than dry doctrinal subjects, over which 'tis more than ten to one, but half the congregation fall asleep'.[87]

The clergy's approach to preaching can provide some insight into what they regarded as a good sermon. The vicar of Flitton and Silsoe, Bedfordshire, provided a simple definition in 1805: 'Preaching is the

[84] Ibid., Walls to Kaye, 28 April 1835.
[85] LAO CorB5/13/15/1, petition from twenty-nine parishioners to Kaye, 7 May 1844.
[86] Ibid., Wilkinson to Paddon, 7 December 1843.
[87] Obelkevich, *Religion and Rural Society* pp. 144–5.

taking of a portion of Scripture, and explaining it; raising some useful doctrine from it, and applying it to the edification of the hearers, to instruct and to reform.'[88] Francis Massingberd, whose diary provides an invaluable insight into the private world of a nineteenth-century country clergyman, found sermon preparation a particular trial. He usually left it to the last possible moment, and would sometimes fail to produce one at all, in which case he would preach an old sermon of his father's. On Sunday 1 July 1838 he recorded:

This morning woke [at] 5 – still time to write sermon, but sl[eep] to 8 – and preach 2 old sermons, with great dissatisfaction.[89]

Matters were no better on the following Sunday, when having again failed to prepare his own, he preached a sermon of Newman's.[90] Sometimes he would rouse himself to write half a sermon only, and would be forced to preach the remainder extemporaneously, a practice of which, as a High Churchman, he strongly disapproved, and which only served to engender further feelings of guilt and inadequacy.[91]

This evidence of sermon recycling is supported by Françoise Deconinck-Brossard's work on the manuscript sermons of an eighteenth-century Durham and Northumberland cleric John Sharp. Her research suggests that Sharp, who performed his professional duties conscientiously, may not have composed more than fifty sermons in the space of thirteen years, and that he used this basic stock repeatedly for a further thirty-one years.[92] To some extent, of course, attitudes to preaching were influenced by considerations of churchmanship. The Evangelical John Rashdall naturally favoured spontaneity above repetition. Four months after his ordination, in January 1834, he abandoned his previous custom of writing sermons, and preached extemporaneously for the first time. Clearly exhilarated by the experience, he scribbled breathlessly in his diary: 'It flings you into your subject so naturally that you only use natural language, and it gives full scope to the excitement and energy of the moment.'[93] Rashdall continued with extempore preaching in his own parish of Orby in Lincolnshire, where he was a curate in sole charge, but he still tended to write the sermons that he

[88] J. Robinson, *The Clergyman's Assistant in the Discharge of Parochial Duties, Especially those of a Private Nature* (London, 1805) p. 17.
[89] LAO MASS8/1, 1 July 1838.
[90] Ibid., 8 July 1838.
[91] Ibid., 12 April 1840 and 13 September 1840.
[92] Deconinck-Brossard, 'Eighteenth-century sermons' pp. 111–12.
[93] Bodl MS Eng. misc. e. 351, 19 January 1834.

preached elsewhere. By June he had further perfected his preaching technique: 'Preached from 10 Rom 20v. with the greatest facility I have yet experienced: 1 hour long and quite extemporary.'[94]

Rashdall's accounts of leading worship in a small rural community provide an interesting commentary on Sunday worship from the clerical point of view. A few days after his ordination, he described in his dairy his first experience of taking a service, which was evening prayer. He seemed little concerned at having transposed various parts of the order of service:

On beginning to read the first discovery I made was that I had a much louder voice than I had calculated upon: and I read much better than I had expected, and during the whole service I stammered only at one word ... my only mistake was in reading the Magnificat before the Psalms, instead of after the First Lesson: an error of no consequence and I should think scarcely perceived. My sermon was fair enough, though I should not expect it would have much effect: I preached with some energy of voice, but little of body. A village preacher ought to have both. Thus ended my first 'duty'.[95]

Rashdall appears to have been the first clergyman to take an interest in the parish of Orby for some years. No doubt sensing this, the congregation – which he described as 'large and attentive' – appeared to increase week by week. After only a month in the parish, Rashdall was preaching to 'a full congregation'. He decided to introduce hymn singing, 'as more simple, and liked by the poor'.[96] Dissent was strong in Orby, and Rashdall's policy towards it was conciliatory. On arrival, he reported that the parish was divided between

Dissenters and no worship-at-all people: this is a bad ground for a Clergyman. However in the absence of a good Parson: a chapel is a good substitute: and perhaps a Wesleyan chapel the best ... I do not think it advisable to oppose their school: but patronize it. I may then draw it to the Church: if I contemplated a long stay then I might pursue a different course ... Nothing effectual can be done I am convinced without a resident evangelical Vicar.[97]

For reasons that he never states explicitly in his diary, Rashdall only held single duty at Orby. He seems to have considered himself better employed conducting services in other places, and would ride off to preach at the surrounding parishes of Gunby, Candlesby, Bratoft, Spilsby, Scremby, Wainfleet, Halton Holgate, Irby and West Keal.

---

94   Ibid., 22 June 1834.
95   Ibid., 30 September 1833.
96   Ibid., 20 October 1833.
97   Ibid., 6 October 1833.

This apparent espousal of itinerancy is a reflection of the shortage of clergy in Lincolnshire available to perform even single duty in many tiny parishes. If a second service was not available, Rashdall thought it 'most desirable' that his parishioners should attend the Methodist chapel.[98] He was a clergyman prepared to sanction and give encouragement to the movement of his parishioners between church and chapel.

THE RITES OF PASSAGE

The Church of England's greatest parochial achievement was perhaps the unrivalled popularity of its occasional offices. Far more people came to church for these than attended Sunday worship, and many who attended for baptism, churching, confirmation, marriage, or burial probably had no other formal links with Anglicanism. Cox uncovered 'evidence of a general addiction to Anglican rites of passage'[99] in Lambeth from 1870 to 1930. Obelkevich concluded that where 'the Church was unrivalled was in its public rites and ceremonies, above all those which marked the principal stages of the life cycle ... Pagan superstition embellished these rites (not necessarily changing their specific Christian meaning) without challenging them.'[100] It was in its role as provider of these rites of passage that the Church was able to impinge to some extent on the lives of the hundreds of thousands of people who would not have considered regular Sunday church-going.

For the majority seeking baptism for their babies, clerical arguments concerning the reality or otherwise of baptismal regeneration – a debate that raged in the middle of the century in the wake of the Gorham Judgment – were entirely irrelevant. For most parents it was a question of giving the child a name and thus an identity in the local community, and more importantly, in heaven; for if the baptised child should die, it could at least be certain of a Christian burial. Baptism served to make the distinction between a baby and an animal, as seen in the example cited in the previous chapter concerning fears for unbaptised children who might be buried in the ground 'like dogs'.[101] The parents' priority was to secure baptism as quickly and with as little

[98] Ibid., 7 October 1833.
[99] Cox, *English Churches in a Secular Society* p. 104.
[100] Obelkevich, *Religion and Rural Society* pp. 304–5.
[101] See also David M. Thompson, 'Baptism, church and society in Britain since 1800' (unpublished Cambridge University Hulsean Lectures, 1983–4) chapter 3.

fuss as possible. For this reason the clerical demand for the appointment of sponsors, or godparents, was particularly irksome. The role of godparents – 'gossips', as they were still known in Lincolnshire[102] – appears to have been relatively ill-defined. The dense and lengthy tracts that SPCK lobbed in the direction of prospective godparents seem to have fallen on largely stony ground. Except, presumably, among the more religious, there does not seem to have been much sense of a spiritual dimension to the godparents' role. It was understood that the child's religious education would be left to parents, teachers and clergy, rather than to godparents. Working people were reluctant to stand as sponsors without some kind of compensation; parents complained that the godparents expected a treat afterwards, or at least some tea.[103]

The necessity for treating sponsors was an often cited reason for preferring that baptism should be privately administered in the home or the parsonage. For most parents, of whatever social standing, the ideal arrangement was for the clergyman to call on them, and the provision in the Prayer Book of a special form appeared to lend an official sanction to this practice, although the rubric warned that it should only be used if there was 'great cause and necessity'. At parish level the debates concerning baptism were centred on the conflict created by the clergy's attempts to introduce public baptism in the face of lay opposition. The insistence on public baptism with sponsors, incorporated into the Sunday service, came from the bishops,[104] and though it was shared by many of the clergy, support for it was not universal.

One of the critics of this policy was George Wilkins, archdeacon of Nottingham and vicar of St Mary's, Nottingham, who in common with some other Nottinghamshire clergy used a shorter, unauthorised form of baptism, the so-called 'naming' ceremony. This involved the babies being brought to the vestry by their parents or nurses, and then 'named' by the sprinkling of water, the use of the baptismal formula and the inclusion of one or two prayers. The child was then registered as the son or daughter of the person whom the bearer stated, and a certificate was issued and paid for.[105] Wilkins defended the practice of

[102] Obelkevich, *Religion and Rural Society* p. 128.
[103] LAO CorB5/4/11, C. S. Bird to Kaye, n.d. (1843); CorB5/4/10/1, White to Kaye, 8 January 1834; CorB5/4/70/1, Winston to Kaye, 31 July 1850; Obelkevich, *Religion and Rural Society* p. 128.
[104] Peter J. Jagger, *Clouded Witness: Initiation in the Church of England in the Mid-Victorian Period, 1850–1875* (Allison Park, Pennsylvania, 1982) pp. 88–90.
[105] LAO CorB5/8/7/6, W. Butler to Kaye, 12 August 1840; CorB5/8A/1, G. Atkinson to Kaye, January 1842.

'naming', claiming that at Nottingham the implementation of the Civil Registration Act in 1837 had already caused an enormous reduction in the number of children being brought for baptism, and if sponsors were always demanded there would soon be no baptism at all:

Out of the 1500 in the year which we have thus named upon an average before the passing of the Registration Acts, not a fifth of them were the children of Church Members. Since the passing of these Acts, not 500 are now brought – but were we to insist upon sponsors we would reduce that number below 50 or 20 and why? The poor people say – "Sir, we can get no sponsors unless we give them a treat, or give them money" – And I may fairly say of all those who have brought sponsors during my 25 year incumbency, that not 100 of them have known what answers to make, or when to look at the books, if they make the response at all, neither consider the sense nor the responsibility, nor ever discharge the duty promised in any way.[106]

The willingness of some clergy to 'name' children rather than baptise them served to reinforce the parental sense that the rite was primarily concerned with conferring identity. In the first half of the nineteenth century there was confusion concerning the significance of naming and baptism. Wilkins, and the other clergy who named children, would presumably have been willing to bury them in the event of death. Other clergy could be less accommodating. Edward Moore of Weston, South Lincolnshire, refused burial to a baby whose mother claimed that 'it had not been baptized, but it had been named' by a Wesleyan minister.[107] Moore's objection seems to have been to what he regarded as the inadequacy of the abbreviated rite, rather than to its having been administered by a Methodist, for most clergy accepted lay baptism as valid. Moore instructed the mother to follow the procession of another funeral that would pass her cottage, and to enter the church with the other mourners to hear part of the service:

She did not appear to me to expect that I should read the service over her child, at all events, she did not evince the least surprise ... There could be no excuse for the child not being properly baptized it was a month old and if it had been sick it is well known that I am ready to baptize privately, and during the time it was alive I must have passed the front of the cottage within easy call on an average twice almost every day.[108]

This is an example of a woman with clear Methodist sympathies, who appeared to value Anglican burial, but not Anglican baptism. Perhaps

[106] LAO CorB5/8/36, Wilkins to Kaye, n.d. (1842).
[107] LAO CorB5/4/67/7, Moore to Kaye, 9 November 1849.
[108] Ibid.

the child's untimely death had shaken her confidence in non-Anglican ceremonies.

In the second half of the century the clerical campaign for public baptism on Sunday became increasingly successful, as an examination of baptismal registers and visitation returns reveals.[109] But predictably, change was not universally popular, and many church-goers must have resented the extended length of afternoon services when baptisms were incorporated. Neither was it always very practical, as in the parish of Whaplode in South Lincolnshire, which was twelve miles long, and where parents were forced to postpone baptism for months on end if bad weather prevented them from getting to church on the one Sunday in the month that the vicar had designated for baptisms.[110] In other parts of Lincolnshire there were reports of lay dissatisfaction from Donington and Kettlethorpe.[111] At South Willingham the incumbent reported in his visitation return for 1873 that 'farmers and others have come to my church *because* Baptism has been administered during service at their own'.[112] Despite the clergy's efforts to transform it into a congregational event, signifying the entrance of a new member into the Church, baptism tended to remain an occasion of greatest significance to the family concerned, 'a convenient ceremony, by which people bestow a name upon their children',[113] or 'a family festival with very few religious associations indeed'.[114] The task of obtaining god-parents hardly became easier. In 1873 the incumbent of Great Stukeley, Huntingdonshire, considered 'that among the poor the profession of sponsorial obligations at baptism is greatly looked on as a *sham*'.[115] At Odell, Bedfordshire, in the same year, the clergyman complained of '*Immense* difficulty in getting sponsors for *children*. The *Fathers* even of the children will not *stand* for them.'[116]

Closely linked with the new emphasis on public baptism was a similar emphasis on public churching, or the 'thanksgiving of women after childbirth', as the Prayer Book called it. The evidence suggests that churching was extremely popular among women of all social groups, although the requirement of public churching caused dissatis-

---

[109] Obelkevich, *Religion and Rural Society* p. 129.
[110] LAO CorB5/4/54/1, T. Tunstall Smith to Kaye, 17 January 1845.
[111] Obelkevich, *Religion and Rural Society* p. 129.
[112] Ibid.
[113] Jagger, *Clouded Witness* p. 80.
[114] John Jackson, *Charge Delivered to the Clergy of the Diocese of Lincoln 1855*, p. 24.
[115] CUL EDR C3/25.
[116] Ibid.

faction among the middle and upper classes. The motives for churching
were predictably mixed, ranging from a pious desire to give thanks for
having survived the dangers of childbirth, to social pressure from
family and friends, and to a general sense of its being a good omen for
the future. Churching was thought to remove the 'uncleanness'
considered to taint women after childbirth, and many believed that any
contact with an unchurched woman would bring bad luck. The
bringing of luck has been identified by Cox as an important element in
rites of passage; baptism was lucky for a child, a church wedding was
lucky for the couple and churching was lucky for the mother.[117] Some
people believed that in the short term, the churching ceremony could
prevent another conception, and that it would ensure that the woman
did not have another child for at least a year.[118] In Lambeth in inner
London the emphasis was rather different; it was thought that
churching would prevent a future miscarriage.[119]

The Prayer Book rubric gave no indication that the thanksgiving
ought to take place in front of a congregation, yet the clergy began to
insist that it should. At Elston in Nottinghamshire in 1850 H. R.
Harrison refused to church women at any other time but immediately
before the general thanksgiving in the Sunday afternoon service, at the
time when babies were brought for baptism. He would make no
exceptions, not even for the wife of the patron of the living, who wished
to avoid the 'novelty and publicity' to which she would be exposed by
sitting in the accustomed churching place in the nave during the
Sunday service. The patron was so enraged at the vicar's attitude, and
by his refusal to give his wife communion at the time of the churching
as she requested, that he threatened to take her elsewhere to be
churched on a weekday.[120] Perhaps if it had been demanded in 1800, a
patron's wife would have been content to sit in the front pew and be
churched in full gaze of her social inferiors. But as the century
progressed Victorian ladies (and their husbands) began to regard the
clerical demand for the public performance of the rite as undignified
and indelicate. For some clergy, however, insisting on the public
performance of the ceremony became something of a personal crusade.
J. F. Ogle, who served as a curate in five parishes over thirty years,
regarded his record for persuading the nobility to accept the public

[117] Cox, *English Churches in a Secular Society* p. 97.
[118] Obelkevich, *Religion and Rural Society* p. 273.
[119] Cox, *English Churches in a Secular Society* p. 99.
[120] LAO CorB5/8A/3, Elston papers, June 1850.

offices of thanksgiving after childbirth and baptism as his greatest achievement, though he had had to 'remonstrate' with the Mexborough family to persuade Lady Pollington to be publicly churched. Presumably worn down by a variety of pressures, she eventually consented to it on eight occasions whilst he was curate of Methley in Yorkshire.[121]

Among working-class mothers the desire to be churched at all costs seems to have remained undiminished. Sensing perhaps that this was an opportunity to punish those whom they regarded as deviant, the clergy's discussions of the topic seem to have centred on the categories of women to be excluded. Rather than remaining a purely religious rite, the withholding of churching became a means of registering social disapproval, and in a manner more frequently resorted to than the associated practices of excluding notorious evil-doers from the Eucharist and the graveyard. The incumbent of Elston not only refused a private churching to his patron's wife; he also withheld the service from a woman at the other end of the social scale who had had a civil marriage and was a leading Primitive Methodist.[122] At Bawtry in Nottinghamshire the clergyman refused the ceremony to a woman who had contravened the deceased wife's sister Act by marrying her brother-in-law.[123] At Padbury in Buckinghamshire churching was refused to a woman who had married her nephew at Northampton registry office.[124] The mothers of illegitimate babies were often also excluded. At the Eton Union Workhouse the Board of Guardians met to discuss the question in 1837. Lord Sidney Godolphin Osborne, rector of Stoke Poges, favoured permitting all the inmates – married or not – who gave birth in the workhouse to be churched in the workhouse chapel. His recommendation took his fellow clergy on the Board by surprise, though his reasoning was straightforward:

The Unfortunate Woman has had to encounter the same Pain and Peril as the rest of her sex under the same circumstances, and she rises from her bed with far more reason to be thankful 'for the safe Deliverance' from the great danger of her Trial, than one for whom death might have been but a change for a better world ...[125]

[121] LAO CorB5/4/73/10, Ogle to Kaye, 27 February 1834.
[122] LAO CorB5/8/28/10, Harrison to Kaye, 6 November 1844.
[123] LAO CorB5/8/31/1, Stockdale to Kaye, 15 October 1842.
[124] LAO CorB5/3/25/4, Eyre to Kaye, 21 July 1845.
[125] LAO CorB5/3/34/11, Godolphin Osborne to Kaye, 2 May 1837.

This reinterpretation of churching as a thanksgiving for deliverance from eternal damnation, rather than for deliverance from the dangers of childbirth, is an intriguing one, and serves to underline the extent to which thoughts of heaven and hell were never far from the minds of nineteenth-century clergy.

Confirmation was another rite of passage with a very broad appeal. It usually took place between the ages of fourteen and nineteen, marked the end of catechism classes and, for those whose religious lives were not circumscribed by their employers, the beginning of choice in religious matters. For some, it was a stage in the process of entry into adulthood. Confirmations were accompanied by treats and festivities, which were very often organised by the clergy – perhaps in an attempt to increase the number of candidates, or perhaps to give young people some harmless enjoyment and divert them from the less edifying activities with which big confirmations were sometimes associated. After the confirmation in Alford in Lincolnshire in 1837, it was reported that many of the young people went straight from the church to the public houses, where the attractions included 'lewd women' and dancing as well as drink. In an attempt to restore order, the clergy were obliged to call in the assistance of constables.[126] There were similar scenes at Lincoln and Louth three years later, where the rural youths of both sexes streamed into the public houses in the town, and then rioted.[127] As they moved between parishes in search of work, it is likely that some were confirmed more than once in order to make the most of the feasting; the tract writers' warnings against repeating confirmation went unheeded.[128] Whatever the ambiguities surrounding the nature of its religious meaning, confirmation was seen as a life-enhancing experience; the bishop's touch could only do one good. In Lincolnshire it was widely believed that confirmation was a cure for rheumatism.[129]

The appeal that confirmation held for Nonconformists was discussed in the previous chapter. Others may have been confirmed without regarding themselves as Christians at all. In 1840, the year of the disturbances at Lincoln and Louth, a total of 10,238 people were confirmed in Lincolnshire. In the smaller county of Buckinghamshire

[126] Obelkevich, *Religion and Rural Society* p. 131.
[127] Ibid.
[128] For example, *The Order of Confirmation: With Instructions for them that Come to be Confirmed and Prayers to be used Before and After Confirmation* (anon.; London: SPCK, 1800) p. 13.
[129] Obelkevich, *Religion and Rural Society* p. 273.

the figure was 4,697 in 1844, and in Nottinghamshire, which was more industrialised, the figure was 3,318 in 1839.[130] At Whaplode in Lincolnshire, an average of thirty people were confirmed at every service held between 1828 and 1846, out of a total population of 2,000.[131] Francis Massingberd managed to field forty-nine candidates out of a population of 400 for the confirmation in 1840.[132] The confirmation figures for 165 parishes in Buckinghamshire, together with the total population, have been preserved for 1838. They reveal an astonishingly high level of participation in confirmation services. In five parishes, Lillington Dayrell, Akeley, Gayhurst, Broughton and Cholesbury, between 11 and 12 per cent of the inhabitants were confirmed in 1838. More typical, however, was a figure of between 1 and 7 per cent of each parish; this occurred in 123 of the 165 parishes surveyed. The smaller the parish, the proportionately greater was the number of the confirmation candidates: a staggering 50 per cent of the inhabitants of Pitchcott were confirmed in 1838, which amounted to fourteen in a population of twenty-eight. At Horsenden it was 35 per cent, or thirteen out of thirty-seven. The picture was predictably different in the larger towns. At Aylesbury, the percentage confirmed was 0.5 per cent, or twenty-five out of 4,907; at Buckingham it was 2 per cent, or sixty-eight out of 3,610; at Great Marlow it was 0.6 per cent, or twenty-seven out of 4,237; at Newport Pagnell it was 1 per cent, or forty-seven out of 3,385. Amersham was the parish producing the largest number of candidates, with 126 out of 2,816, or 4 per cent of the town. Typical of medium-sized villages were Weston Turville, with thirty-nine out of 637, or 6 per cent; Stoke Goldington, with sixty-one out of 912, or 7 per cent; and Milton Keynes, with thirty out of 334, or 9 per cent.[133] It is intriguing that in Buckinghamshire – a county where the population increased by half between 1801 and 1831, and which was recovering from the double blow of the collapse of its lace industry and agricultural depression[134] – such huge numbers were prepared to trek some miles in order to be touched by a bishop. A church that was capable of attracting this number of confirmation candidates was evidently capable of maintaining a wide spectrum of support.

Confirmation declined in popularity in the second half of the

[130] LAO CorB5/9/1–14, Confirmation papers.
[131] LAO PAR1/6. The figures were recorded in the front of the baptism register.
[132] L.AO MASS8/1, 23 August 1840.
[133] LAO CorB5/9/1–14, Confirmation papers.
[134] Richard W. Davis, *Political Change and Continuity 1760–1885: A Buckinghamshire Study* (Newton Abbot: David & Charles, 1972) pp. 16–17, 20.

century, but in the absence of detailed statistical evidence, it is difficult to be certain about when the change came. The attempts of bishops and clergy to invest the occasion with greater decorum had the effect of deterring those who were only there for the beer and the 'lewd women'. When the incumbent of Sixhills and South Willingham in Lincolnshire announced that there would be no feast or reward after the ceremony, none of the villagers in either parish came forward to be confirmed.[135] It was clear that smaller confirmations would be more orderly, even if they had the effect of reducing the numbers with whom the Church made contact. In 1829 Kaye had confirmed 1,090 candidates at once in Bedford, but by 1838 he had been able to reduce the numbers at each service to between 200 and 300.[136] He insisted that confirmations be held in local churches no more than seven or eight miles apart, and that churchwardens provide wagons for the transportation of the candidates.[137] In 1855 Bishop Jackson raised the minimum age for confirmation in the Lincoln diocese from fourteen to fifteen. Under the watchful eye of clergy and churchwardens, and within a few miles of their own village, only the most delinquent were likely to misbehave. Bishops regarded reform of the confirmation service as a key to improving the tone of religious life. Walter Kerr Hamilton, bishop of Salisbury from 1854 to 1869, frequently made notes in his diary concerning the tone of the services he conducted and the demeanour of the candidates, and was particularly disapproving when the candidates failed to kneel, or mumbled the responses. Aware presumably both of social tensions and the dangers of boisterousness, he was willing to hold private confirmations for the children of the upper classes. On 2 November 1856 he held a confirmation at Osmington in Dorset, which accorded well with his High Church principles:

All very nice. Chancel much improved and encaustic tiles and new altar carpet. The confirmation very well ordered. We had the Morning Prayer and Communion S[ervice]. Then 1st charge [Hamilton was combining the confirmation with a visitation, a practice which was becoming less common at this date] – then the Confirmation Service – the Veni Creator was sung just before the candidates came to be confirmed. The candidates kneeling – the amens chanted after each candidates confirmation.[138]

[135] Obelkevich, *Religion and Rural Society* p. 134.
[136] Ibid.
[137] *Gentleman's Magazine*, April 1853.
[138] PH HAM/2/1/1, 2 November 1856.

Hamilton's practice of holding a communion immediately before the confirmation appears to have been an unusual one, and it would be interesting to know whether the confirmation candidates communicated at the service. Generally, people made little connection between confirmation and participation in the Eucharist. As was argued earlier, there was a tendency to regard the Eucharist as appropriate only for those who were far advanced in spiritual things, or who were near to death and therefore unlikely to fall into post-communion sin. The discrepancy between the numbers being confirmed and the numbers participating in the sacrament make it clear that many who were confirmed never communicated at all. Alternatively, they may have seen it as a once-only experience, not to be repeated. Six girls made their first communion at South Ormsby in 1857, but none went back a second time.[139] Pondering lay attitudes to confirmation in his *Charge* of 1855, Bishop Jackson concluded that too much emphasis had been put on knowledge as a prerequisite for admission, and too little on sincerity.[140] He may well have been getting to the root of the matter, for there seems to have been a tendency among catechists to treat confirmation as an examination for which the syllabus was an accurate learning of the catechism, and the service itself as a type of graduation ceremony. After about 1850 the clergy were more likely to urge communion on their confirmation candidates, but this was not universal. In 1851 W. V. Butler permitted only between 40 and 50 out of 158 confirmation candidates to proceed to communion. Others were selected for a further course of instruction.

There may also have been a significant divergence in the subsequent religious practice of men and women, though the evidence here is rather fragmentary. Of thirteen male confirmation candidates in Panton in Lincolnshire in 1854 and 1857, only four subsequently communicated; but of seventeen female candidates, thirteen became communicants. It was probably not unusual for female candidates to outnumber males, and for the male candidates to be younger. St Mary's, Ely sent seventeen girls and six boys in 1825; the female candidates ranged in age from fourteen to twenty-five, the male candidates from fifteen to seventeen.[141] In 1868 and 1869 Bishop Browne held confirmations in the archdeaconries of Ely, Huntingdon and Sudbury. A total of 9,157 were confirmed, of whom 4,193 were

[139] Obelkevich, *Religion and Rural Society* pp. 134–5.
[140] Jackson, *Charge* (1855), p. 26.
[141] CUL EDR C1/6, 1825.

male and 4,964 were female. Obelkevich estimated that about four
boys were confirmed for every five girls in South Lindsey.[142] The
Buckinghamshire confirmation papers provide further evidence for
female candidates in their early twenties.[143] It would be interesting to
know whether these women were seeking repeat confirmations, or
whether they had missed out when younger. Equally, young men
might be hindered from confirmation by the demands of work, as well
as by a feeling that after a certain age they had outgrown it. Bishop
Hamilton noted that at Weymouth most of the male confirmation
candidates had gone to sea.[144] The clergyman at Stoke Golding,
Buckinghamshire, reported: 'Eight more Males commenced cate-
chizing and five more females, but their Guardians would not spare
them about six hours to walk on to Hinckley and back with me and the
warden to be confirmed.'[145]

Admission to the service required a certain amount of religious
knowledge, which was crystallised in the Prayer Book catechism.
Memorising the catechism accurately was a considerable task, even for
a child with a retentive memory who was used to rote learning. Aware
of this difficulty, catechists made use of a variety of teaching materials
that were published in large quantities by Rivingtons, the National
Society and SPCK. The Sunday school mistress of West Wratting in
Cambridgeshire used the *Church Catechism Broke into Short Questions* and
Sarah Trimmer's 'Lectures on the catechism' from her book *The
Teacher's Assistant*.[146] 'Broken catechisms' were also used at St Mary's,
Ely, and SPCK tracts at nearby Stretham.[147] The purpose of these
works was to facilitate the learning of the Prayer Book catechism by
explaining it clause by clause; there was no departure from the Prayer
Book theology. Mrs Trimmer advised that in order to understand the
catechism perfectly, children should first be taught to repeat the words
distinctly, and to make the stops in the proper places. Only once they
had mastered this was its meaning to be explained to them.[148]

The Prayer Book catechism began with the question 'What is your
name?' and continued with 'Who gave you this name?', to which the

---

[142] Obelkevich, *Religion and Rural Society* pp. 132–3.
[143] LAO CorB5/9/9, Confirmation papers.
[144] PH Ham/2/1/1, 11 November 1856.
[145] Ibid.
[146] CUL EDR C1/6, 1825.
[147] Ibid.
[148] Sarah Trimmer, *The Teacher's Assistant: Consisting of Lectures in the Catechetical Form, Being Part of a Plan for Appropriate Instruction for the Children of the Poor* (London: Rivington, 1808) p. 10.

answer was 'My godfathers and godmothers in my baptism; wherein I was made a member of Christ, the child of God, and an inheritor of the kingdom of heaven.' It required the child to recite the Apostles' creed, the ten commandments, and the Lord's prayer, and to draw out certain morals from these, reinterpreting the texts in ways that made them more readily understood. From the Apostles' creed, the child was to affirm belief in the Trinity. From the ten commandments, he or she was expected to commit to heart two paragraphs describing duty towards God and neighbour. Similarly, the Lord's Prayer was used to teach a lesson about dependence on God. The catechism concluded with a lengthy sequence of questions and answers about the two Anglican sacraments of baptism and the supper of the Lord, and the significance that was to be attached to their outward and inward forms. Catechising was a means by which clergy and teachers attempted to inculcate, principally to children and youths, the central tenets not simply of Christianity, but more particularly of Anglicanism. Jeremy Gregory has drawn attention to the extent to which catechising remained a priority in the diocese of Canterbury in the eighteenth century, as the clergy attempted to save their flocks from being seduced by rival creeds.[149] In 1806 Gregory found, most parishes in the diocese still had some kind of catechising.[150] The evidence suggests that during the nineteenth century the majority of clergy made provision for teaching the catechism, although some were handing the task over to teachers in Sunday or National schools. The incumbent of Arrington in Cambridgeshire reported that when he had arrived in the parish in 1806, only two of the poorer children could say their catechism – 'lately with the assistance of the parishioners, who bear half the expense', he had instituted a Sunday school to remedy the situation.[151] By 1865 the Sunday school had disappeared, and the parish clerk had taken over the task of catechising the children.[152]

There is perhaps a distinction to be drawn in some parishes between the on-going catechetical instruction that might be given on a weekly basis – whether in church or in school, or at certain seasons, for example Lent – and the catechising that was intended as an explicit

[149] Jeremy Gregory, 'The eighteenth-century Reformation: the pastoral task of Anglican clergy after 1689' in John Walsh, Colin Haydon and Stephen Taylor, (eds.), *The Church of England c. 1689–c. 1833: From Toleration to Tractarianism* (Cambridge: Cambridge University Press, 1993) pp. 70–3.
[150] Ibid. p. 71.
[151] CUL EDR C1/4, 1807.
[152] CUL EDR C1/12, 1865.

preparation for confirmation. In 1825 the minister at St Clement's, Cambridge, appeared to draw a distinction between catechising and confirmation preparation, reporting that 'From the number of schools now in Cambridge where all are or may be taught it, it is not deemed necessary to catechise children as formerly. They are regularly examined and prepared for confirmation.'[153] The remark is ambiguous, but it could be understood to imply that although the task of teaching the catechism had been handed over to the schools, the clergy ran confirmation classes. The extent to which confirmation classes provided the opportunity for some to stray from the well-trodden ground of the catechism into more speculative or controversial areas is difficult to gauge, and the surviving evidence refers to only the occasional incident. In 1835 John Gould, the rector of Beaconsfield in Buckinghamshire, created a sensation when he questioned a girl in his confirmation class 'on the subject of circumcision, not with respect to its doctrine, but the manner of performing the operation'.[154] The inquiries of other clergy were inspired by the desire to find out about sincerity of motive, in a manner that might have been endorsed by Bishop Jackson. At Lutterworth in Leicestershire the curate J. H. Gurney refused to permit a seventeen-year-old candidate, the granddaughter of a clergyman, to proceed to confirmation because she would not admit to being 'a very great sinner' and was 'quite unconscious of ever having broken the divine law'.[155] Further investigation revealed that Gurney had rejected a number of the confirmation candidates who had applied in previous years,[156] on the grounds that they were ignorant, knew nothing of salvation, never prayed and did not know what confirmation meant.[157] The candidates did not reapply. There remained a general sense that admission to confirmation should be governed by knowledge and not intention.

The passing of Lord Hardwicke's Marriage Act in 1753 meant that for most couples – Jews and Quakers excepted – the parish church became the place where marriage was solemnised, irrespective of religious beliefs. Few seem to have taken the Catholic view of regarding marriage as a sacrament; for most it was essentially a civil rite performed within the church walls. There remained the vestiges of a

[153] CUL EDR C1/6, 1825.
[154] LAO CorB5/3/10/3, J. Du Pre to Kaye, 21 May 1835.
[155] LAO CorB5/5/9/1, W. Jones to Kaye, 25 August 1832; J. H. Gurney to Kaye, 4 September 1832.
[156] Ibid., R. W. Fox to Kaye, 25 August 1832.
[157] Ibid. J. H. Gurney to Kaye, 4 September 1832.

religious attitude in the general disapproval of weddings in Lent, but the legal framework surrounding the marriage ceremony meant that this feeling went little further. During the 1830s the marriage law was altered in two important statutes. The first was Lord Lyndhurst's Marriage Act of 1835, which prohibited marriage between a man and his deceased wife's sister. The second was the introduction of civil marriage in 1837, which provided a real alternative to the ceremony of the Anglican church.

There had been a long tradition of marrying the younger sister of one's deceased wife. The high rates of death in childbirth left many widowers with small children, and it was common for an unmarried sister of the deceased wife to move in and take charge of the home. In such cases, marriage was considered by some as the natural outcome.[158] The Church of England was less comfortable with the custom, arguing that biblical support could not be established, and that if the couple had really become 'one flesh' in the first marriage, the second marriage would be incestuous, as if a man were to marry his own sister. Nevertheless, objections had to be muted; Henry VIII's first wife had previously been his deceased brother's wife, and though this was the reverse of the usual case, the degree of proximity was the same.[159] Lyndhurst's Act was largely ignored or evaded by men who wished to marry their sisters-in-law. Bad feeling about the legislation was heightened because marriages that had taken place before 1835 continued to be perfectly legal, and to those who faced public obloquy for contracting such marriages shortly thereafter, the situation seemed iniquitous. In 1848 a royal commission reported in favour of repealing Lyndhurst's Act, on the grounds that a survey had revealed that 1,364 marriages within the prohibited degrees had taken place since 1835, of which 'upwards of nine-tenths' had involved a deceased wife's sister. Only eighty-eight couples were said to have been deterred from marriage by the legislation, and thirty-two couples were thought to be living in open cohabitation.[160]

The clerical response to deceased-wife's-sister marriages was hostility tempered with a sense of hopelessness at the perceived immorality of the lower orders. At Ravenstone in Buckinghamshire the vicar complained

---

[158] Stephen Parker, *Informal Marriage, Cohabitation and the Law, 1750–1989* (Basingstoke: Macmillan, 1990) pp. 79–87.

[159] Ibid., p. 80; see also Sybil Wolfram, *In-laws and Outlaws: Kinship and Marriage in England* (London and Sydney: Croom Helm, 1987) pp. 30–40.

[160] Wolfram, *In-laws and Outlaws* p. 31.

that if he refused a couple's request, they would simply resort to the superintendent registrar's office, or live together without any ceremony.[161] In the face of couples who ignored the law (it was evidently fairly easy to do, particularly for those prepared to travel to Scotland where a different law prevailed) ostracism seems to have been a result. R. N. Russell of Beachampton in Buckinghamshire was pleased to report that a young woman in his parish was now said to be seriously depressed:

I deemed it my duty to treat the parties in question in a different way after this marriage from that which I manifested before. My conduct towards them has caused them much pain, the more so in all probability from others making it a guide for themselves.[162]

Lord Lyndhurst's Marriage Act remained on the statute book until 1907. Clerical opposition to its repeal was fierce; the deceased-wife's-sister question was one of the most vociferous, though now largely forgotten, of the clerical pamphlet controversies of the nineteenth century.

The Civil Marriage Act was partly intended to give a greater degree of choice, but it could also be used as a means of coercion. Couples retained the option of continuing as before, and marrying in the Church of England with banns or licence. They were free also to marry in the Church of England on the production of a superintendent registrar's certificate, or in a registered building such as a Nonconformist chapel, with or without a civil licence – depending on the fee paid, their residential status and the period of notice given – or in a registry office, with or without a civil licence.[163] The Civil Registration Acts were also part of the movement towards state-administered, non-parochial institutions, a product of the same Benthamite utilitarianism that had created the Poor Law Amendment Act in 1834. Indeed, the structures that the Poor Law had put in place were adopted for the Civil Registration Acts, and it was from the ranks of the poor law guardians that the first generation of registrars of births, deaths and marriages was drawn. This had the effect of permitting the poor law guardians to insist upon marriage as a condition of poor relief; when George Stiffell proved reluctant to marry the pregnant Ellen Barrett, the guardians rejected his protestations and offered to pay for a ring.[164]

Civil marriage made a greater impact in the town than the countryside. Just as the introduction of the civil registration of births had been

[161]   LAO CorB5/3/2/3, W. Godfrey to Kaye, n.d.
[162]   LAO CorB5/3/10/2, R. N. Russell to Kaye, 3 April 1844.
[163]   Parker, *Informal Marriage* pp. 72–3.
[164]   Ibid., pp. 55, 73.

strongly felt by the clergy in the city of Nottingham, so too was the advent of civil marriage. The situation was exacerbated because St Mary's, the ancient city-centre church, was closed during 1843 and 1844 as a result of the church rates dispute described earlier. In consequence, many of the marriages that would have been celebrated at St Mary's were conducted by the superintendent registrars.[165] A clergyman from the Nottingham parish of St Paul's reported in 1839 that the practice of substituting a registrar's certificate for the publication of banns was becoming increasingly common in the city, 'among those who are not yet abandoned enough to be content without the service of our Church'.[166] In an attempt to stamp out this practice, St Paul's injected a note of free marketeering into its relationship with the registrars.[167] Couples who wished to be married after banns were charged four shillings, whilst those who wished to be married on the strength of a registrar's certificate had to pay seven shillings. Even when the cost of publication of banns was included, it was still cheaper to use the church than the registry office.[168]

A continuing problem for clergy in cities like Nottingham, but almost unknown in the country, was that of ensuring that the couples they married were genuine parishioners, did not fall within the prohibited degrees, or were not otherwise ineligible. George Wilkins, archdeacon of Nottingham and vicar of St Mary's, employed the sexton at sixpence a time to check the place of residence of every party making a banns application.[169] Samuel Creswell, the popular administrator of the gardens scheme in the neighbouring parish of Radford, was not so careful. In 1845 his relaxed attitude led to Radford being described by the irate archdeacon as the Gretna Green of Nottinghamshire.[170] As far as establishing the identity and status of the people who applied for marriage, amongst a population of which 'three or four thousand are lodgers or rather wanderers to and from

---

[165] LAO CorB5/8/18, G. Wilkins to Kaye, 11 February 1843. For a fascinating account of civil marriage, see Olive Anderson, 'The incidence of civil marriage in England and Wales' *Past and Present*, 69 (1975) pp. 50–87.

[166] LAO CorB5/8A/16, C. L. W. Armstrong to Kaye, 15 November 1839.

[167] Ibid.

[168] Anderson claims that after 1856, civil marriage was cheaper than a church wedding. The former cost seven shillings, and the latter about twelve shillings; 'The incidence of civil marriage' p. 65.

[169] LAO CorB5/8/20, G. Wilkins to Kaye, 16 January 1845.

[170] There is a touch of irony, conscious or not, in Archdeacon Wilkins' description of Radford. As a curate, he had himself eloped to Gretna with Amelia Auriol Hay, daughter of the incumbent who employed him at Hadleigh in 1811.

Derby, Leicester and other hearts of labour',[171] much information had
to be taken on trust. Another common cause for lament among the
clergy was the conduct of couples at the time of their wedding, largely
it seems because the clergy maintained such different expectations. The
youthful curate John Rashdall officiated at a marriage in Exeter in
November 1835, and commented afterwards in his diary: 'The bride-
groom kissed the bride immediately after the service, for which I
timidly reproved him.'[172]

In the East Midlands, East Anglia and central England there is little
evidence to suggest that the introduction of civil marriage greatly
impinged upon the position of the Anglican clergy as the primary
officiants at weddings.[173] Indeed, there is evidence to suggest that the
innate conservatism of some couples led to their seeking the ministrations of a clergyman even after they had attended the registry office, in
the same manner as some sought to have their babies re-baptised by
the clergy. In 1847 the clergyman at Cowbit remarried a couple who
had already been married by a superintendent registrar. He conducted
the full service as normal, merely omitting the words 'bachelor' and
'spinster' from the banns and the register, and using both the assumed
and maiden names of the bride.[174]

Death and the rituals surrounding burial maintained a central
importance in the nineteenth century. Any shortcomings on the part of
the clergy at the funeral would be noted unfavourably. In 1832, for
example, it was reported that Charles Ash, the curate of Tydd St Mary
in Lincolnshire, had been inaudible and, declining to stand at the
graveside, had sheltered in the porch, though the weather was fine. His
accuser was blunt:

The Poor desire to have the same Service performed as the rich, for though
poor in this world we shall be Rich in another, and, the friends of departed
person feel hurt at anything that may seem slighting to survice which ought to
be performed at that aughfull moment.[175]

To meet the needs of 'that aughfull moment', a significant part of the
publishing industry was devoted to the production of cheap literature

[171] LAO CorB5/8A/16, Armstrong to Kaye, 8 October 1846.
[172] Bodl Ms Eng. Misc. e. 352, 9 November 1835.
[173] Anderson, 'The incidence of civil marriage'. She suggests that significant regional variations
existed, and that civil marriage was most popular in Wales, northern England and the south-
west, where it was appropriated by people who might previously have adopted an informal
approach to the marriage ceremony.
[174] LAO CorB5/4/48/11, W. Hughes to Kaye, 9 July 1847; Kaye to Hughes, 2 August 1847.
[175] LAO CorB5/4/68/3, Robert Burman to Kaye, 8 April 1832.

concerning good deaths. The ideal was to die peacefully and piously in one's own bed, and to be buried in the pleasant surroundings of a country churchyard. Michael Wheeler has drawn attention to the repeated analogies drawn in Victorian death scenes between death and sleep and the bed and the grave, in what was a deliberate blurring of the division between life and death.[176] The theme was echoed in the liturgy of Anglican burial, in which Christ was described as 'the first fruits of them that slept', a passage derived from Paul's letter to the Corinthians.

For many Anglicans the hope of resurrection to which the liturgy testified was shot through with acute anxiety; an anxiety that is also seen in the paradoxical and to some extent simultaneously held beliefs about hell-fire and the recognition of friends in heaven, and in the sharp delineation made between the saved and the damned.[177] For city dwellers the anxiety was not alleviated by the practicalities surrounding burial; Owen Chadwick has provided the classic account of the horror of churchyards in mid-nineteenth-century London, as coffins piled up with no space for burial, and as the bones of the dead were used in the building of new streets.[178] The problem of overcrowded parish grave-yards was not, of course, confined to London. At Radford near Nottingham in 1842 it was reported that 2,292 corpses had been buried in a one-acre plot in the previous twelve years, and that the gruesome sight of broken coffins and skulls could be witnessed daily.[179] Clearly the depiction of a young woman studying the exhumed remains of 'John Faithful' in Henry Bowler's painting *The Doubt: 'Can These Dry Bones Live?'* (1855) was not an over-macabre statement of the case, but rather observed Pre-Raphaelite conventions of realism.

The problem of unwholesome graveyards was brought under control by the Public Health Act of 1848 and the Cemetery Acts of 1852 and 1853. The result was the closure of overcrowded churchyards and the opening of new cemeteries at some distance from the centres of population. In towns, this severed the ancient link between the church-goer and his deceased forebears in the churchyard. In country districts, additional plots of land in reasonably central locations could usually be obtained as they were needed, and the question of overcrowding

---

[176] Michael Wheeler, *Death and the Future Life in Victorian Literature and Theology* (Cambridge: Cambridge University Press, 1990) pp. 33–43.
[177] Ibid., p. 84.
[178] Chadwick, *The Victorian Church*, part I, pp. 326–8.
[179] LAO CorB5/8/32/1, S. Creswell to Kaye, 11 March 1842.

seldom arose. A greater obstacle, in the days before suffragans, could be waiting for a bishop to be in the vicinity to consecrate the land before it was used. The question of a new burial-ground was a potential strain on relations with Nonconformists, particularly if they were asked to contribute to its purchase by means of church rate. In the Lincolnshire town of Gainsborough there was a need for a new cemetery in the mid-1840s. The problem of rate was avoided when 'Mr Hickman and all the gentlemen of the parish' came forward with £300 to purchase a half-acre plot contiguous to the graveyard.[180] C. S. Bird, the mildly Evangelical vicar, resisted attempts to set up a joint cemetery with the Nonconformists, because it would have to have been fenced down the middle, one part episcopally consecrated, the other part left in its natural state. 'I dislike the separation of the Church-people and the dissenters in this way, even after death. A cemetery with a fence down the middle is revealing to all the world our religious divisions and perpetuating them.'[181]

Burial was the last of the Nonconformist grievances to be addressed by parliamentary legislation. Until 1880, if there was not a Dissenters' graveyard in a country parish, Nonconformists were forced to bury their dead according to the service in the Book of Common Prayer, or in silence. After the passing of the Burials Act, non-Anglicans were free to devise their own form of words, and to invite their own minister to conduct the service, provided that it did not give offence to the Christian religion, or to members or ministers of any denomination.[182]

In the earlier period, when tensions ran higher, the clergy had been sometimes involved in skirmishes at the grave-side with dissatisfied Nonconformists. Friendly societies could provide a platform for Nonconformist intervention in Anglican burial services, when members of the society commemorated their deceased member with a special grave-side oration. Rex Russell has established a link between Lincolnshire friendly societies and temperance and Methodism, suggesting that they often developed side by side.[183] At Weston a butcher read an address at the conclusion of the burial of a Wesleyan who was a member of the foresters' club in 1849, despite being warned by the

[180]   LAO CorB5/4/11, C. S. Bird to Kaye, 25 September 1845.
[181]   Ibid., Bird to Kaye, 6 September 1845.
[182]   Chadwick, *The Victorian Church*, part II, pp. 204–7.
[183]   Rex C. Russell, *Friendly Societies in the Caistor, Binbrook and Brigg Area in the Nineteenth Century* (Nettleton WEA, 1975) p. 5. See also, Ambler, *Lincolnshire Returns of the Census* p. xxxii.

vicar that he was committing an illegal act.[184] At Kirton-in-Lindsey a similar incident occurred when the burial took place of a member of a newly-formed lodge of the society of ancient foresters.[185] On this occasion the officiating curate insisted that the address be read outside the churchyard wall. No reference is made to the religious affiliation of the deceased forester at Kirton, but it is likely that societies such as this provided an ideal opportunity for expressing dissatisfaction at the continued Anglican monopoly on burial services, in the period after that monopoly had been ended for births and marriages.

A mood of defensiveness overcame the clergy in the wake of the implementation of the Civil Registration Acts. The evidence for this is seen in Kaye's willingness to sanction an irregular remarriage at Cowbit, in clerical reluctance to church women who had had civil weddings and in the Nottingham clergy's resorting to undercutting the registrars in an effort to maintain the number of church weddings. There was an increasing unease that the poor were happy to do without the Church's ministrations, even if in reality large numbers still continued to come to church to mark the significant moments in life. The clergy did not offer any co-ordinated responses to the advent of civil registration. Many may not have perceived its significance in a wider context than that implied by loss of fees. Nevertheless, by providing an unprecedentedly greater range of legal alternatives to the Anglican rites, the Acts were to play a significant part in edging the Church out of its traditional role. They were a crucial factor in the Anglican adjustment from national church to denomination.

[184] LAO CorB5/4/67/7, E. Moore to Kaye, 9 November 1849.
[185] LAO CorB5/4/79/4, R. Ousby to Kaye, 25 February 1840.

CHAPTER 4

Clerical life

> The Christian Pastor, bow'd to earth
>   With thankless toil and vile esteem'd,
> Still travailing in second birth
>   Of Souls that will not be redeem'd
> Yet steadfast set to do his part
> And fearing most his own vain heart.[1]

The Christian Pastor in Keble's poem experienced the strains of his calling within the world at large as well as amongst those to whom he ministered, and his greatest fear was of his own unworthiness. These verses suggest an accurate perception of the reality of nineteenth-century clerical life. Anglican clergymen were torn between the attempt to maintain what they believed to be their traditional role in society, and the need to respond and adjust to a myriad of new pressures. The extensive literature on the lot of the nineteenth-century clergy, which is concerned to a great extent with such matters as churchmanship, social status and professional development, tends to obscure the stress and insecurity in ordinary clerical lives. It may not have been the same sort of insecurity that resulted from employment in mines or mills, but it was a stress nevertheless. The parochial clergy faced a variety of difficulties that were specific to their calling. These may be broadly divided between those that arose from the structure of the Church and parish, and those that arose from their inner struggles and uncertainties. Evidence in the latter category is harder to extract than in the former, where it is relatively plentiful. In what was for many an already difficult world, from the 1830s onwards the clergy had to contend with a new set of circumstances, the result of ecclesiastical reform. The aims of the church reform movement were to a great extent achieved at the cost of making life less pleasant for the majority of the clergy. This chapter is

---

[1] John Keble, *The Christian Year* (1828), stanza from the Nineteenth Sunday after Trinity.

concerned with the period when the change initiated in the 1830s was beginning to make an impact on clerical lives.

ORDINATION: A TRAP BAITED WITH FLOWERS?

During the eighteenth century about sixty per cent of those matriculating at Oxford and Cambridge were to be ordained in the Church of England.[2] Ordination remained the expected destination of over half of all Oxbridge graduates until the 1840s,[3] a remarkable statistic in view of the expansion of both universities, which doubled in size between the first and third decades of the nineteenth century. There were other routes to ordination as well. The University of Durham began to teach theology in 1834,[4] and King's College London established a theological department in 1847.[5] Like Oxford and Cambridge, Durham and King's were strictly Anglican foundations, with the training of future clergymen among their priorities. In the early years, however, their output of ordinands was overshadowed by that of Trinity College, Dublin, which until about 1870 provided more graduate clergy than anywhere outside Oxford and Cambridge.[6] The result of this rapid expansion in Anglican university education, combined with the continuing expectation that ordination was its sequel, led to a crisis in employment prospects in the Church. A title for orders was an essential prerequisite of ordination, and by the 1820s competition for a title had become intense. A national annual average of 530 men were seeking a first curacy, which was well over double the figure of 245 who had been similarly placed in the 1740s, 1750s and 1760s.[7] The numbers of ordained deacons continued to rise throughout the period, reaching a peak of 814 men in 1886.[8] The crisis came because the increasing numbers were being fed into an ecclesiastical structure that was essentially static. There were about 10,500 livings

---

[2] Alan Haig, *The Victorian Clergy* (London and Sydney: Croom Helm, 1984) p. 31.

[3] Haig, *Victorian Clergy* p. 30; Owen Chadwick, *The Founding of Cuddesdon* (Oxford: Oxford University Press, 1954) p. 2.

[4] E. A. Varley, *The Last of the Prince Bishops: William Van Mildert and the High Church Movement of the Early Nineteenth Century* (Cambridge: Cambridge University Press, 1992) pp. 149–79.

[5] Gordon Huelin, *King's College London 1828–1978: A History Commemorating the 150th Anniversary of the Foundation of the College* (London: King's College London, 1978) p. 19.

[6] Haig, *Victorian Clergy* p. 123.

[7] Peter Virgin, *The Church in an Age of Negligence: Ecclesiastical Structure and Problems of Church Reform 1700–1840* (Cambridge: James Clarke, 1989) p. 136.

[8] Haig, *Victorian Clergy* p. 356; Owen Chadwick *The Victorian Church* (London: A & C. Black, 1972) part II, p. 249.

in 1700, and there were about the same number in 1830.[9] Peel's
Church Building Act of 1843, which eased the path to the creation of
new parishes, alleviated the situation a little, but not dramatically. In
the second half of the century the emergence of the urban 'staff parish',
in which an incumbent was in charge of a team of curates, eased the
problem to some extent by providing more titles for ordinands. Perusal
of the gigantic volumes of Crockford's *Clerical Directory*, published in the
1890s and 1900s, reveals parishes like Christ Church, West Hartlepool,
which employed four curates, and St John's, Kennington, where
employment was found for eight.[10] The most impressive example of
the development was in Leeds, where in 1904 over two-thirds of the
city's ninety-one curates were at work in eighteen staff parishes.[11] Staff
parishes were, however, almost exclusively an urban phenomenon, and
the numbers involved were probably never a large proportion of the
total number of curates employed.

As the competition for titles had intensified at the beginning of the
century, so the climate had become ripe for the exploitation of
potential curates by unscrupulous incumbents or their agents. It was
not unusual for such people to offer a title for orders with a nominal or
non-existent stipend, or to charge an exorbitant rent for the use of the
parsonage house, furniture or outbuildings. Although the Stipendiary
Curates' Act (1813), the Consolidated Act (1817) and the Pluralities Act
(1838) had outlawed such proceedings, the evidence suggests that
plenty of incumbents were prepared to enter into secret, illegal
agreements with desperate potential curates.

John Thorold appears to have been a man who rushed into
ordination with insufficient thought to the problems he was likely to
encounter. He was twenty-four years old, and a graduate of Emmanuel
College, Cambridge when he was offered the title of Bothamsall in
Nottinghamshire, together with the opportunity to do duty at nearby
Clumber Park, which was the seat of the Dukes of Newcastle. Thorold
wrote to the bishop in whose diocese Bothamsall was located in April
1841, stating his determination to obtain ordination 'instantly'. Mr
Champion, agent and son-in-law of the superannuated and senile
perpetual curate of Bothamsall, offered to pay just fifty pounds a year
for the whole duty, and he pressurised Thorold to act quickly.[12] Fifty

---

[9] Virgin, *Age of Negligence* p. 136.
[10] Crockford's *Clerical Directory 1889* (London, 1889).
[11] Haig, *Victorian Clergy* p. 234.
[12] LAO CorB5/8A/4, J. Thorold to Kaye, 7 April 1841.

pounds was the legal stipend, as the living was only worth fifty-two pounds a year, but it was a small sum for a clergyman to live on if he lacked any additional means. Thorold was ordained on the title of Bothamsall on Trinity Sunday 1841. At first his curacy proceeded tolerably well. On arrival he was able to lodge at a farmhouse a mile from the parish; but was then forced to move to the less salubrious environment of Retford when the tenant quit the farmhouse. Shortly afterwards he fell from his horse and broke his arm. This prevented him from performing his clerical duties, and put him to considerable expense in medical bills and horse and gig hire, which was necessary to enable him to visit his parish. By April 1842, his health shattered and his purse straitened, Thorold sought permission to relinquish the curacy.[13] In response, the bishop told him that if he resigned, he would not accept Thorold as a candidate for priest's orders, nor would he ordain another deacon to serve at Bothamsall.[14] Harsh though it seemed, this was the bishop's attempt to enforce some degree of regulation in a system over which he had almost no control. It was a response designed to discourage both incumbents and curates from abusing titles for orders, by ensuring that the titles offered were financially viable, and that curates remained in their first parish for at least two years. Thorold was in any event doomed to remain a deacon until his health improved in 1843, which in itself severely restricted his chances of promotion. The situation in his parish remained tense, with Mr Champion, the agent, objecting not only to Thorold's attempts to resign the curacy in an 'unhandsome manner', but also to the inconvenience of his failure to be in full orders.[15] Thorold appears to have been subjected to a further year of misery at Bothamsall before he could escape from the curacy in 1843. What happened to him next is not clear, though in 1851 he resurfaced as the evening lecturer at St Peter-at-Arches in Lincoln.

In addition to providing evidence of a title for orders, the potential clergyman was expected to supply some evidence of his moral suitability for ordination. All who applied had to provide a testimonial for their conduct for the preceding three years from their college or from three beneficed clergymen. College testimonials, which were frequently printed and followed a set formula, were usually regarded as not worth the paper they were written on, and beneficed clergy could

---

13 Ibid., Thorold to Kaye, 20 April 1842.
14 Ibid., Kaye to Thorold, 22 April 1842.
15 Ibid., Champion to Kaye, 22 August 1842.

be found who would sign papers for men they barely knew.[16] It is of course difficult to assess whether college testimonials became more or less reliable with the passing of years. By the late 1880s certain colleges, notably Christ Church, Oxford were giving bland testimonials that expressed no opinion on the suitability of the candidate for ordination.[17] In the earlier period, however, the testimonial was for some tutors more than a mere formality. Thomas Thorp, who had been Theodore Dunkin's tutor at Trinity College, Cambridge, declined to provide him with a testimonial, not merely because of his unpaid debts, but also because of 'a general impression that he was a stranger to the moral and religious feelings which were necessary to his office as a clergyman, and was independent of the state of his pecuniary relations'.[18] Dunkin, however, must either have reformed himself or have persuaded another tutor to sign his testimonial, for he was ordained in 1838. At about the same period Charles Cotterill was refused a testimonial from J. J. Blunt, senior fellow of St John's College, Cambridge, on account of his 'riotous and drunken habits'. Unlike Dunkin, however, Cotterill was obliged to exhibit a high degree of remorse, remain a layman for a further three years and produce a fresh set of testimonials from three beneficed clergymen in 1837.[19]

The academic preparation considered necessary for ordination was in itself in transition, and it also varied from diocese to diocese. A degree, preferably from Oxford or Cambridge, was always considered highly desirable, and in some dioceses in the earlier period it was indispensable. Later on, however, the numbers of graduate clergy began to decline. By 1879 about one in six had no degree.[20] The approaches adopted before 1850 differed significantly from those adopted afterwards, and reflect the Anglicans' sense of the need to impose more order and uniformity on a system that had been rather haphazard. Bishop Kaye, who had spent nearly thirty years at Cambridge before becoming bishop of Lincoln, had a clear preference for ordaining Cambridge graduates, though, for reasons that are not entirely clear, the numbers of such candidates in his diocese fell by almost one-third during his episcopate. In 1829, 72 per cent of men ordained in the Lincoln diocese were Cambridge graduates; by 1849 it

16   Haig, *Victorian Clergy* pp. 185–6.
17   Ibid., p. 186.
18   LAO CorB5/4/77/2, T. Thorp to Kaye, 4 November 1836.
19   LAO CorB5/19/4/2, Kaye to C. Cotterill, 29 October 1836.
20   Chadwick, *The Victorian Church*, part II, p. 247.

had dropped to 43 per cent.[21] Like other bishops, Kaye believed that preparation for ordination should begin at university. He urged his Cambridge candidates to attend the lectures of the Norrisian Professor of Divinity, and his Oxford candidates those of the Regius Professor of Divinity.[22] In addition to obtaining an attendance certificate from a divinity professor, his ordinands were expected to read some of the classic texts of eighteenth-century Anglicanism – Prideaux's *Connection*, Horne's *Introduction*, Paley's *Natural Theology*, Burnet on the Thirty-nine Articles and Butler's *Analogy* – volumes that were widely regarded as containing all things necessary for ministry in the Church of England.

In the first half of the century, attendance at a dozen or so undergraduate divinity lectures and the perusal of a handful of theological works was the standard academic preparation for ordination. Some ordinands, particularly those who were not yet twenty-three (the canonical minimum age for ordination), might spend a year or so between graduation and ordination studying in the home of a clergyman.[23] For the clergy who offered the tuition, such arrangements provided both additional income and additional parochial help, though the latter was sometimes rather limited. William Butler, master of Nottingham Grammar School and chaplain to the county gaol, was willing to take pupils, either to study for ordination or for the university classics examinations.[24] The tuition that Butler offered appears to have been largely academic. As a High Churchman, he disapproved of the use of lay pastoral agency, and would not have encouraged the ordinands in his care to do more than routine parochial visiting. Even the mildly Evangelical C. S. Bird of Gainsborough appears to have limited the pastoral work of his future curate to visiting the poor.[25] Ordination training could be surprisingly lucrative; in 1857 James Anderson, rector of Tormarton in Gloucestershire, hoped to train six ordinands in his parsonage at a charge of £200 each a year.[26] College-based ministerial training for graduates was not to become commonplace until the 1870s, and even then it was far from universal. Chichester Theological College, founded in 1839, Wells, founded in 1840, and Cuddesdon, founded in 1854, catered for no more than a handful of ordinands, and their alumni were in any case widely

21 *British Critic* 7 (for 1829); *Ecclesiastical Gazette* (for 1849).
22 Kaye, *Charge* (1831) reprinted in *The Works of John Kaye*, vol. VII, pp. 113–14.
23 Chadwick, *Cuddesdon* p. 9.
24 LAO CorB5/8/7/6, W. Butler to Kaye, 30 November 1840.
25 LAO CorB5/4/11, C. S. Bird to Kaye, n.d.
26 PH Ham4/12, H. Drury to W. K. Hamilton, 4 December 1857.

regarded as suspect on the grounds that they had been infected with Puseyite notions.

At the beginning of the period bishops generally seem not to have regarded it as within their prerogative to reject candidates who could provide evidence of a title, a degree and the appropriate testimonials. The widespread practice of ordaining men for other dioceses with letters dimissory (a document from one bishop granting permission for the candidate to be ordained by another bishop) had the effect of distancing the ordaining bishop from the candidates. When the Bishop of Carlisle ordained George Augustus Selwyn for the diocese of Ely in 1833, he can have had little motive for acquainting himself with Selwyn's character.[27] Bishop Joseph Allen was similarly placed when he ordained fifty-three deacons and priests at Ely Cathedral on 27 November 1836, forty-four of whom came from the neighbouring dioceses of Peterborough and Norwich.[28] It would be wrong, however, to suggest a general laxity concerning ordination candidates on the part of bishops in the earlier period. Thomas Burgess, bishop of St David's from 1803 to 1825, spent a whole week before each ordination performing himself all the duties of an examining chaplain so as to 'lay hands suddenly on no man'. He inquired about the motives and the piety of his candidates, as well as testing their theological knowledge, and he even wrote a Hebrew primer to assist them in their academic preparation.[29] In 1822 Burgess laid the foundation stone of what was to become St David's College, Lampeter, which, like St Bees in Cumberland and St Aidan's in Birkenhead, offered theological training to non-graduates.

The use of letters dimissory died out as bishops became younger and fitter and as ordination candidates became more mobile. Bishops took a closer interest in the men they ordained, partly because they knew that they might well become involved in the repercussions which would follow. Like Burgess, Bishop Kaye conducted ordination examinations himself, and seems to have used them as an opportunity to test the orthodoxy, as well as the knowledge, of the candidates. When one of the most Evangelical clergy in the diocese, George Browne, offered a title for orders to H. L. Armitage, Kaye seems to have chosen deliberately contentious topics for Armitage's examination. First he was asked to translate a passage from Augustine on the subject of original sin. Then he was required to answer a series of questions based on

[27] EDR G1/17, Ely Episcopal Acts, 1832–48, fol. 4.
[28] Ibid., fols. 15–16.
[29] J. S. Harford, *A Life of Thomas Burgess D.D.* (London, 1840) pp. 235–6.

Article 27, on baptism: 'What do you mean by the word *"Grace"*?' the bishop demanded of the unfortunate Armitage, 'What is Regeneration?' 'When does Regeneration take place?' These were followed by further questions on the nature of infant baptism.[30] John Rashdall was similarly interrogated, and recorded in his diary accounts of his ordinations to the diaconate in 1833 and the priesthood in 1834. On the Wednesday before the Sunday of his diaconal ordination, Rashdall arrived at Buckden in Huntingdonshire, which until 1837 was the official residence of the bishops of Lincoln, and took a room at the George Inn. On the Thursday he began the examination, and 'answered at some length all the papers', which were chiefly doctrinal, Burnet on the Articles and Paley's *Evidences*. Then followed an hour-long *viva voce* examination with the bishop, during which they discussed the examination papers and 'divers theol. subjects' including the sixth chapter of St John's gospel and Moore's controversial *Travels of an Irish Gentleman*.[31] The examination continued the next day, with more papers on Paley, and one on Pretyman-Tomline, presumably his *Elements of Christian Theology*, which was widely recommended to ordinands but which Rashdall admitted to not having read. The examination concluded with a second, shorter, conversation with the bishop. In the evenings Rashdall dined with the other candidates at the public table in the George. There were only two Evangelicals, and he noted, 'they appeared good men but as usual a good deal bigoted; the rest were apparently everyday persons, and not converted people.' On Saturday Rashdall signed the Thirty-nine Articles, paid three shillings and seven pence and dined with the bishop at a 'sumptuous dinner – venison – all kinds of wine etc.' The next day, in a service that lasted three hours, Rashdall was ordained. The sermon, preached by J. A. Jeremie, moved him and other men to tears.[32] His ordination to the priesthood followed a similar pattern twelve months later. Two days of examinations were accompanied by conversations with the bishop; this time the discussion ranged over politics as well as theology. 'I find he is very afraid of Brougham and the Whigs',[33] noted Rashdall, himself a Whig sympathiser. Perhaps this was a further example of Kaye's tendency to express disapproval of the candidates whose views he did not share.

---

[30] LAO CorB5/8/7/2, H. L. Armitage to Kaye, 23 January 1843.
[31] This was presumably G. H. Moore, an Irish Catholic who had been educated at Oscott, and had entered at Christ's (Bishop Kaye's college) for two terms in 1827 and 1828.
[32] Bodl. MS Eng. misc. e. 351, 24 September 1833.
[33] Ibid., 21 September 1834.

The ordination examinations conducted by Walter Kerr Hamilton at Salisbury in the 1850s were altogether more sombre than those held by Kaye twenty years earlier. There was no question of the candidates staying in a local public house, or of a lavish dinner on the eve of the ordination. In May 1856 Hamilton reflected in his diary on the ordination examination which he had just concluded:

I have delivered a charge every night. The next time I will try to aid the candidates with directions about sermons. It would be well also to arrange about Saturday that they should not be hanging about all the morning. It would be well for one of the chaplains to read through with Candidates the admission service.

N.B. Caution the Butler that there is to be no *beer* next time. If wine is to be abstained from on the Ember Days, so ought beer.

Another subject for my addresses could be the Customs of the Church. The conforming to Customs of each Church. Would it not also be well that my Chaplains and I should every evening join in prayer for the candidates . . .[34]

Hamilton was unimpressed by the quality of many of the men who applied to him for ordination, and he did not hesitate to reject those whom he regarded as unsuitable. He made notes on seven whom he saw for preliminary interviews on 17 October 1855:

Mr Butt – feeble in manner and not much prepared. Mr Falkner – a very strange man, once near Rome – then nearly a sceptic and now doubtful about himself. Mr Leathes – a good orientalist – an odd man – seems to [choose] orders because he must have some definite duty. On leaving he asked for my Blessing and wept on receiving it. I have recommended him for Westbury. Mr Monkhouse – very bad health feels unequal to duty – too much exertion to collect thoughts – has had difficulties about baptism and is ignorant of Doctrine now though he refuses to admit it. I advised his withdrawal. Mr Peppin. Pleasing manners. Quite unsound about III John. Cannot believe *all* children regenerate – because many baptised children have evil tempers. He understood that the [fact] of original sin carried with it the removal of all corruption of nature ... He is evidently thoroughly ignorant of Doctrine. I dismissed him. Mr Troutbeck – A nice young man – going prepared, not shy – His Mother is to live with him – wants agricultural parish. Mr Whitehead – well prepared at Kgs [King's] College.[35]

Hamilton's closest associate on the episcopal bench, Wilberforce of Oxford, founded a theological college next to his palace at Cuddesdon in 1854. The move towards some period of residential training grew in part out of the desire of bishops to ensure that ordinands did not make

[34] PH Ham2/1/1, 17 May 1856.
[35] PH Ham1/1/4, 17 October 1855.

such elementary theological blunders as to equate childhood naughti-
ness with an absence of baptismal regeneration. It grew also from a
realisation that the ancient universities were ceasing to be Anglican
seminaries, and that the admission of non-Anglicans would displace
them from that role altogether.[36] Nor were the *ad hoc* arrangements for
placing ordinands with parochial clergy any longer deemed to be
satisfactory.[37] There was not, however, a revolution in the curriculum
in the new colleges. At Cuddesdon, the academic component remained
very much as it had been before; there were lectures on the Bible, on
early church history, and on the classic texts of Hooker and Pearson.[38]
What was different was the tone. Smoking, for example, was banned as
a 'habit repugnant to the formation of clerical character', and the men
were encouraged to develop clerical rather than undergraduate instincts; to get up early and avoid wearing brightly coloured clothing.[39]
By 1870 the reading list for ordinands in Ely, a diocese that was still six
years away from founding its own theological college, contained a
mixture of the old and the new. Many of the authors had been familiar
for decades – Butler, Paley and Pearson – but some newer scholars
were also being recommended, reflecting a more liberal and critical
tone, among them A. P. Stanley and B. F. Westcott. Francis Massingberd's *The English Reformation*, which he had published in 1843, also
appeared on the book list.[40]

The diaconal year that followed ordination was regarded as a
probationary period, and those who got into difficulty during it were
liable to have their ordination to the priesthood postponed. E. F.
Chamberlayne, ordained deacon on the title of Firsby on Trinity
Sunday 1830, appeared to be progressing well until he committed what
he described as a 'grievous error,' which resulted in a servant in the
house in which he lodged becoming pregnant.[41] Bishop Kaye directed
that Chamberlayne resign the curacy, and then produce testimonials of
good conduct at the end of three years.[42] Chamberlayne moved to
Kent, where he took temporary duties until the Archbishop of Canterbury declared his willingness to licence and priest him in 1833.[43]

---

[36] Chadwick, *Cuddesdon* pp. 7–8.
[37] Ibid., p. 17.
[38] Ibid., pp. 30–2.
[39] Ibid., pp. 27–8.
[40] Ely Diocesan Calendar and Clergy List (1870), pp. 17–18.
[41] LAO CorB5/19/2/8, J. Cheales to Kaye, 19 March 1831.
[42] Ibid., Kaye to Cheales, 22 March 1831.
[43] Ibid., E. F. Chamberlayne to Kaye, 20 March 1833.

Wily parishioners were certainly aware that if they wished to make trouble for a new curate, the most effective moment was immediately before his priesting. The case of M.T. Dupre, the curate of Willoughby with Sloothby in Lincolnshire, well illustrates the point. Dupre's rather aggressive Anglicanism had made him extremely unpopular in certain quarters in his parish. It was alleged that he had refused to alter the times of services to accommodate the Methodist minister, or to subscribe to a Dissenting Sunday school on the grounds that he was establishing one of his own, or to have dealings with non-Anglican tradesmen. He had also attracted hostility by suppressing an unruly beer shop in his parish. His accusers charged him with fathering an illegitimate child and refusing to pray at the church Sunday school, on the grounds that it was under Methodist influence. He appears also to have been threatened with incendiarism.[44] A rural dean's investigation, a petition signed or marked by 106 parishioners and the representations of seven local clergy all proclaimed Dupre's innocence. He was duly priested, but only after suffering considerable anguish that must have left him in little doubt about the way in which his uncompromising views were perceived by the Dissenting radicals of South Lindsey.

CURATES: A CLERICAL UNDERCLASS?

At the beginning of the nineteenth century the term 'curate' was almost always taken to designate a clergyman in whom was vested sole charge of a parish in the absence of a non-resident incumbent. By 1870 a 'curate' was usually understood to mean a clergyman, perhaps recently ordained, who assisted and worked under the direction of a resident incumbent. The transition from sole charge to assistant curacies marked an important change in the character of parochial ministry, and three major causes underlay it. First, the Pluralities Acts of 1838 and 1850, by placing a gradual brake on the holding of plural livings, effectively eliminated a large proportion of non-resident incumbents. Secondly, the rapid rise in the numbers seeking ordination from the 1820s resulted not only in an acute shortage of suitable titles for orders, but also, as time went on, in a shortage of incumbencies. Those who were unlucky in the livings lottery were destined to remain curates, and, as newly-instituted incumbents became obliged to reside on their livings, curates found that, if not dismissed completely, they were

---

[44] LAO CorB5/19/2/7, J. Walls to Kaye, 8 December 1834; curate of Munby to Kaye, 11 December 1834; M. T. Dupre to Kaye, 12 December 1834.

relegated to assistant status. Changes in population distribution were the third force responsible for reshaping the curates' role. In rapidly expanding city parishes, and also in country towns of moderate size, it became impossible for one man, whether curate or incumbent, to undertake the parochial work unaided. By mid-century the proportion of assistant to sole charge curates was expanding rapidly.[45] Nevertheless, the sole charge curates were some way from extinction.

Relations between non-resident incumbents and curates in sole charge were usually governed by strictly formal conventions. Each was aware of the responsibilities that accompanied his side of the contract, and as long as the parochial duties were performed efficiently, the house maintained and the stipend, rates and taxes paid promptly, few difficulties were likely to arise. Nevertheless, the curate's security depended upon the incumbent's continuing to hold office. The death of the incumbent resulted in the termination of a curate's terms of employment, so there was always the possibility that the curate would find himself unexpectedly deprived of his livelihood. This was the fate of John Rashdall; when the non-resident vicar of Orby died in April 1834, Rashdall had completed only six months of his diaconal year. To make matters worse, the bishop initially refused to accept him as a candidate for priest's orders on the grounds that he lacked a title. He relented, perhaps because Rashdall continued to serve the parish until the institution of the new vicar in the following September.[46] Rashdall left Lincolnshire, and did not secure another curacy for almost a year. He spent a great deal of time fretting about his employment prospects until he was finally nominated to St Lawrence's, Exeter in July 1835.[47]

It could be argued that the less a curate and incumbent saw of each other, the more cordial the relationship was likely to be. From the curate's point of view, an incumbent who visited his parish frequently was liable to cause interference, and, if he began to show an interest in residing, he threatened to dispossess the curate altogether. Dispossession was the fate of Richard Wright and Samuel Adams, two curates who at different times in the 1830s served the parishes of North

---

[45] In 1844 the proportion of assistant to sole charge curates was 24 per cent in Lincolnshire, and 53 per cent in Nottinghamshire. By 1853 it was 30 per cent in Lincolnshire, and 57 per cent in Nottinghamshire. See Frances Knight, 'Bishop, clergy and people: John Kaye and the diocese of Lincoln, 1827–53' (unpublished Cambridge PhD, 1990) tables 8, p. 387; 9, p. 388; 10, p. 389; 11, p. 390; 22, p. 402; 23, p. 403; 24, p. 404; 25, p. 405; 33, p. 413. Statistics taken from the Lincoln diocesan specula (LAO SPE 18) for 1832, 1844 and 1853.

[46] Bodl. MS. Eng. misc. e. 351, 13 April 1834; 6 June 1834.

[47] Ibid., 10 July 1835.

Crawley and Astwood in Buckinghamshire. The irascible rector, Robert Lowndes, created havoc for them by moving in and out of residence. Wright had spent £1,000 improving the rectory on the assumption that the aged Lowndes would never return, but they quarrelled about shooting rights and Lowndes gave him notice to leave.[48] The rector appears to have served his parishes unassisted for the next five years, at which point he petitioned for another non-residence licence on the grounds of ill-health.[49] Adams was duly appointed curate, but after less than a year he too was given notice when Lowndes decided to return.[50]

From the curate's point of view greater security was to be found in the service of an old-style pluralist, whose interest in his living was more or less confined to auditing the annual receipts. Robert Ousby, for example, was ordained to the title of Kirton-in-Lindsey in Lincolnshire in 1825, and remained there until his death in 1857. D. S. Wayland, the vicar, was non-resident throughout this period, augmenting the revenues of Kirton (which he effectively split with Ousby) with the perpetual curacy of Thurlby and the curacy of Bassingham, where he resided.[51] Wayland was typical of Lincolnshire pluralists, for despite receiving ecclesiastical income from three sources, he could truthfully describe himself as poor. After the deduction of Ousby's stipend, Kirton yielded £80 for Wayland, Thurlby just £55 and the Bassingham curacy, which he served for an incumbent who was himself resident nearby on Ashby de la Laund, £120. The total, £225, would have been further eroded by rates and taxes, and was certainly modest for a man who claimed that his family increased every year.

In the south of England non-resident pluralists were generally more prosperous. John Young, for example, became rector of Akeley in Buckinghamshire in 1789, but he never resided, preferring his other living in Northamptonshire. His curate at Akeley, John Theodore Reed, entered Young's employment in 1789, and was still at Akeley forty years later. In 1828 Young expressed thorough satisfaction at his

---

[48] LAO CorB5/3/1/4, R. Lowndes to Kaye, 1 January 1830; Kaye to Lowndes, 4 January 1830; Lowndes to Kaye, 6 January 1830; R. Wright to Kaye, 11 January 1830; Lowndes to Kaye, 15 January 1830; Kaye to Lowndes, 18 March 1830; Wright to Kaye, 23 March 1830. Kaye invoked the Consolidated Act to ensure that Wright was given six months notice before being compelled to leave.

[49] Ibid., Lowndes to Kaye, 5 February 1835.

[50] Ibid., S. Adams to Kaye, 10 March 1836.

[51] LAO CorB5/4/79/4, D. J. Wayland to Kaye, 5 September 1831.

curate, and was clearly contemptuous of the bishop's suggestion that he should reside in the parish, instead of a mile away at Leckhamstead. Young made it clear that Reed had no intention of resigning the curacy, and that the parishioners had not complained: 'in the management of my concerns in the Parish I have experienced the greatest assistance and advantage'.[52] Three years later Reed was replaced by another curate, J. G. Littlehales, who served Akeley in conjunction with his own living of Shalstone. Littlehales, like Wayland, was representative of a sizeable, though seldom recognised, body of curates who also belonged to the incumbent class. His eventual resignation of the curacy, in 1837, was precipitated by ill health, and by a conviction that Akeley needed a resident minister

to heal the divisions which the Wesleyan Methodist chapel encourages ... I am sure Mr Young will have no right to complain, as he has had the preferment more than forty years, and I believe has never been ten times in the village. Indeed, though I have now been his curate more than six years, I have never seen him, nor had any kind of communication with him.[53]

Littlehales resigned from the Akeley curacy at a moment when a distinct change was taking place in public attitudes to clerical residence. The Pluralities Bill was under discussion, and it became law in 1838. Disaffected curates had high hopes for this bill and the other legislation that stemmed from the reports of the Ecclesiastical Commission. Edward Price, curate of Steeple Claydon in Buckinghamshire and a Whig sympathiser, expressed the mood with candour in a letter to the bishop in December 1837:

Curates are an order of men who suffer much and say little. Like fags in our public schools, they offer no resistance – some from fear of the powers that are arrayed against them, others perhaps from the hope of one day becoming in their turn Lords and Masters. The system of fagging however is in process of reformation, and perhaps a like fate awaits the present unequal distribution of church revenues, by which a minister of the Gospel is often little better than the serf of his fellow minister.[54]

In fact, as will be shown, much of this optimism was to prove largely unfounded, and the lot of curates became generally harder rather than easier.

It was the Pluralities Act, more than any other piece of legislation,

[52] LAO CorB5/3/3/3, J. Young to Kaye, 5 September 1851.
[53] LAO CorB5/3/6/2, J. G. Littlehales to Kaye, 25 February 1837.
[54] LAO CorB5/3/26, E. Price to Kaye, December 1837.

that set the tone for clerical life in the following decades, though its significance has been little appreciated by historians of the nineteenth-century Church of England.[55] The Act altered all laws concerning the holding of plural livings that had existed since the reign of Henry VIII. It outlawed the possession of almost all third benefices, and of second benefices if they were more than ten miles from the first. The combined value of the benefices was not permitted to exceed £1,000, or the population 3,000. The Pluralities Act was, however, concerned with far more than the holding of multiple benefices. An incumbent could be legally non-resident either by exemption, or by licence. The Act introduced a severe restriction on the qualifications for both categories of non-residence. The exemptions available to chaplains, prebendaries, canons, priest vicars, vicars choral, minor canons, fellows of Eton and Winchester and college fellows were reduced significantly. Licences for non-residence could still be obtained in cases of sickness or infirmity, but it ceased to be possible to renew a licence for periods of more than six months on the grounds of the ill-health of a wife or child. This was significant, as numerous incumbents had remained permanently absent from their livings on the grounds of the ill health of their wives. Stringent financial penalties were imposed on those who persisted in being non-resident without licence or exemption, the ultimate sanction being sequestration and the voiding of the living.

Regulations regarding the employment of curates were also revised by the Pluralities Act. A curate was not normally to be permitted to reside more than three miles from the church to which he was licensed. Incumbents of benefices that exceeded £500, and that had a second church or chapel more than two miles from the mother church, were required to place an additional resident curate there. It also became compulsory to appoint a second curate in parishes where the value exceeded £500 and the population 3,000. If the bishop believed that the parochial duties were being inadequately performed, even when the incumbent was resident, he was empowered, subject to the findings of an episcopally-appointed local commission, to nominate a curate or

---

[55] Owen Chadwick, *The Victorian Church* part I, pp. 136–7, simply states its major provisions, but fails to say that several of them appeared first in the Consolidated Act of 1817. G. I. T. Machin, *Politics and the Churches in Great Britain 1832 to 1868* (Oxford: Clarendon Press, 1977) p. 63, adopts a similar line to Chadwick. G. F. A. Best, *Temporal Pillars* (Cambridge: Cambridge University Press, 1964) p. 306 refers to the Act as marking 'something of a revolution in common clerical life', but this is one of only three very brief references which he makes in the course of his study. Virgin, *Age of Negligence* provides an interesting, if brief, discussion (pp. 102, 209–10).

curates to the parish, and to fix the stipend. These provisions created some alternative employment – though by no means enough – for those curates who were thrown out of their parishes when their incumbent came into residence. The Act maintained the same pay scale that had been laid down by the Stipendiary Curates' Act of 1813, thus retaining a minimum level of income among all curates except those who were employed by incumbents instituted before 20 July 1813. A curate was now obliged to quit his curacy within six weeks if he was given notice by his new incumbent within six months of the incumbent's institution. At all other times an incumbent had to give him six months notice, and have the notice sanctioned by the bishop. Thus the bishops' powers of appointment and dismissal were strengthened, and the security of curates enhanced, at the expense of the rights that incumbents had previously enjoyed. The procedure and cost of being licensed to a curacy was simplified for the benefit of the curate. The Pluralities Act contained other provisions that related to the uniting of contiguous benefices, the disuniting of benefices that had seen large increases in population, and the separating of hamlets and chapelries in certain circumstances. A further significant provision empowered bishops to order the mortgaging of livings valued at over £100 in order to finance the building or repair of parsonage houses. From the episcopal point of view, this was to prove one of the most useful aspects of the legislation. From the incumbents' point of view, it was, as will be shown, one of the most uncomfortable.

The Pluralities Act was highly effective, though its results were gradual. This was because existing interests were respected, and those incumbents who were instituted before the passing of the legislation were exempt from it. In order to appreciate the impact that the Act had, it is necessary to consider separately the residence patterns of those who were instituted before and after 1838. Fifteen years after the passing of the Act, only 3 per cent of those Lincolnshire incumbents who had been instituted after 1838 were non-resident by exemption, compared with one-quarter of those who had been in their livings before the Act. In Nottinghamshire the impact of the legislation was equally marked: 20 per cent of the pre-1838 incumbents were non-resident by exemption as against none of the post-1838 cohort.[56] Each year after 1838 saw a reduction in the number of pluralist incumbents. In 1853 the proportion was a fraction of what it had been fifteen years

[56] Knight, 'Bishop, clergy and people', tables 15, p. 395, and 28, p. 408. The data was derived from the Lincoln diocesan specula (LAO SPE 18).

before, but it was to take another twenty years for the effects of the Act to work themselves out fully. It is difficult for the modern mind to grasp the gradualism of nineteenth-century church reform, devised as it was in order to protect vested interests. Not one of those who framed the 1838 Act lived to see it fully in operation.

Assistant curates who worked in the parishes of resident incumbents became very much more numerous after 1838, a largely unforeseen consequence of the legislation. Because they were virtually a creation of the nineteenth century, they were more or less invisible in law, and tended to fare worse than their brethren in sole charge curacies. Assistant curates had to be licensed, but they had no legal minimum stipend. The plain fact was that the poorer livings could barely support one clergyman, let alone two. When a curate was employed in sole charge, it was assumed that a proportion of the benefice's value could be directed to his payment because the incumbent would be deriving a proportion of his income from elsewhere. As Alan Haig has pointed out, the financial provisions of the Church of England were quite unsuited to the large-scale spawning of the assistant curate class.[57] Although the setting up of the Ecclesiastical Commission's Consolidated Fund had modified the principle of purely local applications for endowments, its funds were entirely taken up with the raising of incumbents' stipends. Until the foundation of the Curates' Augmentation Fund in 1866, the High Church organisation the Additional Curates Society, founded in 1837, and the Evangelical Church Pastoral Aid Society, founded in 1836, were the sole providers of extra financial help for assistant curates.

The grants of both societies could do little more than augment existing sources of income. Rather than funding curates outright, they made a contribution that needed to be matched from other sources. When John Radclyffe Pretyman applied to the Additional Curates Society for a grant in 1844, he envisaged that the parish would raise £50 a year, with the Society making an annual contribution of £20. With the assistance of an additional curate, Pretyman, who was vicar of Aylesbury and already employed one curate there, intended to introduce daily services, which were virtually unknown in the country in the 1840s, and to undertake more visiting of homes and schools.[58] John Smith, of Baldock in Hertfordshire, anticipated that his additional curate would be paid £100, £50 from the ACS and £50 'from a private friend of the

---

[57] Haig, *Victorian Clergy* p. 219.
[58] LAO CorB5/10/3/1, J. R. Pretyman's application to ACS.

incumbent'.[59] E. J. Randolph of Tring requested a grant of £40 or £50 from the ACS; a further £40 would be contributed by the incumbent of a neighbouring parish. Randolph hoped to open a second chapel in one of the hamlets if his application to the ACS was successful. 'The Parish is grievously demoralized, and eaten up with Dissent, there are no less than *seven* dissenting places of worship in the Parish . . .'[60] he lamented. At this time the provision of more clergy and more services was the classic Anglican response to such a state of affairs.

Both societies, however, were obliged to reject many applications due to lack of funds, or because the parish concerned was judged too small to merit help. The Additional Curates Society refused to aid parishes with a population of less than three thousand. Even when applications were successful, grants constituted an insecure source of income. Grants tended to be made for periods of one or two years, and were terminated on the departure of the curate. In 1842 the Church Pastoral Aid Society withdrew its grant from the industrial parish of Mansfield because of its reduced funds, and probably no curate would have been employed there at all had not the bishop intervened to recommend the parish to the Additional Curates Society, who offered £50 towards a stipend.[61] The case of the curate of Lenton in Nottinghamshire, Francis Redford, highlights just how insecure assistant curates remained. In 1848 Redford had encountered considerable removal expenses in order to settle in Lenton, and felt that he was just beginning to become acquainted with the parishioners when his vicar, George Browne, asked for his resignation. Browne had previously received a CPAS grant of £60, and had made up the stipend with £40 of his own. However the grant had been withdrawn, and Browne, who had lost much of his money when his Irish property investments had failed, could no longer afford to pay his curate.[62]

The insecurity that assistant curates experienced was not limited to anxiety concerning their stipends. A curate could be objected to, and sometimes dismissed, on relatively trivial grounds. An unpopular curate who lacked the support of his parishioners seldom survived for long. A curate named Robinson was judged unsuitable for Mansfield on account of his northern accent.[63] At Ison (Hyson) Green near

[59] LAO CorB5/10/3/2, J. Smith's application to ACS.
[60] LAO CorB5/10/3/5, E. J. Randolph's application to ACS.
[61] LAO CorB5/8/1, T. S. Cursham to Kaye, 30 March 1842; 10 June 1842; 30 January 1844.
[62] LAO CorB5/8/40/3, Lenton papers.
[63] LAO CorB5/8/1, T. S. Cursham to Kaye, 5 March 1844.

Nottingham, John Swithenbank was forced to resign because he was disliked in the parish. His vicar, R. P. Blakeney, strongly supported him, and was mystified by his unpopularity. The only tangible criticisms were that 'he wore his college gown too much' and had been perceived as too strict when trying to instil discipline into the school ... ' Mr Swithenbank was greatly liked when a Scripture reader, though not now acceptable as a clergyman.'[64] This is a remark that hints at much; Mr Swithenbank, presumably a local man, was perhaps perceived as having put on airs after he had been to college. He was perceived as not quite a gentleman, but neither was he still a member of the local community. The parishioners appear to have rejected one whom they had once embraced as their own. The curate of Blyth in Nottinghamshire, T. A. Bolton, was also obliged to leave his parish due to unpopularity, and responded with fury. He pointed to the incompatibility between the wording of his licence, which stated that he should remain in his curacy 'until otherwise provided with some ecclesiastical preferment, or lawfully deprived for a crime'[65] and the reality, which was that he could be disposed of at the whim of his vicar on the grounds of 'unpopularity'.

On this rule the poor curate finds himself (like a Dissenting Teacher) almost – nay altogether compelled (contrary to St Paul's directions in Gal.1.10) to 'seek to please *men*' rather than God, lest he and his family should want 'a morsel of bread'. I hope the Church of England is not coming to this![66]

The bishop told him that it was a hardship for a resident incumbent to be required to retain a curate with whom he could not act cordially, and that the spiritual interests of the parishioners must suffer from a 'want of cordiality' between the incumbent and the curate.[67]

'Want of cordiality' was certainly a phrase that summed up relations between many a resident incumbent and his assistant curate. Independence, rather than co-operation, was the attitude that prevailed. The 'one man, one parish' model had become so deeply embedded in the clerical mind that other patterns of ministry seemed awkward and unnatural. Francis Massingberd, rector of South Ormsby with Ketsby, Calceby and Driby, regarded employing a curate as in itself a sign of his own failure to manage his parishes. He found his curate, Mr Bloxam, a source of irritation, although the man appears to have been perfectly competent. 'Curate does nothing in my way' he scribbled

[64] LAO CorB5/8/19, Ison Green papers.
[65] LAO CorB5/8/3/6, T. A. Bolton to Kaye, 13 June 1846.
[66] Ibid., Bolton to Kaye, 22 June 1846.
[67] Ibid., Kaye to Bolton, 29 June 1846.

vexedly in his diary in 1845.[68] Complaints concerning the calibre of curates, and the difficulty of finding reliable ones, were legion, lending weight to the impression that they were regarded by the higher clergy as a clerical underclass, servants rather than independent gentlemen. Archdeacon George Wilkins was particularly damning about the curates who worked in the city of Nottingham: 'Raw, fresh caught Irish curates imported by shoals from Liverpool',[69] he called them, and mostly supported by the Evangelical Church Pastoral Aid Society – Wilkins never made a secret of his contempt for Evangelicals.[70] Even when recommending the curate of Bramcote for the new church of St John the Baptist, Nottingham, his tone was hardly flattering. He described Mr Altham as 'hardworking, straightforward and roughish, but well qualified for hard work'.[71] The reference seemed more appropriate for an assistant gardener than a clergyman.

The so-called 'curate question' was very far from being resolved by the end of the period. By the late 1860s the CPAS and the ACS funded some five hundred curates each, thus to some extent stimulating their continuing expansion.[72] The Curates' Augmentation Fund gave assistance to those who remained unbeneficed after fifteen years. The largely unregulated *laissez-faire* practices that had characterised the relations between incumbents and curates in the earlier part of the century seemed increasingly less acceptable, as did the notion that the curate was a servant of his incumbent, rather than of the Church. J. J. Halcombe, himself a former curate, edited a volume of essays entitled *The Church and her Curates* to highlight their plight in 1874. He isolated four particular grievances – lack of professional status, insecurity of tenure, insufficient prospects of promotion and the absence of a progressive increase of stipend.[73] The thorny question, however, was not so much the best method for augmenting small stipends, but rather whether it was conceivable to give curate A tenure in incumbent B's parish. Whilst the curate was being paid to a large extent out of the pocket of the incumbent, such a situation could hardly be contemplated.

It was natural that those who campaigned for the improvement of the curate's lot should have emphasised their poverty. J. J. Halcombe

68 LAO MASS/8/2, 20 October 1845.
69 LAO CorB5/8/30, G. Wilkins to Kaye, 21 September 1844.
70 LAO CorB5/8/19, Wilkins to Kaye, 29 June 1841.
71 LAO CorB5/8/30, Wilkins to Kaye, 21 September 1844.
72 Haig, *Victorian Clergy* p. 241.
73 J. J. Halcombe, *The Church and her Curates: A Series of Essays on the Need for More Clergy and the Best Means of Supporting Them* (London: W. Wells Gardner, 1874) p. 17.

described the plight of those who were forced to apply to clerical charities for 'out-door relief', and to appeal to their richer brethren for cast-off clothes.[74] The untenured curate, shabby and ageing, was a sad spectacle in the nineteenth-century Church. John Bull, aged sixty-six, was dismissed from a curacy at Aston Clinton in Buckinghamshire on the grounds that he read the service inaudibly. 'I am hitherto without any prospect of another charge' he commented bitterly, 'not with-standing various applications which I have made in answer to adver-tisements. The junior incumbents are unwilling to employ, as a Curate, one who is senior to themselves.'[75] Samuel Oliver appeared to be in an even worse predicament. For forty years he had served the curacy of Whaplode in South Lincolnshire, but was forced to find a new curacy at the age of eighty-seven, when the new vicar came into residence on the living in 1842, as he was now obliged to do by law. The new vicar, T. Tunstall Smith, generously offered to pay Oliver a pension of £50 a year, to top up any curacy that he might manage to secure. Oliver, however, was unexpectedly presented to a living worth £760, whilst Smith found the proceeds of his living equally unexpectedly reduced from £383 to £195. Oliver, who had spent a lifetime at his vicar's bidding, suddenly found that the tables were turned, and demanded a hundred guineas to release Smith from paying the annuity.[76]

The curates who were not actually displaced when the Pluralities Act was implemented tended to fare better from the changes than their incumbents. A case in point was in the parishes of Blidworth and Oxton in Nottinghamshire, which had become densely populated with stocking makers, glove hands, lace weavers and agricultural labourers by the 1840s. The incumbent, who held both livings, was non-resident, and the solitary resident curate had more than enough on his hands; all attempts to secure extra help had ended in failure. When a vacancy occurred on the curate's resignation, the Pluralities Act directed that, because of the size of the population, two curates must be employed at an annual stipend of £135 each. Two curates, Mr Sandback and Mr Roe, were duly appointed, and began to work hard in the busy parishes. Both, however, had considerable independent means, and were willing to agree to a reduced stipend of £110 each. But £220 in

[74] Ibid., p. 31.
[75] LAO CorB5/3/3/6, J. Bull to Kaye, 18 September 1844.
[76] LAO CorB5/4/54/1, S. Oliver to Kaye, 21 February 1842; Kaye to Oliver, 23 February 1842; Oliver to Kaye, 28 February 1842; Oliver to Kaye, 7 March 1842; Oliver to Kaye, 16 March 1842; W. Selwyn to Kaye, 22 March 1842; Selwyn to Kaye, 4 April 1842; G. Oliver to Kaye, 26 April 1842; T. T. Smith to Kaye, 27 January 1843.

annual stipends was still a large call upon a pair of livings, the combined value of which was £385, and the incumbent, C. F. Fenwick, was soon describing himself as 'virtually destitute and beggarly'.[77]

Such reversals in the economic fortunes of curates and incumbents were not uncommon after 1838. The examples of Samuel Oliver, Mr Sandback and Mr Roe highlight the difficulties of generalising about the fortunes of the unbeneficed. It is easy enough to investigate the stipends paid to curates, but almost impossible to know much about their private income. It is evident that in many cases a stipend derived from a curacy was only one component of their total income. A man who looked to the Church for all his financial support was likely to fare adequately whilst young and single, but he needed to ensure that he was presented to a reasonably lucrative benefice if he was to marry a woman without a fortune and avoid poverty in middle age. There were significant local variations in the value of curacies. A curate who accepted a post in Lincolnshire in 1832 was more likely to be paid a paltry £50 a year than any other stipend. Eighty-five curacies were valued at £50 in that year, almost two-thirds more than the second most frequently paid stipend of £80, which thirty curates received.[78] Only 12 per cent of the Lincolnshire curacies were valued at in excess of £100. In Buckinghamshire, by contrast, a curate was as likely to be receiving £120 as £50 in 1832.[79] In the more prosperous southern county there was a far greater evenness in the distribution of curates' stipends, with more or less equal numbers valued at £50, £80, £100 and £120, and 20 per cent of the total in excess of £100.

In 1844 the stipend paid most frequently (the modal stipend) remained £50 in Lincolnshire, whereas in both Buckinghamshire and Nottinghamshire it stood at £100.[80] The greater detail introduced into the parochial returns in the wake of the Pluralities Act means that it is possible to plot separately the fortunes of assistant curates (i.e. those employed by a resident clergyman) and sole charge curates (i.e. those employed by a non-resident) who were in place after 1838. Here too local variations were in evidence. In both Nottinghamshire and Buckinghamshire curates in parishes where the incumbent was non-resident were generally better paid than curates who acted as assistants to

---

[77] LAO CorB5/8/31/5, C. F. Fenwick to Kaye, various dates in 1842.
[78] Knight, 'Bishop, clergy and people', table 5, p. 384. The statistical data in this and the tables which follow was derived from the Lincoln diocesan specula (LAO SPE 18) for the years 1832, 1844 and 1853.
[79] Ibid., table 31, p. 411.
[80] Ibid., tables 6, p. 385; 20, p. 400; 24, p. 404.

resident ministers. In Nottinghamshire, 44 per cent of sole charge
curates received stipends in excess of £100, against 13 per cent of
assistant curates.[81] In Buckinghamshire, the differential was not so
marked – 27 per cent of sole charge curates received stipends in excess of
£100, against 21 per cent of assistant curates.[82] In Lincolnshire,
however, the pattern was reversed, with only 14 per cent of sole charge
curates holding curacies valued in excess of £100, and 23 per cent of
assistant curates. More significant, however, is the discrepancy in modal
incomes: £100 for assistant curates, against £50 for sole charge
curates.[83] At first sight this disparity between Lincolnshire and the other
counties appears puzzling. It would be logical to expect curates in sole
charge of a parish to be paid at a higher rate than those who were
merely assisting a resident minister. Furthermore, both the Stipendiary
Curates Act (1813) and the Pluralities Act (1838) laid down a relatively
generous scale of minimum stipends for sole charge curates leaving those
for assistants to local discretion. The explanation of the Lincolnshire
figures appears to be another reflection of the county's poverty. The
large number of very small, very poor livings led to a higher than
average tenure of multiple benefices; to the existence of incumbents like
D. S. Wayland, whose circumstances were described above. This in turn
resulted in higher levels of non-residence, and in the necessity for curates
being employed in sole charge of two and in some cases three parishes. It
is evident that only by holding two cures could the majority of
Lincolnshire curates scrape together a stipend sufficient on which to live.
It followed that assistant curates could only be employed in the wealthier
parishes, unless the incumbent was willing to pay for one from his
private means. The average value of a Lincolnshire parish employing an
assistant curate in 1844 was a staggeringly high £489.[84]

In 1853 the stipend paid most frequently remained £50 in Lincolnshire and £100 in Nottinghamshire, although by now the differential
was closing and an increasing number of Lincolnshire curacies were
valued at £80 or £100.[85] When the incomes of assistant and sole
charge curates are considered separately the trends that were evident
in 1844 are still pronounced. In Nottinghamshire curates in sole charge
were still generally better paid.[86] Lincolnshire curates continued to fare

[81]   Ibid., table 22, p. 402.
[82]   Ibid., tables 32, p. 412; 33, p. 413.
[83]   Ibid., table 8, p. 387.
[84]   Figures derived from LAO SPE 18, 1844, and the *Clergy List*, 1844.
[85]   Knight, 'Bishop, clergy and people', tables 7, p. 386; 21, p. 401.
[86]   Ibid., table 25, p. 405.

better financially if they worked as assistants to resident incumbents, but the stipend differences were not so large as they had been nine years earlier.[87]

Generalisations made from statistics should however be treated with caution. At least one curate received nothing at all for his services, whilst the highest stipend recorded in the data investigated, an exceptional £270, was paid to an assistant curate in Lincolnshire in 1853. Curates in Nottinghamshire were the best remunerated, though many would have owed their higher stipends to the more densely populated parishes in which they served, and thus would have worked harder than some of their poorer Lincolnshire colleagues. A Nottinghamshire curate in the middle years of the nineteenth century could usually expect to earn at least £100. As less than a quarter of the county's curacies were valued at under £80, it was relatively unusual to be forced by reason of financial necessity to serve more than one cure. In Buckinghamshire stipends were more evenly spread over a wider range than in either of the other counties, but by 1844 (there are no figures available for 1853) the modal stipend had reached the level of Nottinghamshire. Financial prospects were most dismal for curates in Lincolnshire. Although there was some improvement in the number of curacies of £80 and over, average stipends stagnated, and the modal did not rise above £50 until some point in the second half of the century.

Although some correlation exists between the value of livings and the value of curacies, the relationship is not as straightforward as it might at first appear. It was a principle enshrined in both the Stipendiary Curates Act and the Pluralities Act that the salary paid to a curate (or at least to a curate employed by a non-resident) should be in proportion to the value of the benefice served. The legislation of 1813 directed that the salary should in no case be less than £80, or the whole value of the benefice, if that was less than £80. Yet there is little evidence from the sources examined to suggest that the law had prompted a revival in curates' fortunes. In 1832, 62 per cent of curacies in Lincolnshire were valued at under £80, although the percentage of livings worth less than £80 was nowhere near this high figure. The Report of the Ecclesiastical Revenues Commission (1835), which is the sole reliable guide to benefice values at this date, suggests that not more than 13 per cent of Lincolnshire livings were worth less than £80, although 21 per cent were valued at £100 and under, which was

---

[87] Ibid., tables 10, p. 389; 11, p. 390.

significantly higher than the national total.[88] Alternative explanations are necessary to explain the low income of Lincolnshire curates. Three points emerge. First, the figures include a proportion, probably around 15 per cent, of assistant curates exempted from the law, although if this is to form part of the explanation, it needs to be modified by the knowledge that Lincolnshire's assistant curates tended to be better paid. Secondly, a proportion of curacies are included whose incumbents were instituted before 20 July 1813, and they too were exempt from the law. Thirdly, some incumbents of adequate livings continued to make private deals with their curates in ignorance or wilful violation of the law. Benefice values were not therefore directly mirrored in curates' stipends, and apparent correlations may turn out to be false. For example, examining the evidence in purely statistical terms, there appears in the Lincolnshire figures to be a correlation between the frequency of the £50 curates' stipends (31.5 per cent of the total) and the percentage of benefices valued at between £51 and £150 (31.9 per cent of the total).[89] Such an analysis ignores the fact that no curate would have been employed for a good proportion of these poorer benefices.

INCUMBENTS: WINNERS OR LOSERS IN THE LIVINGS LOTTERY?

If it is wise to avoid generalisations about the fortunes of curates, the same wariness is even more necessary in the case of incumbents. Those who were poor tended to attract more attention than those who were financially secure, and as a result are more visible in the surviving evidence. In 1848 a question was asked in the House of Lords about two Lincolnshire incumbents, one at Cherry Willingham and the other at Auborne, who were so destitute that they could have died of starvation. In reply, the Bishop of Lincoln tried to minimise the importance of the incidents, but he issued no denial of the circumstances.[90] These cases, though extreme, were perhaps not isolated examples. Incumbents in poverty, particularly the elderly and frail, were often supported without fuss or publicity by neighbouring clergy. Thus Mr Ison, vicar of Kneesal, Nottinghamshire, who had struggled for years with debt and a sickly family, and who was frequently found with no food or fuel in his house, was aided with £25 a year from a

---

[88] Ibid., table 38, p. 420.
[89] Ibid., tables 5, p. 384; 36, pp. 416–17.
[90] Hansard, *Parliamentary Debates*, 3rd series, vol XCVIII cols. 1222–4.

clerical charity, and by colleagues who performed his duties without charge. Ison was too frail to work himself, and was in no position to contemplate employing a curate. His living yielded just £90 a year.[91]

In 1830, 16 per cent of the total English benefices were valued at £100 and under. The situation was bleaker in the counties on which attention is being focused in this study. In Lincolnshire 21 per cent were valued at £100 and under, in Buckinghamshire it was 18 per cent, in Nottinghamshire it was 20 per cent and in Cambridgeshire it was 19 per cent. By contrast, 4 per cent of the total English benefices were worth between £1,000 and £2,000. In Buckinghamshire the figure was 1 per cent, in Lincolnshire 1 per cent, in Nottinghamshire 2 per cent, but in Cambridgeshire it was 7 per cent. In the low-income range of values of £300 and under, all four counties significantly exceeded the figure of 54 per cent, which was the percentage in England as a whole. In the high-income range £301–£2,000, Buckinghamshire and Lincolnshire lagged behind the rest of the country, whilst Nottinghamshire and Cambridgeshire were slightly above the national percentage, which was 29 per cent of livings in that range. The mean average benefice values varied between the counties, but were not particularly typical of actual incomes because the figures were skewed by the inclusion of the handful of livings worth in excess of £1,000. In Lincolnshire the mean benefice value was £285. In Nottinghamshire it was £293. In Buckinghamshire, where only two livings were worth more than £1,000, it was just £262. In Cambridgeshire, where the average was swollen by the inclusion of Doddington, with the exceptional value of £7,781, and by ten other livings worth over £1,000, it was £374. If these eleven livings are excluded from the calculations, however, the average drops to £244.[92]

Alan Haig has suggested that in the mid-Victorian period £300 marked the boundary between keeping up a respectable middle-class appearance and having to struggle.[93] If £300 is taken as the benchmark that points to prosperity, £200 is the line that separates a modest from an impoverished benefice. In 1834 Bishop Kaye had suggested that an

[91] LAO CorB5/8A/11, G. Wilkins to Kaye, 14 June 1842; T. Sampson to Kaye, 22 June 1842.

[92] The figures for individual counties have been derived from the *Ecclesiastical Revenues Commission Report*, 1835, and comparison has been made with Peter Virgin's table 6, 'The structure of the annual ecclesiastical income of the English Beneficed Clergy in the year 1830' in Virgin, *Age of Negligence*, p. 277. See also Knight, 'Bishop, clergy and people', table 38, p. 420, for a detailed analysis of the structure of annual benefice incomes in Lincolnshire and Buckinghamshire, and comparison with Virgin's figures.

[93] Haig, *Victorian Clergy* p. 304.

income of £200 was the absolute minimum which a clergyman needed to discharge his parochial duties. Indeed, in 1834 the principle that the clergyman should relieve the poor was still taken as an axiom, although this attitude was changing. 'The possessor of a living even of £500 a year, with a family and without any private source of income, if he administers as he ought to the temporal wants of his parishioners, has little or nothing to spare.'[94] In 1830, 37 per cent of English benefices were valued at £200 or under, 16 per cent between £201 and £300 and 49 per cent at £301 and above.

Even the income of a moderate benefice could be seriously eroded by a variety of factors that did not impinge upon a layman in a similar economic and social position. Curates had to be paid, and this expenditure amounted to a sizeable proportion of the value of many benefices. Rating and taxation imposed a further burden, and after tithe commutation was perceived as being unfair. This was because the tithe rent charge into which tithes had been commuted was rated as though it was land. Opponents of this practice argued that clergy were not only liable to income and indirect taxes, but were rated on their professional income as well. Furthermore, they were allowed few deductions for necessary expenses – not even their curates' stipends were deductible. Difficulties were compounded because the valuation was almost invariably performed by the farmers who owned the land in question, and who had a vested interest in under-estimating its value. It was not unknown for rates and land tax to absorb between a quarter and a third of modest gross incomes.[95] Glebe houses also had to be maintained, for any scrimping or economising on repairs could result in a clergy widow's modest legacy being eaten away by heavy dilapidations payments that had to be made to the incoming incumbent. Any mortgages on the living, taken out to build or repair a parsonage house, had to be paid. In the earlier part of the period it was expected that a proportion of the benefice's revenues would be used for relieving the poor, particularly if there were no other resident gentlemen in the parish. It was incumbents who bore the brunt of financing parochial charities and schools, as well as being the source of an endless stream of small donations in individual cases of hardship.

A further example from the parish of Whaplode illustrates the expectations of the parishioners in this respect. Tunstall Smith, the new vicar who displaced Samuel Oliver, soon found that the Fens gave him

[94]   Kaye, *Charge* (1834) reprinted in *Works*, vol. vii, pp. 143–4.
[95]   Ibid., pp. 302–3.

ague. After a few years he moved to Barnet, to serve a curacy for an incumbent who was himself non-resident. Smith appointed a curate, John Fleming, and was obliged under the terms of the Pluralities Act to pay him a stipend of £150. A dispute broke out when it appeared that this stipend was merely notional, and that Smith intended to deduct £50 for the use of the vicarage furniture, to force Fleming to pay the rates and taxes and not to allow him the surplice fees, which were paid for his attendance at baptisms, marriages, churchings and funerals.[96] This situation aroused unfavourable comment among the parishioners, who got up a petition to protest about the effects of Smith's non-residence. They complained that the curate's finances were so straitened that it was 'quite impossible for him to relieve the wants of the needy or the distress of the suffered'.[97] Their argument is interesting – the parishioners claimed that the parish was worth £550 per annum (clearly an exaggeration) and yet the curate was receiving only £70. The accuracy of these figures is largely immaterial; what is important is the implication that they felt themselves entitled to their share of the living's wealth through *ex gratia* payments in times of hardship, and were resentful at what they saw as 'their' money being spent elsewhere. The parishioners petitioned the bishop, unsuccessfully of course, to 'oblige the vicar to relinquish his living' and to give it to one who would be more solicitous in looking after their interests.

Alan Haig is surely correct in his judgement that 'what kept the clergy – and hence the parochial system as a whole – afloat financially, was the amount of their private means'.[98] An independent income was widely regarded as an essential prerequisite for ordination, although the proportion of clergy who had private means is impossible to assess. In 1854 W. J. Conybeare asserted that 'the clergy, while poor as a profession, are rich as a class; a fact which goes to account for the popular notions of "the vast wealth of the Church"'.[99] If Conybeare was correct in his estimation that few clergy lived on less than £500 a year, then it is evident that it was the 'vast wealth' of the English upper and middle classes, more than any other economic factor, which maintained the Church of England in the nineteenth century. An instructive comparison may be drawn with the salaries of civil servants in the mid-1850s. An incumbent living on £500 a year was in a similar

[96] LAO CorB5/4/54/1, J. Fleming to Kaye, 3 January 1848.
[97] Ibid., Whaplode parishioners' petition to Kaye, December 1849.
[98] Haig, *Victorian Clergy* p. 307.
[99] W. J. Conybeare, *Edinburgh Review* 99 (1854) pp. 105–6. Cited in Haig, *Victorian Clergy* p. 308.

bracket to an assistant clerk, who earned between £350 and £600, but who would not have faced the same sorts of expenses as a clergyman. The starting salary for a chief clerk in the civil service (alias principal officer) began at around £1,000 in the mid-1850s, a figure that the clergy could rarely match.[100]

The system was, as Sydney Smith famously remarked, one of blanks and prizes. But for those who had to make their way in the world without the advantages bestowed by independent means, the Church could indeed resemble a trap baited with flowers. It held undoubted attractions. In comparison with some other careers, it was relatively cheap to enter, and it was perceived as offering an elegant, leisured and gentlemanly style of life. It promised sizeable prizes for the lucky, the talented and the well-connected. But it was also the case that huge numbers of obscure clergy were destined to wear away their lives in tiny benefices or curacies. For curates so placed, the chief problem tended to be insecurity of tenure. For incumbents, it was meeting from their own resources all or most of the costs involved in running a parish. Debt, which was all too common among those who had attended Oxford or Cambridge, was the fear that haunted them most. William Day, vicar of Hawridge, Buckinghamshire (valued at £156) found himself catapulted from Merton College, Oxford to Hertford gaol in the space of two years because of his unpaid debts.[101] Charles Reay, vicar of Swanbourne, Buckinghamshire (valued at £160) was apparently filled with an urgent missionary zeal, and sailed to New Zealand with Bishop Selwyn in December 1841.[102] After his hurried departure it emerged that he had left debts with local businesses amounting to £105.13.6½d. His wife, whom he had left behind in Swanbourne, promised to discharge the debts, but the episode proved deeply embarrassing for Henry Venn, who had arranged Reay's passage under the auspices of the Church Missionary Society.[103] J. W. Butt, vicar of King's Langley, Hertfordshire (valued at £264) and Lakenheath in Suffolk (valued at £136) was perhaps the most deeply indebted clergyman in the country. He owed £7,000, having lost a tithe suit at Lakenheath in about 1825. By 1845 the parties who had advanced him large sums during the suit had become restive for

[100] Geoffrey Best, *Mid-Victorian Britain 1851–1875* (London: Weidenfeld & Nicolson, 1971) p. 89.
[101] LAO CorB5/3/14/10, G. Sandby to Kaye, 26 October 1836; J. Browne to Kaye, 22 October 1838.
[102] LAO CorB5/3/5, G. A. Selwyn to Kaye, 20 December 1841.
[103] Ibid., G. Cowley to Kaye, 24 March 1842; H. Venn to Kaye, 7 April 1842.

payment,[104] and his Hertfordshire living was sequestrated at the creditors' request. His furniture was seized by a solicitor, his house cleared and the contents sold, and the grates, kitchen range and shutters (which belonged, as in all glebe houses, to the living and not personally to Butt) were ripped out. Butt was particularly mortified that this action should have taken place on Good Friday:

That most solemn day was desecrated by the packing up and taking away of every article that I possessed in the world – and the peace of the village was broken on a day which I had laboured to teach my people to consider as the most sacred of the whole year – and which I had, at length, brought them to observe strictly and with becoming solemnity.[105]

Butt was rescued from total destitution by the kindliness of his churchwarden, who took his dying son into his own home, rented and furnished a small house for the rest of the family and set in train a subscription fund for their relief that raised £210 in about a fortnight.[106] It appears that Butt still maintained the confidence of many of his parishioners, and the poor in particular. Despite an attempt by a group of twenty-seven householders, tithe and ratepayers to drive him out of the parish, Butt succeeded in staying in King's Langley until his death in 1855.[107]

The provision and maintenance of a suitable house for the living was the responsibility of the incumbent, although housing was obviously a matter of considerable interest to curates as well. In the counties of Lincolnshire, Nottinghamshire and Buckinghamshire there existed something of a crisis in the Church's housing stock in the early years of the nineteenth century. To a great extent it was ameliorated by the single-minded efforts of the clergy themselves, though sometimes the coercion of the bishop and his archdeacons played an important role. It was an act of unselfishness for an incumbent voluntarily to mortgage his living, and thus reduce his own income, in order to build or rebuild a house that would benefit his successors as much as himself. If he was unwilling to be generous, and if he had been instituted after 1838, clause 62 of the Pluralities Act could be invoked against him. Clause 62 empowered the bishops to demand that a house be built or an existing one repaired on all livings worth more than £100 a year. To pay for this,

---

[104] LAO CorB5/19/14, J. W. Butt to Kaye, 18 March 1845.
[105] Ibid., Butt to Kaye, 24 March 1845.
[106] J. Butts to Kaye ,22 March 1845 and 4 April 1845; D. Jenks to Kaye, 31 March 1845.
[107] Petition sent to Kaye, 1 May 1845; Toovey, Hartley and Groome to Kaye, 20 May 1845, 28 May 1845 and 17 December 1845.

bishops were given extensive powers to mortgage the glebe, tithes, rents, rent charge and other profits arising from the living over a period of up to thirty-five years. The sum borrowed was not to exceed four times the annual net income of the benefice, after the deduction of outgoings.

Although provision was made for the incumbent to raise initial objections, once the mortgage had been entered upon it remained binding upon him and his successors. A mortgage could all too easily become a crippling financial millstone around the incumbent's neck, and be deeply resented. At Foscott (Foxcote) in Buckinghamshire there had been no resident minister for years, although a house belonging to the church existed, and was thought capable of repair. In 1843 a newly-instituted rector, E. A. Uckwatt, proved as reluctant to reside as had his predecessors. Initially he assented to repairs sufficient to make the house habitable by a curate, but as the time drew near to begin the building he became increasingly hostile to the idea.

I never for a single moment supposed I should be called on to build. In point of justice I considered myself exempt when my predecessors never spent 6d. but put people in the parsonage charging them an exorbitant rent.[108]

A dispute between the rector and the bishop dragged on until mid-1845. Kaye remained determined to enforce clause 62, undeterred both by Uckwatt's plea of ill health and by the reluctance of the patron, the Duke of Buckingham, to allow clergy houses close to his own.[109] Uckwatt did not succumb until July 1845, when he claimed to be repairing the house out of his own pocket. The case well illustrates the way in which the clergy could find themselves quite unexpectedly and personally liable for the costs imposed by the wider reform movement.

The provision for mortgaging livings dated from Gilbert's Act of 1777, which empowered the Queen Anne's Bounty to make loans for the building and repair of parsonages. The clergy had therefore come under pressure from the Church hierarchy to rebuild their houses well before clause 62 made it legally compelling. Robert Phillimore, rector of Slapton in Buckinghamshire, was coerced into massive debt by Archdeacon Hill, who was a zealous campaigner for the restoration of glebe houses and churches, with an arrogant manner that made him unpopular. Hill visited Slapton in 1826, and finding that the parsonage was very dilapidated, he gave orders for its immediate repair.[110]

---

[108] LAO CorB5/3/22/5, E. A. Uckwatt to Kaye, 21 February 1845.
[109] Ibid., Kaye to Uckwatt, 19 June 1845; R. N. Russell to Kaye, 28 June 1845.
[110] LAO CorB5/3/6/6, Hill to R. Phillimore, 25 June 1830.

Making return visits in 1829 and 1830, he discovered that his instructions had been ignored, and told the churchwardens to inform the rector that if immediate steps were not taken, he would issue a sequestration against the living.[111] In response to this serious threat Phillimore began repairs, on the understanding that the costs would not exceed the estimate of £200, and that this sum would be forthcoming from the Queen Anne's Bounty. He claimed that the archdeacon had given this assurance to the surveyor.[112] Unfortunately, the expenses quickly doubled to £400, and subsequently soared to in excess of £900.[113] No grant was forthcoming from the Queen Anne's Bounty because the application did not reach the governors until the work had commenced, thus making it ineligible.[114] No funds were available from diocesan sources.[115] The living, which was worth only £192, was already heavily mortgaged as a result of the construction of a farmhouse and outhouses by Phillimore's predecessor. Faced with a deepening financial crisis, Phillimore's tone became desperate:

Mr Archdeacon Hill ordered the repairs himself and told my surveyor he would get all the money for me ... is a clergyman who has no private property (and very few of them have any) to be brought to a condition of absolute ruin by being compelled to rebuild his parsonage?[116]

By the following year, 1834, the hapless rector felt certain that he would be 'sent to gaol and confined there perpetually because I cannot keep buildings in repair from lack of income to do so'.[117] It does not appear that Phillimore ever went to gaol, though it is not possible to establish how, or indeed if, the bills were eventually paid. Four years later Phillimore was complaining of £1,000 worth of bills, and that the house was still unfinished. The painting was incomplete and the only water supply came from a pond.[118]

The examples of Uckwatt and Phillimore illustrate the most dire scenario that could unfold for an incumbent who was forced to repair or build. In the majority of cases the restoration of the parsonage was adequately financed and accomplished to the satisfaction of all con-

[111] Ibid.
[112] Ibid., Phillimore to Kaye, 22 February 1833.
[113] Ibid., Phillimore to Kaye, 17 September 1834.
[114] Ibid.
[115] Ibid., Kaye to Phillimore, 19 April 1833.
[116] Ibid., Phillimore to Kaye, 18 April 1833.
[117] Ibid., Phillimore to Kaye, 17 September 1834.
[118] Ibid., Phillimore to Kaye, 11 September 1838.

cerned. At Hawridge in Buckinghamshire, for example, where the rectory had been 'only an old cottage', it was put into 'perfect repair' along with the outbuildings, barn and stables, for about £450.[119] Mortgages were the most usual method of financing large building projects, but dilapidations payments were useful when smaller sums were required. Grants from the Queen Anne's Bounty were more problematic. The Bounty tended to refuse aid unless it was met by a subscription of similar size independent of dilapidations,[120] or was to aid parishes that were judged to be too poor to pay a curate after the mortgage and interest payments had been met.[121]

What emerges is the generosity of many incumbents in paying the bills themselves without resort to mortgages, as well as their changing standards of what was fitting for a clergyman. The case of Thomas Hayton is instructive. He spent sixty-six years as perpetual curate (which meant he had the same legal rights as an incumbent) of Long Crendon in Buckinghamshire. When he arrived in the parish, in 1821, the glebe house was uninhabitable; no money was available for dilapidations, and the living was regarded as too small to be mortgaged. For the first five years he lodged in the village, 'in one small apartment less than the least of a Cambridge or Oxford attic'.[122] He described the state of the parsonage in a letter to Bishop Kaye in 1827:

The Glebe House for the Benefice of Long Crendon is perhaps one of the meanest edifices of the same nature in the whole range of your diocese. There is a kitchen & a parlour (about 8 feet by 10 each) with a small pantry below stairs; above there is the same number of rooms, such as I am sure your Lordship would scarcely deem suitable for your lowest menial. Indeed no clergyman within the memory of man, previous to myself ever resided in the village of Crendon, much less in the Glebe House.[123]

In addition to his duties at Long Crendon, Hayton served the curacies of Winchendon and Chearsley, neither of which had a glebe house as both had been previously served from Oxford, about fifteen miles away. With an income from all sources of £210,

[119] LAO CorB5/3/14/10, R. Sandby to R. Smith, 5 August 1828; Sandby to Kaye, 16 January 1832.
[120] As for example at Normanton, Notts (LAO CorB5/8/34).
[121] As for example at Laneham, Notts (LAO CorB5/8/35/3) and Upton, Notts (LAO CorB5/8/33/1).
[122] LAO CorB5/3/21/1, T. Hayton to Kaye, 23 April 1827. An edition of Hayton's correspondence during his time at Long Crendon has been published by the Buckinghamshire Record Society: J. Donald (ed.), *The Letters of Thomas Hayton: Vicar of Long Crendon, Buckinghamshire 1821–1887* (Aylesbury, 1979).
[123] Ibid.

Hayton had become engaged to be married, and rented a house four miles from Long Crendon but within ten minutes walk of Winchendon and Chearsley.[124] Four years later, in 1831, Hayton decided to repair his glebe house, initially with a view to attracting a 'respectable' tenant.

I pulled down an old parlour with the intention of making it to the tenant's wishes. Finding nearly the whole of the building in sorrowful decay, I was determined to make a sacrifice of one year's income, I have accordingly done so; – and, to my present embarrassment & my deep-seated grief – much more has been expended. The house I have actually remodelled! – and in the first place to fulfil my agreement with the Tenant, and secondly with a hope of eventually living there myself.[125]

Hayton moved into his glebe house at Michaelmas 1832. He calculated that he had spent £500, or over three years income on it, and despite rebuilding 'the cottage in the plainest style & at a most moderate cost', still felt that he had failed 'to render it decently suitable for a humble pastor'.[126] Hayton rebuilt the house without assistance from the Queen Anne's Bounty, and without mortgaging the living under Gilbert's act. He borrowed the money from friends, repaying them over twenty years.[127] He requested, and received, five pounds from the bishop to purchase fixtures and grates. He remained in the house until his death in 1887.

Hayton's concern to attract a 'respectable' tenant is interesting. As a house became dilapidated, respectable tenants moved out and the poor moved in. In about 1830 Archdeacon Hill sent Kaye a memorandum detailing thirty-one glebe houses in his archdeaconry (out of a total housing stock of about 150) that were either dilapidated or in need of repair or rebuilding, or which had been divided and inhabited by paupers.[128] Pauper occupation of glebe houses was indicative both of low levels of clerical residence and of a shortage of alternative accommodation for labourers. At Fleet Marston, Buckinghamshire, where the population amounted to just forty-one in 1841, all the land in the parish was divided into four farms, with the exception of one acre attached to the rectory. Besides the rectory and three farmhouses, there were no other houses or cottages. The rectory

[124] Ibid., Anon. to Kaye, 22 March 1831.
[125] Ibid., Hayton to Kaye, 28 March 1831.
[126] Ibid., Hayton to Kaye, 26 May 1832; 4 April 1833.
[127] Ibid.
[128] LAO CorB5/3/32/19, J. Hill to Kaye, n.d., but probably 1830.

had become split into three tenements, occupied by three families, a total of about eighteen people. In 1832 Archdeacon Hill directed the rector of Fleet Marston to give the labourers notice to leave, thus precipitating furious protests from the parish landowners, who objected that if their labourers were evicted they would be obliged to walk six miles each day to and from work, and would not be on hand at night to watch over cattle and guard against incendiarism.[129] Hill appears to have failed in his attempt to evict the labourers, for no clergyman ever resided at Fleet Marston during the first half of the nineteenth century. By 1842 Fleet Marston rectory had disappeared from the official records; the benefice was listed in the parochial returns as having no house in that year.[130]

It was obvious that the more dilapidated a house became, the greater was the sum that had to be raised for its restoration. At Oving in Buckinghamshire, where in the late eighteenth century the house had been let to the poor at an annual rent of five pounds, it was estimated in 1828 that between £400 and £500 would need to be spent before it could be made fit for a gentleman.[131] At Archdeacon Hill's own living of Tingewick, the glebe house was 'only a farmhouse', and, although he had spent £1,000 on repairs to it, Hill regarded it as unsuitable for his curate, for whom he rented another property a hundred yards from the church.[132] The enhancement of the social and economic fortunes of the clergy during the late eighteenth and early nineteenth centuries resulted in modest glebe houses, which had been regarded as commodious in 1740, being rejected as totally inadequate in 1840, even when they had been in more or less constant clerical occupation. At Pilham in Lincolnshire, William Dunkin described how, when he came to the living in 1792, the parsonage was of 'mud walls and mud accommodation neither safe nor decent for a clergyman'.[133] Dunkin claimed to have spent considerable sums converting it into a comfortable parsonage. His successor in the benefice did not, however, share his standard of comfort. Shortly after presentation in 1839, Charles Newmarch made plans to raise £270 by mortgaging the living to the governors of the Queen Anne's Bounty, in order to improve the 'wretched' glebe house.

[129] LAO CorB5/3/32/11, landowners' and occupiers' memorial to Kaye, 3 April 1832.
[130] LAO SPE 18, 1842.
[131] LAO CorB5/3/25/3, E. M. Willan to Kaye, 19 September 1828.
[132] LAO CorB5/3/28/6, Hill to Kaye, 20 August 1828.
[133] LAO CorB5/4/77/2, W. Dunkin to Kaye, 2 December 1833.

The walls are in parts very damp and need battening, caused by defective drainage. The Floors on the ground storey are all brick and need to be replaced with board. The upper storey floors are very weak.[134]

The complexity of legal procedures surrounding the construction of new parsonages meant that restoration, even when so extensive as to render the original building unrecognisable, was almost always favoured to total demolition.[135] During Bishop Kaye's episcopate at Lincoln from 1827 to 1853, 214 parsonage houses were built, rebuilt or made fit for clerical residence.[136] Analysis of the parochial returns reveals that the level of housing stock remained fairly static, and that the emphasis was on rebuilding existing parsonages. In Lincolnshire 72 per cent of parishes had a glebe house in 1832, of which 60 per cent were in clerical occupation. In 1844, 72 per cent of parishes had a glebe house, but the figure in clerical occupation had climbed to 71 per cent. By 1853, 75 per cent of parishes had a house, and the figure in clerical occupation had reached 80 per cent.[137] The overall rise in glebe houses was just 3 per cent in twenty-one years, but the overall rise in clerical occupation was 20 per cent. In Nottinghamshire the pattern was strikingly similar. There are no figures available for 1832, but in 1844, 75 per cent of parishes possessed a glebe house, of which 73 per cent were in clerical occupation. In 1853 the percentage of glebe houses had actually fallen slightly (though not in real terms) to 75 per cent. Of these houses, 82 per cent were occupied by clergy.[138] Buckinghamshire was best served in terms of both parsonages and resident clerics, which was perhaps in part due to the relentless efforts of Archdeacon Hill. In 1832, 88 per cent of parishes had glebe houses, of which 76 per cent had clergy living in them. The percentage had dropped to 86 per cent in 1844, indicating that the disappearance of Fleet Marston rectory was not an isolated example. The level of clerical occupation had however risen to 82 per cent.[139] There are no figures available for 1853.

TWO CLERGYMEN: A GLIMPSE INTO THE INTERIOR

There was of course more to being a clergyman than worrying about money, housing and job prospects, important though these were.

[134] Ibid., C. F. Newmarch to Kaye, 6 October 1839.
[135] Best, *Temporal Pillars* p. 205.
[136] *Gentleman's Magazine* (April 1853) pp. 428–31.
[137] Knight, 'Bishop, clergy and people', tables 1, p. 380; 2, p. 381.
[138] Ibid., table 16, p. 396; table 17, p. 397.
[139] Ibid., table 29, p. 409; table 30, p. 410.

'Fearing most his own vain heart' as Keble put it, the parochial clergyman, perhaps newly-isolated in his rural glebe house, pondered on what his life should be. For men who had been acquainted with the bustle and stimulation of university life, or who had lived among other clergy in busy towns like Louth, nicknamed the 'nest of rooks' because of the numbers of clergy who resided there in the 1820s and 1830s,[140] the role of a resident country clergyman could be a hard one to assume. Francis Massingberd, a graduate of Magdalen College, Oxford, tried to devote himself to scholarship, but found a commitment to regular study difficult in the isolation of South Lindsey. By 1838 he seems to have recognised that the academic world was passing him by. 'Great learning is now hopeless for me. My excellence must therefore be as a Parish Pastor "unstable as water, thou shalt not excel".'[141] Nevertheless, his scholarly ambitions revived in the following year, when his Oxford friend Edward Churton invited him to contribute a volume on the English Reformation to a series of which Churton was editor. This volume became the *English Reformation*, which by 1870 had found its way on to the reading list of the Ely ordinands. But Massingberd's initial pleasure at the invitation disappeared when Churton advertised the book as to 'appear shortly' before it was even begun, and the project became a burden.[142] For John Rashdall, the transition from Trinity College, Cambridge, and Cheltenham, where he had a wide circle of Evangelical friends, to 'the lonely usefulness of a Country Curate's Life' scarcely seemed easier. A few days before his ordination he wrote, 'could I but feel the spirit of "a Sent one" filling me I should despise all the difficulties, and consider the pleasures to be given up but as dross: at present I am in the darkness of unbelief: mine at least is a fruitless faith.'[143]

The survival of the diaries of Massingberd and Rashdall provide a rare glimpse into the interior world of the parish clergy, and also a valuable corrective to the impression – which can all-too-easily be

---

[140] It was Bishop Kaye who coined the phrase to describe Louth. In 1832 there were nine parishes whose incumbent lived in Louth, and eleven whose curate lived there – excluding, that is, the two parishes in Louth itself. These parishes were up to seven miles from Louth, indicating that the surrounding countryside was largely devoid of resident clergy. Allowing for some pluralism, the total number of out-of-town clergy may not have been quite as high as twenty. By 1844 the number was down to one incumbent and five curates. By 1853 there were, excluding the clergy who served Louth itself, just one incumbent and one curate residing in the town.

[141] LAO MASS/8/1, 15 December 1838.

[142] Ibid., 6 August 1839.

[143] Bodl MS Eng. misc. e. 351, 24 August 1833.

gained from the study of diocesan papers – that the clergy were little concerned with spiritual matters. Between September 1833 and September 1834 both men ministered within about six miles of each other – Massingberd at South Ormsby and Rashdall at Orby. They had a slight social acquaintance, and even courted a pair of sisters (Massingberd married Fanny Baring in 1839 and Rashdall considered Rosa Baring 'the prettiest and most elegant girl I was ever intimate with').[144] There were further similarities: both men had substantial private means, and could be considered fortunate in worldly terms. But both suffered from an intermittent sense of isolation, and were subject to fits of depression, self-doubt and spiritual unease. Massingberd's diary is undoubtedly the darker document, shot through with self-reproach and anxiety about money, his marriage, his inability to pray or to write sermons on time. It contrasts with Rashdall's more positive treatment of his spiritual life. During his Lincolnshire curacy, he was a serious yet relatively unburdened young man, still in the process of Evangelical conversion. Living in lodgings in Spilsby, he seemed less isolated than Massingberd. After leaving Lincolnshire, he served a couple of Exeter curacies, and later at Eaton chapel in Eaton Square, London. He ended his ministry as vicar of Dawlish in Devon, and died in 1869.

The unstructured nature of the parochial clergyman's life was burdensome for Massingberd, but not for Rashdall, who had read avidly at Cambridge, and simply transferred his university habits to Spilsby. He spent a great deal of each day with his books, and read widely, from Hooker, Jeremy Taylor, Butler and Horne to Southey, Hazlitt, Locke, Goethe, Byron and Jane Austen. Rashdall fitted easily into local society, and continued to enjoy the company of his college friend, Alfred Tennyson, who lived at Somersby – though he despaired privately about the state of Tennyson's soul. Just as his Evangelical sensibilities did not prevent him from reading plays, novels and the writings of High Churchmen, neither did they preclude him from attending balls and parties, though he was careful to maintain a balance between solitude and sociability. After he left Lincolnshire, Rashdall seems to have become less tolerant and more serious. He read more selectively, and gave up many of the social and cultural activities that he had previously relished, although the decision to do so was accompanied by a considerable tussle, as he tried to separate his own motivations from the expectations of others.

---

[144]   Ibid., 3 November 1834.

London is a dull place to me now ... and the old style has lost its attractions, even if it would not be improper for a clergyman. No Operas, no Theatres, no Balls. But it was prudence, the wish not to give offence – the fear of injuring the character of a Xn minister, that has kept me away, and by no means the want of interest, or the pleasurable expectation: in fact on the contrary I should have done better to have gone, than to have remained listless at home as far as my own state of mind is concerned. It would have been, as it always is, benefited by such things – they afford food for thought ... but then I see evidently that the feeling of delight and interest connected with these things betrays a state of mind anything but elevated ... when a man ceases to pray his spirituality is gone.[145]

Massingberd also found an equilibrium difficult to achieve. 'Always tempted to go to books or other studies first, and neglect parish: but it never answers. Should do just the contrary: parish first, then as much else as possible. Wickcliffe *spent the morning of every day in his parish*.'[146] Massingberd seemed to fritter away his time, and if his self-accusations bore any relation to reality, it is difficult to know how exactly he did fill his days. On 7 July 1830, when he was twenty-nine years old and apparently in good health, he wrote a typical entry in his diary:

Now again am I sunk in sloth. I do not rise betimes, I do not read the bible. I do not pray effectually, I do not visit my flock regularly. I do not write my sermons, or I scribble them without premeditation. I do not study *at all*. I do not attend to my affairs, I do not regulate the occupations of my family. My mind is full of vain and frivolous thoughts, and abstracted from my duties ...[147]

Similar litanies punctuate the pages of his diary. At the age of forty-seven he concluded that his neglect of the Bible had been throughout life one of his 'most crying sins'.[148] He frequently made new resolutions to study the Bible, to pray more regularly, to get up earlier, and just as frequently abandoned them with a growing sense of self-disgust. Typical is his entry for 15 December 1848:

Resolve, please God, to begin this day morning and evens. to read the lessons for the day. What a thing to resolve upon, having been 23 years a priest, when the Church enjoins the clergy to do it every day.

In less than a fortnight Massingberd had lapsed in his Bible reading.
       Massingberd found talking about religion with parishioners difficult

[145] Ibid., 4 July 1835.
[146] LAO MASS/8/1, 23 October 1840.
[147] Ibid., 7 July 1831.
[148] LAO MASS/8/2, Ash Wednesday 1848.

and embarrassing, and this made his desire to retreat into his study, or to seek convivial society far away from his parish, all the stronger. He addressed the dilemma in a revealing entry in his diary of 12 January 1845:

Dined yesterday (Saturday) at the Bp. of Exeter's – and several times of late dined out with people who live in 'the world' – connexions indeed – but somewhat dissatisfied with myself. Is it a *morbid* feeling? Or is it from ye want of sufficiently strong views one side or another? I belong in fact to no party and oscillate between both. I have a conception of the line I wish to take, but qn. [question] whether it be a practicable line. In prayer this morning, repeating – Lord Thou Knowest that I love Thee – the answer came forcibly to my mind – *Feed my Sheep – Feed my Lambs*. Christ's ministers ought surely to be occupied in this – not merely as hirelings, when they are with their own flock, but wherever they are. To do some good to the souls of people is a much more obvious duty than to write speculative books about religion; and my shyness and love of speculation and abstraction together make this peculiarly difficult for me.[149]

In common with other well-connected country rectors, Massingberd was expected to play a closely defined part in society, and had little freedom to reinterpret his role. He found it a hard one, sensing a contradiction between a Christian call to poverty and simplicity, and the social imperative of maintaining his position as a gentleman. He was quite capable of reflecting upon the chasm between the life of Jesus and that of the well-to-do nineteenth-century clergyman. From time to time he introduced austerity measures into his household, although the emphasis on the spiritual benefits that these were supposed to promote was usually rather ambiguously fused with an attention to the financial savings that would also be achieved. On New Year's Day 1841, he recorded:

I intend this year to reduce my establishment, to submit to the humiliation of having no regular man servt. in ye house etc – *Humiliation?* Think of Christ! But it will help to pay off debts, and restore or rebuild Driby church, and pay curate – and will answer other good purposes of self-denial. Dear wife quite willing.[150]

The social necessity of entertaining could also be a trial:

Yesterday had a large dinner party, 12 – too many, vulgar and inelegant in itself, and q? [questioned] the lawfulness to a clergyman, even if not too expensive, of setting this example. 'Call not thy rich neighbors, but call the Poor etc.'[151]

---

[149] LAO MASS/8/1, 12 January 1845.
[150] Ibid., 1 January 1841.
[151] Ibid., 12 September 1839.

Marriage was another obligation that Massingberd was expected to fulfil, for an unmarried clergyman who could afford a wife was an object of suspicion on Puseyite grounds. After years of searching for a suitable bride, Massingberd's choice fell upon Fanny Baring, a member of the banking family who lived in Lincolnshire and Putney in London, and whom he seems to have known only very slightly before the wedding. From the beginning of their marriage, Massingberd set about moulding his new wife in conformity with his own notions, but Fanny seems to have been reluctant to co-operate in this attempt to reshape her personality. They quarrelled violently and seemingly unceasingly. Massingberd regarded his wife as obstinate, quick-tempered and lacking in religious sympathy. The unhappiness that resulted is at the root of much of the anguish which pervades his diary. Typical is the entry for 8 August 1841: 'Quarrel again at breakfast with poor F. She is astonished and cannot understand why such things as she says annoy me so.'[152] In 1847 he was filled with remorse after swearing at her during a particularly bitter altercation: 'I think this was the worst unkindness I ever committed: and how great the sin – *oaths* too, in the mouth of a presbyter of Xt's [Christ's] Church – And how little like a gentleman.'[153] This was but one of the many conflicts that Massingberd experienced between the roles which he was expected to assume. 'Difficult always to keep up the thought and wish in society to be taken for a *clergyman* and nothing else – Apt to desire to be taken also for a *gentleman*. How much more *dignified*, as well as humble, the opposite course.'[154]

It was the Eucharist that helped Massingberd to make some sense of his life. He usually made a point of recording when he participated in it, and his state of mind before and after the service. In November 1838 he described himself as 'indolent, procrastinating and very much inclined to despond, until today, administered ye Holy Communion to Rebecca Pridgson, and was cheered and refreshed and happy'.[155] By 1840, he seems to have started holding monthly communion services at South Ormsby,[156] and in 1845 he thought of introducing a 'regular' (presumably weekly) early communion, but gave it up, probably for fear of being considered a Romaniser.[157] When in London he would

152 Ibid., 8 August 1841.
153 LAO MASS/8/2, 4 August 1847.
154 LAO MASS/8/1, 5 August 1842.
155 Ibid., 14 November 1838.
156 Ibid., 4 March 1840.
157 LAO MASS/8/2, 25 October 1845.

attend the sacrament at the Margaret Street chapel,[158] after which he would typically describe himself as 'much refreshed'. In 1848, in what seems to have been a notable departure from contemporary convention, he celebrated communion at the baptism of his second child. 'Methought Angels and departed friends were present – my Mother especially.'[159] In the following year he held a private communion, probably in the rectory, at which only his wife, sister and four servants were present. 'Very blessed time and yet I was *peevish*.'[160]

John Rashdall, in contrast, made little of the Eucharist, at least initially. He does not appear to have received the sacrament at all during his diaconal year, nor to have made arrangements for a priest to be present at Orby at Christmas or on Easter Day. Several weeks after his ordination to the priesthood he made a passing reference to having administered the sacrament at West Keal, but it is not clear that he was the celebrant on that occasion, and he does not appear to have regarded it as having any particular significance. It was not until he had been a priest for a year, and was living in Exeter, that he remarked 'at the Sacrament in the morning experienced that Xt is present at his ordinances'.[161] Later, he favoured the introduction of monthly communion services. In his first year as a clergyman, Rashdall's spiritual life pivoted around his quest to be fully converted. He had cultivated a solid Evangelical faith prior to ordination, but he believed that the experience of 'perfect regeneration' had eluded him. Indeed, the harder he pursued it, the more elusive it appeared to become. In his first year as a curate he recorded the peaks and troughs of his religious life with remarkable candour; in later years he became a little more reticent. A few days after his diaconal ordination he recorded:

My soul is clogged in its spiritual flight, and even alone in the fields, my eyes fixed upon the blue sky, I could not fix my mind on God ... O, what is 'regeneration': the work I trust in God has been begun in me; but the chains of sin are still tight around me: The light of life within me is dim and distant.[162]

Rashdall continued to use this imagery of his soul being 'clogged' and 'bound' until the evening of 13 October 1833, when he 'enjoyed an hour or two of the most delightful contemplation and communion, that

[158] LAO MASS/8/1, Palm Sunday 1841; MASS/8/2, 5 February 1848; 17 April 1848.
[159] Ibid., 18 June 1848.
[160] Ibid., 19 May 1849.
[161] Bodl MS Eng. misc. e. 352, 20 September 1835.
[162] Bodl MS Eng. misc. e. 351, 30 September 1833.

ever helped a poor sinner from the earth'.[163] This seems to have been a decisive experience, for he dwelt upon it for several days. On 17 October he declared, 'I can now pray, think and read like a Christian, though the flesh terribly lusteth against the Spirit!'[164] On 2 November, however, he still felt that there was 'a great gulf between me and perfect regeneration'.[165]

Rashdall's quest for regeneration turned out to be less straightforward than he had supposed. He likened his faith to a 'boat upon the swelling waves' of his uncertain heart. 'With them it rises and with them it sinks: the winds of doctrine and of passion blow upon it like a storm.'[166] He became conscious of himself as 'yet a mere babe in Christ: though a Minister of the Gospel, I feel I am only in its first principles both of doctrine and practice.'[167] His struggle continued into the new year. On 13 February 1834 he wrote:

Last two or three days have been most undeserved manifestations of the love of God in a renewal of heavenly thoughts, desires, and affections, after a strange coldness, and fearful and miserable alienation. I am still perplexed about the nature of regeneration.[168]

Matters became worse in March:

I am now in the state of the most desperate sinner, only that my lot is the worse from a knowledge of the excellence of the state from which I have driven myself. Satan is fearfully successful against me.[169]

But there was an improvement in April, and on 17 April he felt the 'power of a Servant of the Lord'.[170] By May he was beginning to become doubtful about the value of recording any observations about his inner state:

Since last entry to the contrary have been in spiritual matters, dark, estranged and wilful. This morning have experienced a change, but of which the previous notices herein written bid me doubt the reality ... I am too much inclined to self-confidence, and to enjoy before the time the peculiar joys of the righteous ...[171]

[163] Ibid., 13 October 1833.
[164] Ibid., 17 October 1833.
[165] Ibid., 2 November 1833.
[166] Ibid., 31 December 1833.
[167] Ibid., 24 November 1833.
[168] Ibid., 13 February 1834.
[169] Ibid., 10 March 1834.
[170] Ibid., 17 April 1834.
[171] Ibid., 20 May 1834.

The diary suggests that a greater spiritual confidence developed in Rashdall during 1835. By the beginning of 1836 a decisive change had occurred. 'Desperate as I am, I do not seem to feel alarmed for my final salvation. I cannot help feeling myself a child of God from whom his father's countenance is hid ... I know that is a groundless confidence, that I have no right to trust thereto – yet I do – & I cannot help it.'[172]

John Rashdall believed that the direct intervention of the Holy Spirit would regenerate his soul. He was striving for a very particular religious experience; it was a state that he sometimes achieved, though he considered that the experience was usually all too fleeting. He was much troubled by his inability to attain a consistent state of holiness, which was the ideal for which he strove. Like Massingberd, he had some difficulty in integrating his spirituality with his public life, and would frequently complain of how unspiritual he felt after an evening spent in society, or in the company of 'Fred' Tennyson. This underlay his loss of interest in being in London. He decided theological questions on the basis of personal experience, rather than Anglican orthodoxy. This is reflected in his attitude to the Eucharist, and in his failure to assent to the doctrine of baptismal regeneration. He held an open ecclesiology that allowed friendly relations with Nonconformists; he considered Mr Harris, the Independent minister at Alford chapel, as 'the most heavenly minded Christian' he had ever met.[173]

Francis Massingberd's approach was significantly different. He sought to avoid the labels of party, though many of his attitudes seem characteristic of the High Church. His ecclesiology was exclusively Anglican, not pan-Protestant. In common with many other clergy, he found Newman's conversion to Roman Catholicism in 1845 an unsettling episode, but when Manning seceded five and a half years later, he noted that 'the deep affliction of others did not seem to touch me. Whether from a more hopeful spirit or indifference, or a mind too much set on this world – or else from the blessing of a more abiding love for the Ch. of E.'[174] It was characteristic of Massingberd that in striving for heaven he tried to ignore the reality of the world. This is reflected in the priorities he set himself in 1845:

To guard against (1) vain thoughts (2) ambition (3) vain regrets (4) unkindness to F (5) cowardice (6) extravagance, especially as regards any sudden impulse

[172] Bodl MS Eng. misc. e. 352, 7 January 1836.
[173] Bodl MS Eng. misc. e. 351, 14 April 1834.
[174] LAO MASS/8/2, 3 December 1850.

(7) fear of man, especially in sudden impulses – To acquire Love, pervading love, of God and Christ, to seek his Glory, desire his praise, long for his Presence, Look for his Salvation, *Labor in His Service.*

Massingberd strove to love God; he did not suppose that God would love him. To a great extent his image of God was of a wrathful, remote, retributive deity; grace, love, forgiveness and redemption were not freely available. The terror of Judgement was writ large. Increasingly torn apart by a sense of his own failure, Massingberd began to worry about problems that do not appear to have existed, for example that God would punish him and his wife for their continual rows by inflicting illness on their son, although the boy always seems to have been healthy.[175] His parochial responsibilities became oppressive: 'How little visiting of my flock. The flock of Christ! Every one of whose souls cost his precious blood, and *will be required at my hands!*'[176] Massingberd believed quite literally that an account of every day of his life would be required at the judgement-seat,[177] and in the context of such a belief his shortcomings as a parish priest came to weigh on him almost intolerably.

[175] Ibid., 24 September 1846.
[176] Ibid., 22 October 1845.
[177] Ibid., 16 December 1850.

CHAPTER 5

Relations remoulded

Last Monday sent to Rivingtons 'Church Reform Without Legislation' for publication and received answer that they have
declined to publish any thing else upon the subject.

This was Francis Massingberd's diary entry for 3 July 1831. Undeterred
by the rejection, he published his pamphlet privately, and persuaded
Rivingtons to take a revised version of it in 1833, entitled *Some
Considerations on Church Reform, and on the Principles of Church Legislation.*
Massingberd's approach was characteristic of the rage to participate in
the reform debate that swept through the Church in the early 1830s.
Geoffrey Best has suggested that 1833 was the peak year for publications of this sort.[1] 'Untold dozens of churchmen buckled down to the
self-imposed task of communicating to the world their views, and their
views on other writer's views, on this engrossing subject.'[2] The writings
of the most influential and often cited contributors, Thomas Arnold,
Edward Berens, Edward Burton and Lord Henley, represent just the
tip of an iceberg;[3] church reform was an issue on which no clergyman
was likely to remain indifferent.

Among the labyrinth of proposals, it was Henley's suggestion that
the Church's capitular, collegiate and episcopal property would be
more efficiently managed by a body of commissioners, who should be a
mix of both senior churchmen and politicians, which was to find
particular favour with his brother-in-law Sir Robert Peel, when he
became prime minister in 1835.[4] The body that Peel brought together
in that year as the Ecclesiastical Revenues and Duties Commission
transformed itself into the Ecclesiastical Commission in 1836, and

---

[1] G. F. A. Best, *Temporal Pillars: Queen Anne's Bounty, the Ecclesiastical Commissioners, and the Church of
England* (Cambridge: Cambridge University Press, 1964) p. 278.
[2] Ibid., p. 280.
[3] For a discussion of these works see ibid., pp. 278–90.
[4] Ibid., pp. 285–8.

acquired permanent status.[5] It was to assume a critical role in reshaping the Church of England; nothing else had as marked an impact on common clerical life as did the implementation of the Commission's policies. Its reports became blueprints for the redrawing of diocesan boundaries and the reallocation of episcopal funding, and for radical changes to the rules on residence and pluralities, and on cathedral finance. They gave substance to the Established Church Act (1836), the Pluralities Act (1838) and the Dean and Chapter Act (1840), and they contributed to a shift from largely parochial and local forms of church government to more centralised and episcopally-dominated styles.

In the previous chapter it was argued that the parochial clergy bore the brunt of the sometimes painful adjustments which were necessary in order to put the Commission's policies into practice. Financial hardship and isolation were not uncommon, as clergy became legally compelled to go into residence and build parsonages in parishes that in reality were too small and too impoverished to support a resident incumbent. This chapter considers some further effects of the Commission's policies, as well as other developments. It begins with an examination of the changing status of the bishop, and considers in particular the questions of patronage and clergy discipline. As about half of the livings in the Church of England were in the gift of lay patrons, the bishops' acquisition of greater amounts of patronage for themselves became a potent symbol of the attempt to increase episcopal influence, although lay patronage remained a force to be reckoned with throughout the period. Another change aimed at strengthening the authority of bishops was in their powers to discipline recalcitrant clergy, although parliamentary attempts to make disciplinary measures more effective were not particularly successful, as will be shown. The bishops' influence was, however, to be bolstered by the emergence of a strengthened middle tier in the diocesan hierarchy, seen in the greater importance given to rural deans and archdeacons. The implications of this for the parochial clergy are fully explored in the second part of the chapter. The third section considers the consequences of the beginnings of the shift from parochial to diocesan forms of church government for the laity, particularly for those who had fulfilled the traditional roles of churchwarden, parish clerk, sexton and schoolteacher. The chapter concludes by reflecting upon the implications of the laity's inclusion in

[5]   Ibid., p. 298.

diocesan church structures, which was a new development in the period from 1860.

BISHOPS, PATRONS AND RECALCITRANT CLERGY

At the beginning of the nineteenth century a bishop's disciplinary powers over his clergy were more or less confined to issuing ultimatums with the non-residence and curates' licences, and to dangling the prospect of the augmentations from the Queen Anne's Bounty as a carrot to prevent clergy from misbehaving.[6] If a bishop received a request to order an incumbent into residence, to defend the interests of a curate or to remove a notoriously wicked rector, his response was almost invariably the same, that he possessed no powers of interference and, if the parties concerned would not respond to gentle persuasion or stern rebuke, he could do little. Critics who heaped scorn on what they perceived as the vacillation of bishops at the beginning of the period, usually failed to appreciate just how limited their powers were. The Stipendiary Curates' Act of 1813 and the Consolidated Act of 1817 went some way towards strengthening the authority of bishops, but it was not until the Pluralities Act, in 1838, that they achieved the far wider range of powers discussed in the previous chapter. The bishops had emerged from the constitutional revolution of 1828–32 with their confidence dented, and they found themselves confronted with a new set of problems that they viewed in almost apocalyptic dimensions. 'We cannot be surprised at being told' said Kaye in his Charge for 1831, 'as we repeatedly are, that [the Church's] days are already numbered, and that it is destined to sink at no distant period before the irresistible force of enlightened public opinion.'[7]

In the context of a constitutional relationship between Church and State that accorded bishops the status of peers of the realm, it was inevitable that they should be expected to assume the lead when the government decided that the time was ripe for church reform. To politicians, anxious to regain the initiative by ensuring that the Establishment functioned more efficiently, the bishops seemed ideally qualified for the task.[8] The result was that from the mid-1830s episcopal influence in the Church of England began steadily to increase, as

[6]   Ibid., p. 215.
[7]   John Kaye, *Charge* (1831), printed in W. F. J. Kaye (ed.), *The Works of John Kaye*, 8 vols. (London, 1888), vol. VII, p. 47.
[8]   Best, *Temporal Pillars* p. 264.

Bishops Blomfield, Kaye and Monk became the prelates who set the agenda for the Ecclesiastical Commission. They were the prominent bishops on the Commission in the crucial first five years of its life. Archbishops Howley and Vernon Harcourt, though also present, did not assume a significant role.

The three scholar-bishops – Blomfield, Kaye and Monk – were sufficiently similar to classify them as of a type.[9] They had been close friends for over twenty years before they were summoned to the Ecclesiastical Commission by Peel. Born within four years of each other in the 1780s, and sharing similar middle-class, non-clerical backgrounds, the three had been drawn together at Cambridge.[10] They all became bishops between 1820 and 1830; Kaye at Bristol and then Lincoln, Blomfield at Chester and then London, and Monk at Gloucester, after a spell as dean of Peterborough. It was perhaps the sense of a common mind that had grown out of their long friendship, and the self-assurance that came from the conspicuous success which they had enjoyed in their academic and ecclesiastical careers, which led them to suppose that they could reform the church without reference to anybody else. As J. A. Venn put it (without apparent irony) when describing the career of Blomfield, he 'set himself to reorganise the established Church'.[11]

The view of politicians that the bishops were pre-eminently qualified to carry out the task of church reform unaided by their junior colleagues was not one generally shared by the clergy. Clerical distrust of the episcopate was hardly new, but intensified in the period after 1835, as the bishops were seen to be apparently accumulating powers unchecked.[12] Whilst the Ecclesiastical Commission was welcomed by some of the Whig-sympathising curates who hoped that it would bring them a better future, for most of the clergy the magnification of the

---

[9] For Blomfield, see A. Blomfield, *A Memoir of C. J. Blomfield*, 2 vols. (London, 1863); Olive Brose, *Church and Parliament: The Reshaping of the Church of England 1828–1860* (Stanford: Stanford University Press and London: Oxford University Press, 1959); P. J. Welch, 'Blomfield and Peel: a study in co-operation between Church and State 1841–46', *Journal of Ecclesiastical History*, 12 (1961). For Kaye, see Frances Knight, 'Bishop, clergy and people: John Kaye and the diocese of Lincoln 1827–1853' (unpublished Ph.D thesis, University of Cambridge, 1990). There is little available on Monk, beyond the entries in J. A. Venn, *Alumni Cantabrigienses* and the *Dictionary of National Biography*.

[10] They had a shared interest in classical scholarship. Monk became Regius Professor of Greek; Kaye was elected Regius Professor of Divinity; Blomfield resigned his fellowship in order to marry, but maintained a considerable scholarly output in the 1810s.

[11] Venn, *Alumni Cantabrigiensis* (Cambridge: Cambridge University Press, 1940) vol. 1, part 2, p. 300.

[12] Best, *Temporal Pillars* pp. 261–4.

episcopal office seemed unwelcome. When Henley had formulated the idea of a commission, he had not intended it to be subject to episcopal domination. In order to avoid this from happening, Peel had made an early attempt to widen its membership to include a few archdeacons, but Blomfield and Kaye had resisted fiercely.[13] If the bishops had acceded to Peel's request, much of the clerical antagonism might have been dissipated.

One example will illustrate the difficulties that resulted from the attempts to implement the Commission's policies at diocesan level. The relationship between the Lincoln chapter and its reforming bishop appears to have become extremely strained, and even a chapter member who had initially welcomed the Commission became hostile to it. In 1835 Archdeacon Bayley of Stow had written supportively to Henry Goulburn, who was Peel's adviser on church matters, 'Be assured that the best part of us [the Lincoln chapter] are most willing to have a good and ample reform – and any of us would be glad to give information on any question proposed, in writing or viva voca.'[14] Bayley's connection with Lincoln was strong; he had served as sub-dean between 1805 and 1828. As a conscientious churchman, he was aware that the unseemly domination of the close by the discredited Pretyman brothers, whose father, Bishop Pretyman-Tomline, had conferred multiple preferments on them in the 1810s, did nothing to enhance the standing of the cathedral or the Church.[15]

Bayley's promise of co-operation with the Commissioners proved to be short-lived. It was the Commissioners' second and fourth reports, which became the substance of the Dean and Chapter Act, that threw Lincoln and other chapters into turmoil.[16] The core of the proposals was the suppression of all non-resident prebends (there were fifty-two at Lincoln, and about 360 in the Church as a whole), all sinecure rectories and, with certain exceptions, the equalising of resident canonries at four each per cathedral. The revenues released as a result of this reorganisation were to be transferred to the Ecclesiastical

[13] BL Add. MSS 40418 fo. 14, Peel to Howley, 22 March 1835; fo. 83, Howley to Peel, 25 March 1835. Blomfield and Kaye were alleged to have claimed that 'no selection could be made which would not give rise to jealousies'.

[14] BL Add. MSS 40333 fos. 293–4, Bayley to Goulburn, 28 January 1835; also cited by Best, *Temporal Pillars* p. 292.

[15] For an account of the life and times of the Pretymans, see David M. Thompson, 'Historical survey, 1750–1949' in Dorothy Owen (ed.), *A History of Lincoln Minster* (Cambridge: Cambridge University Press, 1994) pp. 224–42.

[16] A selection of the petitions and protests that were addressed to Kaye against the fourth report and the subsequent bill have been preserved at the LAO as CorB5/10/16/1–36.

Commission's Common Fund, which would redirect the money to parochial work in the densely populated and so-called spiritually destitute parts of the country. In place of the non-resident prebends, up to twenty-four honorary canonries could be created at the discretion of the bishop in each cathedral. It was further proposed to transfer the patronage of individual members of each chapter to the bishop, whilst maintaining the patronage of the dean and chapter as a corporate body. Other changes, conceived, no doubt, with an eye on the progeny of Bishop Pretyman – who had been appointed to their string of lucrative posts shortly after ordination – related to the minimum age, modes of appointment and income of chapter members.[17]

The *Memorial* of protest that the dean and chapter of Lincoln sent to the Ecclesiastical Commissioners in January 1837 was couched in wounded tones.[18] The memorialists regretted that no discussions had taken place between bishops and their deans and chapters, and they were fearful of the concentration of episcopal patronage, which they believed would result in toadying to bishops: 'If so many different streams are converted into one straight channel of preferment, much obscure merit must be overlooked; and we fear, encouragement given to indirect methods and unworthy endeavours to procure interest with those who have so much to distribute.' They were deeply critical too of the principle that permitted endowments given in one place to be switched to another locality.

The dean and chapter's *Memorial* was a clearly contrived snub to their diocesan on the Ecclesiastical Commission, but as such it was not the end of the matter. Archdeacon Bayley began to organise his own crusade in the parishes, a campaign that was to split the normally close-knit ranks of the archdeacons. In June 1840 he circulated a petition to the clergy of his archdeaconry, asking them to support a motion in opposition to the Dean and Chapter Bill. On a surviving copy of the petition now at Lincoln is written a note to George Wilkins, archdeacon of Nottingham, from Charles Hoare, archdeacon of Winchester.[19] Hoare had been asked by Bayley to send a copy of the petition to every archdeacon in England and Wales, to ascertain whether he had considered writing to his clergy in a similar vein, and if

---

[17]   Owen Chadwick, *The Victorian Church*, 3rd edn (London: A & C. Black, 1971), part I, p. 137.
[18]   LAO CorB5/10/16/19, *A Memorial addressed by the Dean and Chapter of Lincoln to His Majesty's Commissioners Appointed to Consider the State of the Established Church with Reference to Ecclesiastical Duties and Revenues*, 24 January 1837.
[19]   LAO CorB5/10/16/27, Bayley's petition to the archdeaconry of Stow, 1 June 1840.

not, requesting him to do so. Thus it appears that Bayley was attempting to orchestrate a nationwide clerical protest against the Dean and Chapter Bill. Wilkins, however, seems to have felt a greater loyalty to his bishop than to his fellow archdeacons on this question, and he presumably forwarded the circular to Kaye in order to alert him to Bayley's proposals.

It was awkward for a bishop to find that a sizeable proportion of his clergy, as well as his cathedral chapter, had petitioned against a legislative measure with which he was closely associated. When Bayley's petition was presented to the House of Lords, Kaye did his best to shrug it off. Blomfield acted as his spokesman, though his intervention was concerned not with the substance of the petition, but with whether or not all its signatories were indeed clergy in Bayley's archdeaconry.[20] The report of the debate in the following day's *Times* prompted Charles Goddard, archdeacon of Lincoln, to offer Kaye some thoughts concerning the conduct of his fellow archdeacons:

Now all I know of the matter is what I told you three weeks ago in the Strand, namely that Archd. Hoare wrote to me sometime ago, and *as he said* by advice of Bayley and transmitted a copy of a petition which I was to recommend to the clergy of my archdry, as Bayley intended to do to those of Stow. I made *no* answer to either ... because whatever may be the private opinions of an Archdeacon ... yet I hold it a gross indecency for an Archdeacon to attack or arrange attacks upon a scheme which his Diocesan has more or less approved ... so as to *work up* the clergy to oppose it. What the clergy choose to do of their own hands without consulting their Archdeacon or being set in motion by him, I do not hold myself at liberty to enquire; but the *loyalty* of an Archdeacon to his Bishop (and one forcefully consistent with entire freedom of opinion) is I conceive this ... not to abuse or undermine what his Diocesan is known to support.[21]

This incident concerning Bayley's petition illustrates in a vivid manner the new dilemmas of archdeacons, as well as those of bishops who were also Ecclesiastical Commissioners. Though Goddard may have sympathised with Bayley in private, he expressed strong disapproval of what he regarded as Bayley's abuse of office.

The affair raised significant questions about the extent to which an archdeacon should bow to the authority of those above him, and the extent to which he might act as a free agent, or take the part of the clergy. One of the central concerns of the Lincoln dean and chapter,

[20] Hansard, *Parliamentary Debates*, vol. LV, cols. 115ff., 30 July 1840.
[21] LAO CorB5/10/18/6, C. Goddard to Kaye, 31 July 1840.

the threat that the Bill posed to their patronage rights, highlighted the larger question of which clergy should be rewarded by whom. Clive Dewey has suggested that 'patronage was the organising principle of English society',[22] and has argued convincingly that in the right hands it could be a great instrument of reform. In order to advance in the Church, a clergyman had to catch the eye of a patron. Every living in the Church had a patron, or patrons, in whom was vested the right to present an incumbent to the living when a vacancy arose. Patronage was exercised by bodies, such as cathedral chapters, as well as by individuals; large amounts were controlled by the Crown, church dignitaries, colleges, schools, trustees and various public bodies.

Individual lay people formed the largest category of patrons. In the period from 1821 to 1901 private individuals, or trustees, made up between 42 and 52 per cent of the whole.[23] Perhaps one-fifth of the patrons were women. It followed that about half of the incumbents in the Church of England had to thank a lay person for promoting them. Although the extent of lay patronage did not diminish during the period, its character underwent some significant shifts. In 1823 it was estimated that the core of the political elite, 300 peers and baronets, owned between them the patronage of 1,400 livings.[24] The attitudes of this body of noble patrons to their ecclesiastical responsibilities naturally varied significantly. Noble patrons included the Earl of Scarbrough, who possessed eleven livings and resided at Glentham in Lincolnshire in a 'house filled with illegitimate children, and a Lady, still not his wife'.[25] Scarbrough's selection of clergy could raise eyebrows; one of his nominees was regarded as so undesirable that nobody could be persuaded to sign his testimonials, as the law required.[26] At the other end of the spectrum, and rather more typical, was the Duke of Newcastle, who took such care over the appointment of incumbents to his numerous livings that they were rarely able to live up to his exacting standard. In 1842 he set out in an eleven-page letter the qualities he sought in the new incumbent of Worksop. The man appointed should be around forty years of age, a gentleman, but not an unapproachable fine gentleman. He must be

22 Clive Dewey, *The Passing of Barchester* (London: Hambledon Press, 1991) p. 143.
23 A. Haig, *Victorian Clergy* (London and Sydney: Croom Helm, 1984) p. 249.
24 Richard Yates, *Patronage of the Church of England* (London, 1823) p. 110; cited by M. J. D. Roberts, 'Private patronage and the Church of England, 1800–1900', *Journal of Ecclesiastical History*, 32:2 (April 1981) pp. 199–223.
25 LAO CorB5/8/7/3, G. Wilkins to Kaye, 10 May 1839.
26 LAO CorB5/8A/9, Wilkins to Kaye, 12 December 1839.

Remarkable in piety ... learning, good sense, judgement, justice and sound discretion. A good preacher with a good voice and agreeable and persuasive delivery ... His opinions should be *anchored*, not floating about on a voyage of discovery – not a Tractarian, or Evangelical or an anything else, but sound, orthodox ... the best of the old school of Church of England divines.[27]

In 1847 it was once more necessary for the Duke to find a new incumbent at Worksop. He asked the bishop to recommend a man of the 'old church stamp', neither Tractarian nor Evangelical. Kaye suggested James Appleton. As a litmus test of Appleton's orthodoxy, the Duke demanded to know which of the church societies he supported, a significant, if perhaps rather irrational, means of selecting a suitable minister for a large urban parish. Satisfied that he gave his support exclusively to the societies under the patronage of the Archbishop of Canterbury and the bishops, Newcastle was prepared to nominate Appleton to the living.

The Duke of Newcastle's attitude to candidates for Worksop highlights two important respects in which the exercise of lay patronage was changing. First, Newcastle was more interested in knowing that a man supported SPCK, the Additional Curates Society and the National Society, rather than inquiring if he would vote Tory at the next election. As the votes of individual clergy became less significant in an extended franchise, politics ceased to play the important role that it had done in securing patronage in the eighteenth century.[28] Secondly, the Duke referred the choice to his bishop, rather than exercising it entirely independently. It was being increasingly seen as the hallmark of responsible lay patronage that the patron should defer the decision to the bishop. This had the effect of further enlarging the bishops' influence, and of eroding that of the lay patrons, though not in ways that admit to statistical analysis.[29] Patrons were, in effect, being encouraged to do what the bishop considered best for their parishes, rather than to assist their own family and friends.

As a consequence of the Dean and Chapter Act, and of the efforts of the bishops themselves, the bishops' share of patronage rose from 12 to 20 per cent of the total between 1835 and 1878.[30] The most dramatic example of the effects of this policy may be seen in the case of Samuel Wilberforce; he succeeded in raising the patronage of the Bishop of

[27] LAO CorB5/8A/4, Newcastle to Kaye, 6 September 1842.
[28] Haig, *Victorian Clergy* p. 258.
[29] Ibid., pp. 268–9.
[30] Ibid., p. 249.

Oxford from 14 livings to 103 between 1845 and 1869.[31] The achievements of other bishops were more modest, but significant nevertheless – the patronage of the Bishop of Lincoln increased from 66 in 1835 to 88 in 1865. At Ely, however, the bishop's patronage fell from 131 in 1835 to 43 in 1865.[32] This was because the bishop of Ely had large patronage holdings in the neighbouring diocese of Norwich, which were transferred. The stated aim of the policy was to allow bishops to exercise greater control over their own dioceses by the promotion of deserving clergy. It had, however, a secondary purpose – that of curbing lay patronage, though this was seldom alluded to publicly.

Despite the existence of generous and responsible lay patrons in his own diocese, Kaye referred disparagingly to the 'very inadequate notions which laymen entertain of the obligations incident to the Possession of Patronage'.[33] As far as he was concerned, the most desirable lay patron was the one who dug the most willingly into his purse to build a new parsonage or to repair the church, but who did not expect to gain any special influence in return for his gift. Lay benefactors were encouraged to provide the money for new churches, but if they then expressed an interest in claiming the right of patronage they were firmly dissuaded. In 1844 Hannah Carter gave £2,000 to build a church in the neglected Buckinghamshire hamlet of Hazlemere, where three hundred people lived 'in wretched huts which they have themselves built upon the waste ... and without one resident neighbour able to assist them in their sufferings'.[34] She declared that she wished the patronage of the new church to be vested with herself or her representatives in perpetuity, although she would delegate the actual task of appointment to trustees. Kaye, however, communicated his reservations about the creation of new lay patrons to the rector of Chenies, and Hannah Carter was persuaded to relinquish her right of patronage in favour of the rector of Chenies.[35] A similar situation developed when a layman offered £2,500 for a church at Lane End in Buckinghamshire. In this case, the perpetual presentation was vested in the rector of Hambleden.[36] The solution of placing the patronage in the hands of a neighbouring incumbent was less controversial than

---

[31] Ibid., p. 268.
[32] R. A. Burns, 'The diocesan revival in the Church of England *c*. 1825–1865' (unpublished Oxford DPhil. thesis, 1990) p. 180.
[32] LAO CorB5/3/11/1, Kaye to E. O. Smith, 26 November 1832.
[34] LAO CorB5/3/18/3, H. Carter to Kaye, n.d.
[35] Ibid., Wriothesley Russell to Kaye, 6 March 1844; 27 June 1844.
[36] LAO CorB5/3/18/4, Lane End papers, 1830.

conferring it directly on the bishop would have been. Nevertheless it still amounted to a form of episcopal and clerical encroachment on what had previously been regarded as the unquestioned rights of the laity.

Other factors militated against the further accumulation of lay patronage. When new parishes were carved from old ones, the new patronage created seldom went to lay people. In the rural deanery of Leeds in 1905 only three of the fifty-seven parishes were in private patronage; the great majority were in the hands of the vicar of Leeds, the bishop, the Crown and bishop alternately, or trustees.[37] As the nineteenth century progressed, lay patronage became a phenomenon increasingly confined to rural areas, but this did little to lessen clerical hostility. A comfortable rural rectory was considered a more desirable commodity than a newly created and poorly endowed slum parish.[38] It was the thought of such plums being jealously guarded by lay patrons that caused clerical hostilities to grow, and the lay patron ran the additional risk of being beached by a change in the tide of public opinion. The mid-Victorian world was one in which merit, rather than connection, was becoming viewed as the only appropriate grounds for promotion. After the virtual end of direct patronage in the civil service in 1870, and the abolition of the purchase of promotion in the army in 1871, the Church stood alone in reserving large areas of its preferment to those with private connections.[39] Whereas the meritorious but unconnected curate might eventually be appointed to an urban vicarage in the gift of his bishop, the rectory drawing-room could still be permanently reserved for the squire-patron's brother. The rise in the number of patron-incumbents who presented themselves to their own livings was part of the clerical reaction against lay patronage. By 1878 one ninth of privately owned patronage was in the hands of patron-incumbents.[40]

The handful of avaricious patrons who traded in livings by advertising them in the papers in the 1870s were as easy a target for the Church's critics as the relatively few rapacious pluralists of the 1830s had been to the previous generation. Nevertheless, Bishop Magee's parliamentary attempts to reform the ecclesiastical patronage system

[37] Haig, *Victorian Clergy* p. 251.
[38] Ibid., p. 252.
[39] Ibid., p. 254; Roberts, 'Private patronage' p. 214.
[40] Rosemary O'Day, 'The clerical renaissance in Victorian England and Wales' in Gerald Parsons (ed.), *Religion in Victorian Britain: Traditions* (Manchester: Manchester University Press, 1988) p. 197.

ended in failure, with the hostility coming from the House of Commons rather than the Lords.[41] Opposition to Magee's bill was focused by an anti-clerical body of Disraelian Conservatives, who regarded the defence of the patronage system as necessary to protect the rights of protestant laymen like themselves. For them, the possession of patronage was a form of property ownership, and its abolition would be the thin end of a large wedge. They also felt threatened by the rise of ritualism[42] – not an unreal fear in view of the bishops' tendency to veto the prosecution of ritualist incumbents. Thus what had started as an argument about the need to offer professional rewards to hard-working clergy became entangled in one about the attitudes of Anglo-Catholics to secular authority.

Outwardly, the patronage system seemed little changed, although, as has been shown, the climate in which lay patronage was exercised did alter. The only measure to find its way on to the statute book in the nineteenth century was the Benefices Act of 1898. This act abolished resignation bonds, which had sometimes been used to compel an incumbent to resign his living after a stated period, so that the patron might present another person to it – perhaps one of his relatives. It also made the sale of next presentations illegal, and prevented the public auction of advowsons (the right of appointment) unless they were attached to a nearby estate of at least 100 acres[43] – which was a concession to the propertied classes. The rights of bishops were strengthened under the Act so that they could refuse the patron's candidate on the grounds of inadequate professional experience, as well as on the basis of character or physical or mental incapacity. The possibility of parishioners participating in the choice of their clergyman was only minimally recognised; the bishop had to give the parishioners one month's notification of his intention to institute, but the Act specified no method of appeal.[44] Thus it remained the case that it was usually only by becoming a patron himself that a person could take part in the selection of a clergyman. There were occasional radical experiments, but these were rare, as in 1869 when the Duke of St Albans transferred the entire responsibility for selecting an incumbent for the Lincolnshire parish of Redbourne to a representative group of parishioners.[45]

[41] Roberts, 'Private patronage', pp. 215–16.
[42] Ibid., p. 216.
[43] Ibid., pp. 221–2.
[44] Ibid., p. 222.
[45] Ibid., p. 218.

The bishops' lack of power to take effective sanctions against recalcitrant clergy was another matter that exercised them. The traditional method was for the bishop to try to persuade the offender to withdraw from his parish and appoint a curate in his stead. It was technically possible to have recourse to the Ecclesiastical Courts, but in practice the expenses involved were too great, and neither bishops, archdeacons nor churchwardens were willing to bear the costs. The passing of the Church Discipline Act in 1840 was intended to give bishops powers to suspend incumbents whose mode of life was deemed unsuitable, although, as will be shown, its impact was limited. The Act is significant in the present context because it confirmed the diocesan bishop, rather than the archbishops' courts, as the source of jurisdiction. The time-honoured methods had, however, often dealt effectively with offenders, whereas following the letter of the new legislation sometimes produced an outcome that was less satisfactory. Some examples of clergy discipline cases dealt with by Bishop Kaye before and after the passing of the Act will illustrate these contrasts.[46]

In 1833 charges were brought by a parishioner against John Bewicke, rector of Hallaton and vicar of Loddington in Leicestershire. It was alleged that he never wore a black gown or bands, that he had administered the sacrament in coloured gaiters, and despite excellent health he never knelt for prayers and seldom preached. Furthermore, he had formed a connection with a Mrs Hickman, who had been observed climbing through his bedroom window by means of a ladder. As a result of his preoccupation with Mrs Hickman, he had failed to conduct a service on a Sunday and on Ash Wednesday. In a parish of 800 people, only seven or eight attended church.[47] Bewicke denied the charges, but the allegations were confirmed by the archdeacon, who also attested to the respectability of the parishioner who had made them. The bishop demanded that Bewicke appoint a curate at Hallaton and that he relinquish his duties there. A curate was already employed in his other parish of Loddington, and the bishop insisted that his stipend be raised in accordance with the law.[48] Bewicke co-operated, and although he retained both livings until his death in 1843, he does

---

[46] For a fuller discussion of this topic, see Frances Knight, 'Ministering to the ministers: the discipline of recalcitrant clergy in the diocese of Lincoln 1830–1845' in W. J. Sheils and Diana Wood (eds.), *The Ministry: Clerical and Lay*, Studies in Church History, 26 (Oxford: Blackwell, 1989) pp. 357–66, and Burns, 'The diocesan revival' pp. 181–219.

[47] LAO CorB5/5/1/2, T. Vowe to Kaye, 4 January and 25 February 1833; T. K. Bonney to Kaye, 3 April 1833.

[48] Ibid., Kaye to J. Bewicke, 4 April 1833.

not appear to have exercised any spiritual functions after the bishop's intervention. Kaye adopted similar strategies in the cases of the rector of Beachampton, who assaulted a tithe payer in 1833,[49] and the vicar of Selstone, who in 1839 was reported to have been constantly drunk for the previous eight months.[50]

The case of John Willis, rector of Haddenham with Cuddington in Buckinghamshire, throws some light on the effects that the passing of the Church Discipline Act had on the Church's attempts to restrain dissolute clergymen. When Willis' misdemeanours first became apparent, in the mid-1830s, a curate was appointed by the bishop to perform his duties in the manner described above.[51] But when he offended again in 1843, the provisions of the new legislation were used to their fullest extent. A commission of enquiry, consisting of two rural deans, and two local incumbents, was granted powers to examine Willis, his accusers and the witnesses upon oath. Initially an attempt was made to enhance the atmosphere of legal gravity by holding the proceedings in the Magistrates' Chamber in Aylesbury, but this was abandoned, probably for fear of incurring unnecessary expense.[52] Willis was found guilty of having visited a brothel in Aylesbury, of being drunk in the pulpit and later in a hayrick. A charge of his having been thrown out of an inn in High Wycombe was dropped on the grounds that the only person who could have formally identified him could not be found.[53] Willis pleaded guilty to the charges. A full report of the proceedings was transmitted to the bishop by one of the rural deans, John Harrison, who had taken the initiative in bringing the prosecution. The bishop consulted with John Haggard, a lawyer at Doctors' Commons and chancellor of the diocese of Lincoln. Kaye took the course that Haggard regarded as safest, and suspended Willis from his benefice for one year.[54]

This was by any standards a very moderate sanction to take against someone who had had a damaging influence in a large parish for at least fifteen years. Harrison alleged that Willis enjoyed a private income of £800 in addition to his preferment, which was worth £370.[55] In such circumstances it was hardly surprising that Willis

---

[49]   LAO CorB5/3/10/2, J. Hill to Kaye, 26 June 1833 and following.
[50]   LAO CorB5/8/7/3, G. Wilkins to Kaye, 10 May 1839.
[51]   LAO CorB5/3/14/1, G. Cracroft to Kaye, 27 May 1835.
[52]   LAO CorB5/19/11, J. Harrison to Kaye, 23 December 1843.
[53]   Ibid., Harrison to Kaye, 3 February 1844.
[54]   LAO CorB5/3/14/1, R. Swan to Kaye, 24 March 1845.
[55]   LAO CorB5/19/11, Harrison to Kaye, 29 September 1843.

greeted the twelve-month break from his clerical labours with equanimity.[56] Despite having followed the provisions of the Church Discipline Act to the letter, a year or so of suspension appears to have been the gravest penalty that a bishop could impose. This was because the concept of the parson's freehold emerged unblemished from the Act. It seemed that despite the complexity of the new procedures, the practical measures available to a bishop differed little from those before 1840, when offenders would be asked to leave their office and appoint a curate. Further, it could be argued that the formality and publicity surrounding a commission of enquiry (a procedure required by the Act) could considerably harm the reputation of the Church. The clamour of public attention could inflict greater damage than the quieter, more private proceedings of the old days.[57] Once it became necessary to adopt quasi-legal forms of cross-examination, it became correspondingly more difficult to obtain sufficient evidence for an indictment. The charge against Willis of unruly behaviour at High Wycombe was dropped because the woman in whose company he had allegedly been at the time could not be found to identify him. Witnesses who might have been prepared to make informal statements in private to neighbouring clergy, were less willing to be sworn in court.

The point is further illustrated by the case of Henry Dashwood, vicar of West Wycombe. He was alleged to have been heard to 'damn the church', to have boxed with prize fighters, to have been intoxicated in public and to have breakfasted with women at a fair.[58] John Pigott, the rural dean, recommended that a commission of enquiry be established to investigate the allegations in November 1844. The bishop agreed, but by the following March it had to be abandoned. The accused vicar was a baronet whose father owned most of the parish and whose brother was the MP for Wycombe. Almost all of those who could have been called as witnesses were tenants on the family estate, and declined the invitation to give evidence.[59] Once more Kaye had to resort to the time-honoured method of delivering a stern lecture upon the necessity of living up to the sacred calling of a clergyman.[60] On this occasion, it had the desired effect, for the following month Dashwood resigned the living.[61]

[56] Ibid., Willis to Kaye, 5 April 1844.
[57] Ibid., P. Wilmot to Kaye, 30 October 1843.
[58] LAO CorB5/3/16/2, J. R. Pigott to Kaye, 4 and 12 November 1844.
[59] Ibid., B. G. Parker to Pigott, 26 November 1844.
[60] Ibid., Kaye to H. Dashwood, 12 March 1845.
[61] Ibid., Dashwood to Kaye, 9 April 1845.

The Church Discipline Act represented a victory for the continuation of the parson's freehold; that is to say it permitted no permanent deprivation of livings, even those of notoriously dissolute clergy. The Church in 1840 was not ready for a measure that would have struck at the heart of its belief in the supremacy of the freehold, even though it might have reduced the level of public opprobrium over clerical scandals, which, though relatively few, attracted wide publicity. Lord Sidney Godolphin Osborne, rector of Stoke Poges in Buckinghamshire, expressed the feeling in 1841: 'Puseyism and Noetism are bad enough, but neither do in my opinion the mischief that the ill conduct of the clergy do when that conduct is allowed to pass unnoticed.'[62] As it was, the 1840 Act turned into almost as big a failure as the Public Worship Regulation Act of 1874. As Burns has pointed out, it was drafted when the threat to church discipline was perceived as coming from drunks and adulterers, but it was on the statute book at a time when discipline problems were increasingly likely to involve disputes about the nature of the Church itself. Those with grievances began to seek attention in the courts; even Keble and Pusey tried to get themselves prosecuted under the Act.[63]

The Church Discipline Act increased the bishops' powers to a relatively modest extent. Despite the efforts of the Ecclesiastical Commission to impose a greater degree of rationalisation, and to focus authority in the person of the bishop, the Church of England remained a complex institution in which devolved power was maintained by the continuation of ancient privileges. The bishops had to accommodate the rights of incumbents, just as they had to continue to live with lay patrons. As late as 1878 they had control of only one appointment in four. Bishops could try to assert their authority by being more active, and in doing so they were assisted by the coming of the railways, which brought hitherto inaccessible places within reach for confirmations and visitations, and made attendance at meetings in London and elsewhere easier and therefore more frequent. The railways also provided the means for clergy (and laity) to attend on their bishops. Nevertheless an increase in busyness should not be mistaken for a corresponding increase in power. The worst fears of the early opponents of the Ecclesiastical Commission, that it would result in an episcopally-dominated Church, did not come to pass. Bishops continued to adopt a higher public profile, but they still had to rely on moral exhortations

---

[62]   LAO CorB5/3/12/4, S. Godolphin Osborne to Kaye, 8 April 1841.
[63]   Burns, 'The diocesan revival' p. 215.

and on securing goodwill from a variety of sources. In reality Blomfield, Kaye and Monk were unable to change the Church on their own.

The office of archdeacon was an ancient one in the Church, but in the early nineteenth century it began to assume a greater importance. The archdeacon ranked immediately below the bishop in the diocesan hierarchy, an ordinary possessing a jurisdiction independent of the bishop's, though subordinate to it. He was naturally conscious of his position as the bishop's lawful representative at the local level. Self-designation as the 'eye of the bishop', the term borrowed from canon law and a common medieval description for an archdeacon, was a favoured metaphor.

Before the implementation of the Dean and Chapter Act, the funding of archdeaconries was generally insufficient, and this proved to be the greatest obstacle to archdeacons' attempts to fulfil the demands of their office. They had to rely on the income of the fees they received at visitations, and out of these they had to pay the expenses entailed in managing their archdeaconry. The Report of the Ecclesiastical Revenues and Duties Commission in 1835 found that the average net annual income of an archdeaconry in England and Wales was just £87.[64] In 1837 Archdeacon Hill of Buckingham complained that he had a total ecclesiastical income of less than £350 a year from which to meet all the administrative and legal costs of his archdeaconry. Like other archdeacons, he was forced to supplement the meagre revenues of his archdeaconry, in his case just £74 a year, by holding other livings in plurality. Hill held Tingewick and Shanklin, which he claimed brought him about £120 each.[65] He complained, with some justification, that among the clergy he was 'reviled as a pluralist'.[66] This in itself was a sign of the times; before the 1830s the holding of a few livings in conjunction with an archdeaconry would have aroused little comment. That recourse to such pluralism was necessary was tacitly acknowledged in the Pluralities Act of 1838, which exempted arch-

---

[64] The data for individual archdeaconries is presented in a tabluated form in the *Clerical Guide* for 1836.
[65] LAO CorB5/19/2 and 3, Hill to Kaye, n.d., but sometime between the 7th and the 12th of April 1837.
[66] Ibid.

deacons from the rules that governed the lower clergy. The archdeacons had to wait for the Dean and Chapter Act of 1840, and the
Amendment Act of the following year, to place them on a more secure
footing. As existing interests were always respected, the legislation only
benefited newly appointed archdeacons. Pluralism was not effectively
eradicated among archdeacons until about 1860.[67]

It was the archdeacon who shouldered much of the responsibility for
superintending the day-to-day administration of the Church at a local
level, and it was by means of the archidiaconal visitation that he was
brought into most direct contact with his archdeaconry. Two distinct
types of visitation existed. At the general (or ordinary) visitation, clergy
and churchwardens were summoned to one of the principal churches
in the neighbourhood, and the proceedings were conducted in a
manner that echoed the bishop's own visitation. The clergy and
wardens took part in a service, and one of the clergy would preach.
They would then all answer their names and listen to the archdeacon's
charge, which was normally concerned with topical and local issues.
Afterwards the archdeacon received fees and presentments from the
churchwardens (questionnaires that they completed concerning the
state of their parish) and he then formally admitted them into their
annual term of office. Traditionally the proceedings were followed by a
dinner, but the custom was on the wane by the mid-nineteenth
century, a casualty of the loss of common ground not only between
clergy themselves, but also between clergy and churchwardens.[68] As
party tensions increased, visitations were more likely to become
acrimonious rather than social occasions. In theory at least clergy and
churchwardens were supposed to attend a general visitation on an
annual or biennial basis.

At the parochial visitation, in contrast, the archdeacon visited each
parish individually, inspecting buildings, making directions, ordering
repairs and completing a visitation return. He also made enquiries
about the provision of services and schools, about the residence of the
incumbent and curate, and about the activities of Dissenters in the
parish. The toil of a parochial visitation could occupy at least a month
each summer, and although canon law required that each parish be
visited once in three years, in most places this was impractical. Samuel
Butler, as archdeacon of Derby, undertook a complete visitation of his

[67] Burns, 'The diocesan revival' p. 74.
[68] The visitation dinner was also dying out at episcopal visitations. It shrank to a buffet at
Peterborough in 1854 and at Norwich in 1858. See Burns, 'The diocesan revival' p. 33.

archdeaconry over forty-seven days in the summers of 1823 and 1824. He covered 1,200 miles and visited 166 churches, completing an 86-article questionnaire at each.[69]

Between 1817 and 1822 Charles Goddard conducted visitations at about 400 of the 516 parishes under his jurisdiction in the archdeaconry of Lincoln. He could not afford to visit the remaining parishes, as the value of his archdeaconry (£30) was only sufficient to pay the expenses of the general visitations, and his other Lincoln preferment, the prebend of Louth, produced just £14.[70] By 1827 he had decided reluctantly that he would have to abandon the plan of systematic parochial visitations, though he declared himself willing to visit any parish that was unknown to him, if requested to do so by the bishop. 'In regard to those which I *have* visited, I have generally a very clear recollection.'[71] Goddard had to rely very much on his recollections, though he continued to visit parishes sporadically until his resignation in 1844. He resigned in order to make way for H. K. Bonney, who became Archdeacon of Lincoln under the terms of the Dean and Chapter Act, with a stipend of £500 a year and collation to the newly-created fourth canonry in the cathedral.[72] Bonney began a strenuous systematic visitation of his archdeaconry, which took place mainly in the summer months between 21 May 1845 and 12 June 1850.[73]

Goddard's achievement in inspecting 400 churches in five years had been formidable, and he claimed that he was the first archdeacon to conduct a parochial visitation for forty years, though this may have been an exaggeration.[74] His work had been further hampered because the office of archdeacon's registrar was occupied by the notoriously neglectful Richard Pretyman. Though officially required to attend the visitations, he (predictably) never appeared in person, delegating the duties to a scantily paid deputy. Goddard lamented:

I am often prevented doing my own duty fully; because, if I stay out a day or two longer, I am aware that I am keeping his [Pretyman's] deputy registrar

[69] M. R. Austin, (ed.), *The Church in Derbyshire in 1823–4: The Parochial Visitation of the Rev Samuel Butler, Archdeacon of Derby in the Diocese of Lichfield and Coventry* (Derbyshire Archaeological Society, 5, 1974) p. 10.

[70] LAO CorB5/140, Goddard to Kaye, 7 June 1827. See also Goddard's evidence to the Ecclesiastical Courts Commission, PP(1831/2) xxiv, p. 134.

[71] LAO CorB5/140, Goddard to Kaye, 7 June 1827.

[72] Thompson, 'Historical Survey, 1750–1949' pp. 236–7.

[73] For an account of this visitation, see N. S. Harding, (ed.), *Bonney's Church Notes: Being Notes on the Churches in the Archdeaconry of Lincoln 1845–1848* (Lincoln, 1937).

[74] Ecclesiastical Courts Commisson Report, p. 134. A Dr Gordon had held a visitation in the 1780s.

out, who can ill afford the expense, although he is very liberal ... I have often
wished to stay at places to inspect churches, but I have not done it, because I
felt that it was not right to keep him out.[75]

The Archdeacon of Lincoln's court, though it no longer transacted any
business, had as its official John Pretyman, and he too pocketed a sum
that should have been directed to the work of the archdeacon.[76] Not
all archdeacon's courts were similarly moribund. The Archdeacon of
Derby's court was still functioning in the 1820s, and heard causes
ranging from the enforcement of repairs to churches to moral and
ecclesiastical offences.[77]

If they lacked a sympathetic relationship with their bishop, archdeacons tended to feel unsupported, for they found few friends among
the lower clergy. Goddard worked under three bishops of Lincoln,
Pretyman, Pelham and Kaye. He had clearly suffered as a result of
Pretyman's nepotism, and he despised Pelham, who had failed to act
on his representations. With Kaye he enjoyed a far more cordial
relationship, and he had no hesitation in adopting the bishop's
reforming agenda as his own. Like his bishop, he identified non-
residence as the 'great evil' in his archdeaconry,

Though not much to be wondered at since for the last seven years the licences
have been renewed as *matters of course*; [a reference to Pelham's episcopate]
and the ground stated was frequently *unfitness* of house, that unfitness which in
many instances might before this time have been removed has been thus
perpetuated.[78]

Some of Kaye's other archdeacons, notably George Wilkins of
Nottingham[79] and Justly Hill of Buckingham,[80] also declared that the
elimination of non-residence was their first priority, and in this respect
they identified themselves closely with episcopal policy.

It was hardly surprising that archdeacons lacked popularity among
the generality of the lower clergy and parish officers. Parochial
visitations became occasions to be dreaded, for the clergyman and the
churchwardens knew that the archdeacon might order expensive
repairs, and that he would report to the bishop on every aspect of the
church and the parsonage house and outbuildings, as well as on the

[75] Ibid., p. 138.
[76] Ibid.
[77] Austin, *The Church in Derbyshire* p. 5.
[78] LAO CorB5/140, Goddard to Kaye, 30 March 1827.
[79] George Wilkins, *Charge Delivered to the Clergy in the Archdeaconry of Nottingham* (1832).
[80] LAO CorB5/3/6/6, J. Hill to R. Phillimore, 25 June 1830.

clergyman's own conduct and abilities. This did not, however, cause them invariably to act on the archdeacon's instructions. A precise record of one Staffordshire parish's response is supplied by the minute-book of Cheadle vestry meeting.[81] One month after the visitation of George Hodson, archdeacon of Stafford, his letter to the churchwardens was read at a vestry meeting on 12 August 1830. Hodson's orders for repairing and whitewashing the belfry and for repairing the pews were put into effect. Instead of repairing or replacing the covering on the communion table, the vestry decided to dye it blue, and instead of removing the earth from the north side of the church, they ordered that that side of the church be spouted, ('it appearing that the soil on the North side of the Church cannot with propriety be removed'[82]). Hodson's recommendation for the construction of a suitable vestry was met by a resolution to widen the existing one. An order for the replacement of the outer door of the church porch by a light gate was unanimously rejected. Thus, even the most indefatigable archdeacon could be thwarted by the alternative proposals of the vestrymen, who were likely to be better informed than he about the precise state of the fabric and the suitability of particular proposals.

It was Goddard's custom, when confronted with a dilapidated church, to order the churchwardens to summon a vestry to levy a rate sufficient to cover the cost of repair. If they refused to comply, he threatened the parties concerned with legal action; though this was a bluff, for Goddard was perfectly well aware of the expense and uncertainty of the Ecclesiastical Courts, and in no case did he ever actually resort to them.[83] Securing repairs to chancels, where responsibility rested either with the rector or with a lay impropriator, and to parsonage houses, where it lay with the incumbent, was even more problematic. Goddard admitted to the Ecclesiastical Courts Commissioners that he knew of no way of compelling repairs to be carried out.[84] Unlike Archdeacon Hill in the case at Slapton cited in the previous chapter, he does not seem to have threatened sequestration in order to effect repairs to glebe houses, or to have ordered the repairs himself without the incumbent's consent.

As he went out on his parochial visitations, a knowledge of surveying

[81] David Robinson (ed.), *Visitations of the Archdeaconry of Stafford 1829–1841* (London: Staffordshire Record Society, 1980) p. xxviii.
[82] Ibid.
[83] Ecclesiastical Courts Commission Report, p. 135.
[84] Ibid., pp. 136–7.

and a sound understanding of ecclesiastical architecture were the qualities that an archdeacon most needed, and perhaps also a thick skin to withstand the occasionally rebarbative comments of clergy and churchwardens. Given the absence of any formal training in practical skills, the archdeacons appear to have managed surprisingly well, although some blunders occurred, as for example when H. K. Bonney recommended iron for the pipes at Wyberton.[85] All archdeacons agreed that when botching local workmen, as opposed to skilled craftsmen, were employed by churchwardens in the interests of economy, hideous results followed. Disagreement over what constituted a repair was a further difficulty that frequently arose, as W. B. Stonehouse, archdeacon of Stow, remarked in 1845:

For the practice of putting a piece of new cloth into an old garment, by which the rent is made worse, is too often met with. [This was surely every archdeacon's favourite scriptural allusion.] The answer evidently is to place any part of the fabric in that state in which it was before it became impaired. Thus it is not a repair to remove the decayed stone tracery from a church window and to replace it with a wood mullion, nor is it a repair to take off the lead, and to remove the decayed though in many places fine old Gothic beams and to replace them with a flat plaster ceiling and a covering of tiles.[86]

There is evidence here of an underlying conflict between Gothic and classical taste, which was a feature of many church restorations. The archdeacon preferred Gothic-style open roofs, moulded beams and stone windows; the vestry appeared to have expressed a preference for 'traditional' moulded plaster ceilings and wooden window frames.

It is evident that in the course of his parochial visitations an archdeacon had the opportunity to influence the character of worship by trying to make the church furnishing and fixtures conform to his particular ecclesiastical tastes. When the ecclesiologist Edward Churton became Archdeacon of Cleveland in 1846, it has been suggested that the doctrines of the Camden Society reached the remotest parishes.[87] Contrasting approaches can be seen between the High Church H. K. Bonney, archdeacon of Lincoln, and the Evangelical George Hodson, archdeacon of Stafford. Bonney always paid particular attention to the communion table, although he was not fanatical about it. At Lusby he

[85] Harding, *Bonney's Church Notes* p. 200.
[86] N. S. Harding (ed.), *A Stow Visitation: Being Notes on the Churches in the Archdeaconry of Stow, 1845 by The Venerable W. B. Stonehouse* (Lincoln, 1940) p. 12.
[87] Graeme Drewery, 'Victorian church building and restoration in the diocese of York, with special reference to the archdeaconry of Cleveland', (unpublished PhD thesis, University of Cambridge, 1994) p. 129.

ordered that two mats be removed, and a proper covering procured.[88] At North Elkington, Nettleton, Kelsey St Mary and Tealby he noted that there were drawers in the tables, though he seemed not to think that this impinged upon their liturgical function.[89] At Nocton, however, he ordered that a shelf with large folio books, which stood over the communion table, be removed to the vestry.[90] At Kirkby Green he was horrified to discover that the communion table was movable, and set at the north-east corner of the nave, whilst the east end was occupied by charity seats.[91] Whatever the style of the table, Bonney sometimes directed that it be treated with a little boiled oil, presumably to preserve the wood.[92] Hodson, by contrast, though clearly a most conscientious archdeacon who conducted four visitations between 1829 and 1841, paid little attention to either the appearance or covering of communion tables.[93] At Chilcote, the table was an 'old oak frame with moth-eaten cover',[94] at Darlaston it was a 'plain painted shelf, on brackets'[95] and at Drayton Bassett it was 'an old oak cupboard'.[96] Hodson was more concerned with the general structural soundness of churches, and in particular floors and roofs. Church furnishings were of little interest to him, though he paid careful attention to the condition of Bibles and prayer books.

Like the bishops, the archdeacons were a small but influential group in the Church. In 1836 there were just fifty-eight of them in the whole of England and Wales, and in 1865 the number had risen to only sixty-nine.[97] They could exercise wide powers, and before the revival of suffragan bishops in 1870 the archdeacon was usually his diocesan's chief ally and assistant. In most cases personally selected by the bishop, the archdeacon provided him with a constant flow of information about the parochial life of his diocese, and the conduct of the clergy, as well as conveying the views of the bishops to clergy and churchwardens in the parishes. After this formidable grounding in diocesan administration, it is perhaps curious that so few archdeacons ever became bishops themselves. In the period from 1825 to 1865 only Samuel Wilberforce

[88] Harding, *Bonney's Church Notes* pp. 139–40.
[89] Ibid., pp. 116, 85, 58, 67.
[90] Ibid., p. 21.
[91] Ibid., pp. 18–19.
[92] Ibid., p. v.
[93] Robinson, *Visitations of the Archdeaconry of Stafford* p. x describes Hodson's churchmanship.
[94] Ibid., p. 6.
[95] Ibid., p. 7.
[96] Ibid., p. 8.
[97] Burns, 'The diocesan revival' p. 115.

was promoted successively to the offices of rural dean, archdeacon and bishop.[98] A greater number, including Blomfield and Butler, moved from archdeaconries to bishoprics. Nevertheless, 90 per cent of the archdeacons in this forty year period remained in office until overtaken by death or incapacity. It was not a route to future advancement.[99] An archdeacon's career usually began with a respectable performance at university, and he typically held a college fellowship before moving into an incumbency in his late twenties or early thirties. In the earlier period at least future archdeacons appear to have attracted the attention of the bishops who promoted them as much through personal ties of friendship, or through their writing, as through any conspicuous success as parochial clergy.

The spectrum of churchmanship was comprehensively represented among the archdeacons.[100] In the early decades of the nineteenth century the domination of the episcopate by the High Church Hackney Phalanx was reflected in the bishops' choice of archdeacons. All eight of Bishop Kaye's archdeacons were High Churchmen in a similar mould to himself, though he had inherited half of them from his predecessors.[101] Other High Church archdeacons of the 1820s included J. J. Watson, George Cambridge, Charles Daubeny and J. H. Pott. Evangelicals were barely represented until the end of the decade, when Bishop Ryder appointed Edward Bather, William Spooner and George Hodson, and Bishop Charles Sumner promoted Charles Hoare. The number of Evangelicals increased still further in the 1840s and 1850s. Tractarians also figured prominently as archdeacons: men like Benjamin Harrison, George Prevost and Thomas Thorp, and also more maverick characters: for example Henry Manning and Robert Wilberforce, both of whom converted to Roman Catholicism, and George Denison, who became one of the Church's sternest defenders of both church schools and of the doctrine of the real presence.

The rise of party among churchmen brought the clergy into conflicts with each other that would have been undreamed of even a few decades earlier. There is little evidence of archdeacons moderating their church-

[98] Ibid., p. 75.
[99] Ibid.
[100] For a fuller discussion, see Burns, 'The diocesan revival' pp. 62–4. I have drawn upon his work in this paragraph.
[101] The archdeacons Kaye appointed were J. B. Hollingworth to Huntingdon in 1828, T. K. Bonney to Leicester in 1831, W. B. Stonehouse to Stow in 1844 and H. K. Bonney to Lincoln in 1845. Kaye inherited C. Goddard at Lincoln from Pretyman, G. Wilkins at Nottingham from Vernon Harcourt and from Pelham, J. Hill at Buckingham, H. V. Bayley at Stow and H. K. Bonney at Bedford.

manship upon appointment, although the Evangelical Walter Shirley ceased to take a prominent role in the Church Pastoral Aid Society, the Church Missionary Society and the Bible Society, or to support strong measures against the Tractarians, after becoming Archdeacon of Derby in 1840.[102] Most, however, seem to have remained very much party men. One of Shirley's predecessors at Derby, Samuel Butler, firmly resisted an attempt by Evangelical clergy to gain control of a new clerical society proposed for the archdeaconry in 1826, and he used his charge of 1829 to attack the 'morbid sentimentality' of Evangelicals.[103] The conflicts between the High Church archdeacons of the diocese of Lincoln and those clergy who were Evangelical further illustrate the point. In a letter he wrote to Peel, Charles Goddard sheds a revealing light on his churchmanship in a passing reference to his achievements whilst a curate: 'I took the lead in establishing District Committees of Soc for PCK at Wycombe, Aylesbury etc, and what I did was without Ultraism on the one hand or Evangelism on the other.'[104] Goddard appears to have used the term 'Evangelical' exclusively as a term of abuse: he described Dr Guburgh of Sleaford as 'a rank Evangel'.[105] and Mr Glover of Freeston as an 'Evangelical of the worst stamp'.[106]

Goddard's vitriol was shared by the Archdeacon of Nottingham, George Wilkins, whose novels, *Body and Soul* (1822), *The Two Rectors* (1824), *The Village Pastor* (1825) and *The Convert* (1826), were chiefly concerned with the defence of High Church orthodoxy and a sustained attack on Evangelicalism. In *Body and Soul* the hero, Dr Freeman, rector of a large manufacturing town bearing a suspicious resemblance to Nottingham, encounters the unsavoury Mr Griper, a Calvinistic Evangelical and a representative of an insidious party responsible for subverting a large proportion of the town. The book was so poorly constructed that it failed both as fiction and as theological polemic. It did, however, attract the attention of the Archdeacon of Ely, the Evangelical J. H. Browne, who described it as 'a labyrinth of error' and trusted that 'the shallowness of its reasonings and the inaccuracy of its statements, would rapidly consign it to merited oblivion'.[107]

---

[102] Burns, 'The diocesan revival' p. 64.

[103] Austin, *The Church in Derbyshire* p. 7.

[104] BL Add. MSS 40417 fo. 237, Goddard to Peel, n.d. [1835].

[105] LAO CorB5/140/15, Goddard's remarks to Kaye on his visitation of 1827.

[106] Ibid.

[107] J. H. Browne, *Five Letters Addressed to Revd G. Wilkins, Containing Strictures on Some Part of a Publication Entitled 'Body and Soul'* (London, 1823) letter 2, p. 2; letter 1, p. 2. See also, J. H. Browne, *A Sixth Letter to Revd G. Wilkins in Reply to a Chapter in the Second Volume of 'Body and Soul' Entitled 'Evangelism'* (London, 1823).

Wilkins' literary efforts were clearly offensive to the Evangelical clergy in his archdeaconry, as were some of his more conventional archidiaconal publications. In his charge of 1841 he accused the Calvinistic Evangelicals, who fraternised with Dissenters, of promoting a climate favourable to the reception of Tractarianism, and he singled out the Bible Society, the Church Missionary Society and the Church Pastoral Aid Society, all organisations supported by Evangelicals, for particular criticism. The Evangelical clergy were vociferous in response. Robert Simpson of Christ Church, Newark, described the charge as libellous and a collection of 'gross falsehoods ... not only unchristian, but also illegal'.[108] He lobbied the bishop (unsuccessfully) to prevent its publication, and threatened Wilkins with legal action if he went ahead. At Clarborough, a Simeon Trust living, Charles Hodge described the charge as 'objectionable both for its sentiments and also (more particularly) for imputing wrong motives to a particular section of the Church'.[109] Hodge wondered if attendance at archidiaconal visitations was compulsory, and, if the clergy were bound to attend, whether it would be sufficient for them merely to answer their names and not stay for the charge. 'If we are bound to hear every thing and any thing that an archdeacon may choose to say on such occasions, without the means of protesting on the spot or absenting ourselves at future visitations, we are placed indeed in a hard situation.'[110] Kaye was predictably hostile to this request, for he supported his archdeacons as firmly as they usually supported him. 'There can be no doubt whatever', he replied, 'that the clergy are bound to attend the visitation of the archdeacon, and that they put themselves to ecclesiastical censure by non-attendance.'[111]

The archdeacons were, as Arthur Burns has noted, 'responsible for turning into concrete achievement the schemes of the bishops and the Ecclesiastical Commission'.[112] The close proximity to the parochial clergy into which this brought them was a further cause of distrust, and they were perceived, rightly, as being on the side of the bishops. Lack of warmth and over-formality were the complaints most frequently levelled at the Lincoln archdeacons by the clergy. Goddard

[108] LAO CorB5/8/2, R. Simpson to Kaye, 28 May 1841; 1 June 1841.
[109] LAO CorB5/8A/6, C. Hodge to Kaye, 9 July 1841.
[110] Ibid.
[111] Ibid., Kaye to Hodge, 12 July 1841.
[112] Burns, 'The diocesan revival' p. 77.

was described as 'austere'.[113] Hill was accused of having 'a cold stare'[114] and of being a 'persecutor'.[115] Wilkins was universally disliked by those who did not share his theological position. Despite their personal experience of parochial life, the archdeacons could seem remote from and unsympathetic to the day-to-day problems of the lower clergy.

In an attempt to ease the burden on the archdeacons, and to increase the superintendence of individual parishes, bishops from the 1820s onwards began to revive the ancient office of rural dean. At the beginning of the nineteenth century Exeter appeared to be the only English diocese where rural deans were still engaged in their customary activities.[116] In Wales there is evidence of their being active from 1717.[117] A rural dean was an incumbent in whom was vested oversight of the parishes in the deanery in which he lived. He could inspect the churches and parsonages of his neighbours, but he could not hold visitations, for unlike an archdeacon he did not possess an independent authority.[118]

The rural deans emerged as important personnel in the nineteenth-century Church. Their restoration represented an experiment in clerical deployment that spawned an entirely new stratum of ecclesiastical middle management. It was a change instigated by the bishops, independent of the promptings of the Ecclesiastical Commission and of parliamentary legislation. Kaye reinstated them in the Bristol diocese in 1824, and then in the archdeaconry of Lincoln, apparently at the suggestion of Archdeacon Goddard, in the summer of 1829.[119] At Exeter rural deans were democratically selected by clerical election, but in other dioceses the appointment was made by bishops acting on the advice of their archdeacons.[120] This was the case at Lincoln, where Kaye was very much dependent upon the archdeacons' personal knowledge of the individuals involved. In 1829 Goddard recommended candidates for the twenty-three deaneries in his archdeaconry, prepared their letters of appointment and delivered them in the course of

[113] LAO CorB5/19/15, G. Watson to Kaye, 1 January 1835.
[114] LAO CorB5/3/14/10, Anon. [paper torn] to Kaye, 23 April 1839.
[115] LAO CorB5/3/28/4, J. Brigges to Kaye, 10 September 1830.
[116] Ibid., p. 86.
[117] F. C. Mather, *High Church Prophet: Bishop Samuel Horsley (1733–1806) and the Caroline Tradition in the Later Georgian Church* (Oxford: Clarendon Press, 1992) pp. 164–5.
[118] Burns, 'The diocesan revival' p. 101.
[119] William Dansey, *Horae Decanicae Rurales*, 2 vols. (London, 1835), vol II, p. 413.
[120] Burns, 'The diocesan revival' p. 98.

his visitation.[121] He looked for active, competent, locally-respected resident incumbents, whose ecclesiastical opinions conformed to his own. Francis Massingberd, who had first caught his eye in 1827 (when he preached a sermon 'beyond the common' at the archidiaconal visitation),[122] was selected for the deanery of Hill. Charles Worsley was another chosen, who according to Goddard had much improved the formerly wretched village of Thurlby, and now resided there in a 'new and very neat parsonage house'.[123]

The Lincoln archdeacons were generally unreserved in their support for the rural deans. As early as 1826 Bayley had pressed for their revival, and in April 1829 had written to Kaye recommending various candidates. 'I rejoice that you will restore R. Deans; I am persuaded that great good will ensue.'[124] His sentiments were echoed by Goddard,[125] and by Stonehouse, who remarked that the rural dean was 'ever at hand to prevent abuses, to advise with and direct church-wardens, and to attend to the wishes and suggestions of the clergyman'.[126] Wilkins seems to have been alone among the Lincoln archdeacons in experiencing difficulty and disappointment with his rural deans.

Our Rural Deans do not work well – Mr Vaughan is gone away for some weeks – Mr Anderson is willing but not very active, and John Vernon excuses himself from attending the District Meetings – saying he has enough to do in his own parish and that too much is required of the Rural Deans. I must therefore act for them and push on business by myself and rely upon none.[127]

Kaye's response was that more rural deans should be appointed, but Wilkins was scornful.

It is no request of mine that more Rural Deans should be appointed than two to each of the deaneries now existing. There are no duties incumbent upon me which I cannot fully discharge with their aid alone, or without, whenever necessary.[128]

Here was an example of an archdeacon who, unable as he was to delegate or share responsibility, felt that his jurisdiction was being eroded.

[121] LAO CorB5/4/140, n.d. [1829].
[122] Ibid., Goddard's remarks to Kaye on his visitation of 1827.
[123] Ibid., Goddard's remarks to Kaye on his visitation of 1829.
[124] Ibid., Bayley to Kaye, 25 April 1829. See also his Charge for 1826.
[125] Goddard, *Charge* (1833); see also his Charge for 1836.
[126] Harding, *A Stow Visitation* pp. 12–13.
[127] LAO CorB5/8/36, Wilkins to Kaye, 15 February 1842.
[128] Ibid., Wilkins to Kaye, 25 February 1842.

There was a palpable sense of surprise and confusion among those incumbents who were suddenly called upon to become a new generation of rural deans. Bishop Kaye did not handle the business of the rural deans' appointments particularly skilfully. Once he had approved the names submitted by the archdeacons, he wrote a brief note informing each of his appointment, but apparently saying nothing of what the office entailed. The replies of the startled recipients, preserved for the Leicester and Nottingham archdeaconries, reveal that most did not have the faintest idea what would be expected of them.[129] Typical were the responses of W. W. Greenaway: 'I am not exactly sure of the nature of the office, or the extent of its duties . . .',[130] and John Vernon 'Perhaps Archdeacon Wilkins will be able to give me an outline of what I am or ought to do with this new office.'[131] Amongst the replies preserved from Leicester, the general consensus was one of pleasure at having been honoured with the appointment. In Nottingham, however, a greater reluctance prevailed. A higher proportion of men declined the office, pleading ill health, inexperience and, in one case, that the state of his own parish was insufficiently well ordered to permit him to scrutinise and report on other people's. The new rural deans were naturally anxious about the reception they would receive when they embarked upon their tours of inspection, and requested the bishop to make their appointment widely known. William Selwyn of Branstone (Branston) in Leicestershire, requested the bishop to notify the clergy by means of a circular letter, which he offered to deliver in person.[132] John Robinson of Cotgrave, Nottinghamshire, was concerned about the effect of ruridecanal inspections upon churchwardens, whom he feared would 'take alarm and stand upon the defensive', although he planned to approach them first with 'a civil note'.[133]

The letter of appointment received by every rural dean in the Lincoln diocese specifically stated that his duties were to report to the archdeacon or bishop on 'all things relating to the churches, chancels, churchyards and to the glebe houses of non-resident incumbents, and their fences and enclosures',[134] to visit these premises annually and to scrutinise the conduct of churchwardens. It is, however, apparent that the duties of rural deans were by no means confined to checking up on

[129] LAO CorB5/5/16 and CorB5/8A/39.
[130] LAO CorB5/5/16, W. W. Greenaway to Kaye, 2 January 1839.
[131] LAO CorB5/8A/39, J. Vernon to Kaye, 10 October 1839.
[132] LAO CorB5/5/16, W. Selwyn to Kaye, 18 February 1839.
[133] LAO CorB5/8A/39, J. Robinson to Kaye, 13 October 1839.
[134] Dansey, *Horae Decanicae Rurales*, vol II, pp. 420–1.

their non-resident neighbours. The superintendence of National schools became an early and important priority, with the rural deans assuming the lead in the plethora of education committees that were spawning by the late 1830s.

In addition to becoming educationalists, the rural deans were expected to take the lead in mediating in any disputes and disciplinary problems concerning the clergy in their neighbourhood. The Church Discipline Act of 1840 assigned them a special role in the investigation and prosecution of offenders, as has been shown. The clear preference of the majority of the clergy for having any difficulties arbitrated by their rural deans or neighbouring incumbents pointed strongly to the need for a locally-based tier of middle management in the diocesan hierarchy. The archdeacons, though invested with greater legal powers than the rural deans, could not attempt to exercise a continuous personal surveillance of the many parishes within their jurisdiction, particularly when some could not afford to reside within their archdeaconries.

The revival of rural deaneries afforded an unparalleled opportunity for making use of those incumbents who were known to be conscientious and reliable, whose services were secured without the necessity of additional expenditure. Their role was flexible because it was not defined in law. They had first-hand knowledge of people and places, and they could adopt a less formal approach. Archdeacon Bayley expressed it well in a letter to John Carr, rural dean of Lawres, in 1843: 'True it is you have no direct power to order the church-wardens but by residence and proximity you have a better thing – influence by persuasion and good management.'[135] When an archdeacon might resort to a threat of legal action, a rural dean had to rely on his own good example. Their presence brought particular stability to places where a high proportion of incumbents were out of residence, and whose parishes were in the hands of a body of transitory curates. Investigation of rural deans in the archdeaconry of Leicester reveals that their presence provided an important thread of continuity. Of ten appointed in 1838–9, a decade later one had died and one had resigned, but the other eight remained in office. Random sampling amongst Leicestershire incumbents who were not selected as rural deans suggests that only 57 per cent were still in office after a decade in the archdeaconry.[136]

---

[135] Harding, *A Stow Visitation* p. 13.

[136] This figure is based on a sample of forty Leicestershire incumbents from four deaneries between 1841 and 1851. The information is extracted from the *Clergy List*.

The rural deans seem generally to have adapted well to their duties. They were selected with a view to their willingness to work, but their duties – with responsibility for about ten parishes apiece – do not appear to have been unrealistically onerous. It was not unusual, however, for a rural dean to display signs of discomfort at the powers that his new office gave him in relation to those whom he had previously regarded as friends and neighbours. W. W. Greenaway, rural dean of Sparkenhoe in Leicestershire, expressed his anxiety at the outset. He described himself as 'on the best terms' with his clerical neighbours, and connected to many

By ties of closer intimacy ... [which] ... in some instances might be entirely severed by my communications with your Lordship, if those communications were made known to the individuals in question.[137]

Greenaway requested that all his disclosures be treated with strict confidentiality, not from 'cowardly motives; but ... *conflicting* feelings'.[138] If the rural deans expressed a personal dilemma, the question of divided loyalty was clearly at the heart of it. The question was not one of such obvious concern for the archdeacons, whose natural alliances tended to be with their bishops and, as their archdeaconries became annexed to canonries, with their cathedral chapters, rather than with the parochial clergy.

That the rural deans soon began to venture beyond inspecting their neighbours' fences to taking a lead in local education and in the arbitration of disputes between clergy, is a measure of the respect that they had swiftly earned. They began to revive ruridecanal chapters, or deanery meetings, at which local clergy would gather to discuss topics of interest. The effectiveness of these gatherings presumably depended upon the dispositions of the clergy involved, and the judiciousness with which the agenda had been drawn up. It was not unusual for the bishop to be invited to suggest items for the agenda, or to give his approval to one put forward. More neutral topics like education and church rates were preferred to contentious theological or party questions.[139] But even when the clergy confined themselves to Bible study, tensions could arise, as Walter Kerr Hamilton, bishop of Salisbury, noted in his diary in 1856:

[137] LAO CorB5/5/16 W. W. Greenaway to Kaye, 9 March 1839.
[138] Ibid.
[139] Burns, 'The diocesan revival' pp. 107–8.

Mr Watts [a rural dean] came to tell me of his troubles with his neighbour Mr Copley Saunders 'a most wild and unmanageable person' and also to express his great fears about the meetings of the clergy in their R. Deaneries. He says that Huxtable's H.Sc. [Holy Scripture] readings do not prosper – that the clergy are themselves startled at finding how great the differences are between them. He also does not like the notion of having the H.C. [Holy Communion] before the meetings – says it will lead to formalism.[140]

In the later 1850s and 1860s the focus of debate in the deanery chapters, as in the Church as a whole, turned to the question of relations with the church-going laity, and the extent to which they might be invited to participate in what had previously been clerical bodies. In the diocese of Exeter it was decided to associate leading laymen with the deanery chapters; in other places two completely separate meetings were set up.[141] The development of diocesan assemblies in the 1860s was further evidence of the desire to harness the talents and energies of articulate laymen. It was accompanied by a relative decline in the status of the parish officers. It is these changes in the formal roles available to lay people that will be considered next.

THE ECLIPSE OF LAY AUTHORITY: CHURCHWARDENS, PARISH CLERKS, SEXTONS AND SCHOOLTEACHERS

Traditionally, a number of specific roles were assigned to the laity within their own parishes, but – unless they happened to be members of Parliament or patrons – they had no opportunity to participate in the activities or management of the Church beyond their own parish boundaries. Churchwardens were the most important officers in the ecclesiastical parish. They were required to become the legal representatives of the parish at large, to provide all that was necessary for public worship, to repair and protect the church and its contents, to raise church rates and to spend them to the satisfaction of the vestry, to propose and carry out parochial regulations and to suppress profaneness and immorality.[142] Until 1834 they had responsibility for arranging poor law relief in conjunction with the parish overseers. They were also expected to report to the archdeacon or the bishop any deficiencies in their clergymen. Certainly this was no task to be undertaken by the faint-hearted, for, in large parishes at least, churchwardens might be

---

[140] PH HAM1/1/4, 7 January 1856.
[141] Burns, 'The diocesan revival' p. 112.
[142] James Shaw, *The Parochial Lawyer*, 4th edn (London, 1833) p. 1.

expected to devote considerable amounts of time and energy to their duties. Unlike the other parochial offices of parish clerk and sexton, which were remunerated and regarded as freeholds, churchwardens worked voluntarily, and were elected for a period of one year, though re-election was possible, and in some parishes quite usual. Once elected and sworn in, a process which normally happened at the archdeacon's visitation, churchwardens enjoyed a considerable degree of autonomy, and were remarkably free from both clerical and parochial restraint. They were not bound to obtain the advice or consent of either the minister, the parishioners or the archdeacon before carrying out the majority of repairs, although they needed the support of the vestry if they wished to set a rate to pay for them.[143]

Any adult male of good standing who resided in the parish could stand for the office, although there were exclusions for peers of the realm, clergy, MPs, members of certain professional bodies, serving officers in the military and ale-house keepers. Teachers and preachers of Nonconformist congregations were excluded, but not other Dissenters, and Roman Catholics and Jews were eligible, provided they were prepared to swear the necessary oaths.[144] The customary, though not universal, means of selecting wardens was for one to be nominated by the clergyman and the other by the parish. This system gave scope for parishioners to register their contempt for the Establishment, if they so wished, by selecting a Dissenter for the office, and this was not unknown, particularly in places where there was hostility to church rate. A Nonconformist radical might well block all attempts to impose a rate, as in the case of St Mary's, Nottingham, described in chapter three. Neither the bishop nor the archdeacon could refuse to admit a warden who had been duly elected by the parish. It needs to be remembered, however, that more evidence has survived concerning the activities of a few flamboyant Nonconformist wardens than for the majority of inconspicuous, conscientious Anglicans.

Many different sorts of people were elected as churchwardens, and they displayed a correspondingly wide range of attitudes to the Church. Among those who expressed hostility to the clergy may be included the people's warden at Bawtry in Nottinghamshire, a Dissenter who tried to have the curate dismissed because he would not administer communion to a woman who regularly attended an

---

143 Ibid., p. 20.
144 For further details of who was eligible and who was excluded, see Shaw, *The Parochial Lawyer* pp. 2–6.

Independent chapel on Sunday evenings.[145] Disputes with the clergy about the celebration of the Eucharist were a common cause of contention, the motives underlying them apparently ranging from obstructiveness to firmly held theological differences. At Stokeham in Nottinghamshire the wardens seem to have been in the former category, and they refused to provide a sacramental cup or to wash the curate's surplice, as they were supposed to do; in the neighbouring parish of East Drayton they would not provide bread and wine, and the surplice remained unwashed for two years.[146] At Whaplode St Mary in Lincolnshire the churchwarden was a Dissenter who claimed he had no wish for the post, but had nevertheless been unanimously elected by the parish. He refused to abstain from administering the Lord's supper in the local meeting-house, but, to the consternation of the vicar, he proved quite willing also to accept the Anglican communion.[147]

There is evidence of disputes arising when wardens had been influenced by Tractarianism. At Boston the churchwardens, in an attempt to increase the level of ceremonial, outraged the clergy by purchasing a deep puce altar cloth embroidered with a large white cross, and by draping it over the altar at the beginning of Lent.[148] At St James', Standard Hill in Nottingham, the warden was described by a clergyman as 'highly respectable' but 'of late years [he has] unfortunately drank in Tractarianism'.[149] A ferocious dispute broke out about the way in which the Eucharist was to be celebrated, which came to a head when the defiant curate commenced a communion service by walking up to the altar with a black bottle in one hand and bread wrapped in a paper in the other.[150] These examples are suggestive of wardens who were taking an active interest in directly liturgical matters. Given that they possessed such a high degree of autonomy once elected, Tractarian churchwardens may have played a significant role in the reshaping of worship; one which has not previously been acknowledged.

Other churchwardens had no hesitation about offering clergy their

[145] LAO CorB5/8/31, The churchwardens of Bawtry to Kaye, 17 October 1845; T. A. Bolton to Kaye, 4 November 1845.
[146] LAO CorB5/8/28/1, J. Goodacre to Kaye, 28 January 1847.
[147] LAO CorB5/4/67/7, J. Hutchinson to Kaye, 10 November 1849; E. Moore to Kaye, 30 September 1849.
[148] LAO CorB5/4/130, J. H. Oldrid to Kaye, 29 April 1850.
[149] LAO CorB5/8/5, H. Bolton to Kaye, 21 April 1847.
[150] Ibid., Wilkins to Kaye, 30 June 1847.

unqualified support. Thomas and Robert Stone proved staunch allies to Mr Fane, the temporary curate at Radnage in Buckinghamshire, when it was thought that he had been neglecting his duties:

I Can asure is Lordship that there Rang about the duty of the Church Mr Fane is well be likd at Radnage Sir the Church was Every Puew was quite full yesterday afternn Sarist Sir the Church Sarist cant be in Better Hands than Mr Fane . . . Sir I am sory to send you such Bad riting.[151]

George Rogers was another churchwarden prepared to provide a glowing testimonial; he gave it for Mr Atkinson, curate of Arnold in Nottinghamshire, who had incurred the bishop's irritation for failing to live in the vicarage:

He gives great satisfaction and although the population is nearly five thousand he certainly exerts himself very much, performs two full services on the Sabbath, visits his parishioners and particularly those that are needy and distress'd, of which there are a great number at this time.[152]

A few churchwardens were the principal landowners in their parish; others were barely literate. Tradesmen and farmers predominated. In the Bedfordshire deanery of Shefford in 1850, among twenty churchwardens whose occupation can be identified, there were thirteen farmers. Others included a beer retailer, an auctioneer, a baker, a grocer and postmaster, a plumber, painter and glazier, a relieving officer and registrar for births, deaths and marriages and the steward and surveyor to Lord Olney.[153] It seems doubtful that churchwardening was widely regarded as a suitable occupation for a gentleman. There were only a handful of gentry holding the office in the archdeaconry of Stafford in the 1830s, among them the Tractarian A. J. B. Beresford Hope, who claimed to have been a neglectful churchwarden of Sheen, where he was also patron.[154] In his charge of 1839, George Hodson, archdeacon of Stafford, urged gentlemen of rank and property to come forward for the office. Hanley, Lane End and Stoke each had a pottery manufacturer as churchwarden. At Stoke it was Herbert Minton, whose encaustic tiles were to become such a prominent feature of Victorian church restorations. At Burton, the brewing trade was represented by a member of the Worthington

---

[151] LAO CorB5/3/2/2, T. and R. Stone to J. Symons, 6 December 1841.
[152] LAO CorB5/8A/1, G. Rogers to Kaye, 30 January 1840.
[153] CUL EDR C1/9, list of Bedfordshire churchwardens, 1850, with information about occupations extracted from the *Post Office Directory for Berkshire, Northamptonshire, Oxfordshire, West Bedfordshire, Buckinghamshire and Huntingdonshire, 1847.*
[154] Robinson, *Visitations of the Archdeaconry of Stafford* pp. xxiv–xxv.

family, and the other churchwarden was an iron founder. The election of men of this sort was mirrored in other industrial towns in Staffordshire, perhaps an indication that the office of churchwarden was seen to confer additional status on a man whose worldly fortunes were rising. In rural areas the social standing of wardens was noticeably lower.[155]

C. E. Mayo, complaining to Bishop Kaye about the irregularities of a clerical colleague, believed that the Church suffered much evil from 'the diffidence of uneducated churchwardens who feel themselves incapable of making a complaint'.[156] It is apparent that although churchwardens were expressly empowered to report upon the misdeeds of the clergy,[157] complaints were as likely to be received from individual parishioners or other clergymen as from the wardens themselves. An examination of 350 churchwardens' presentments in the diocese of Ely at ten-year intervals over the period 1805 to 1864 reveals a high level of satisfaction with the clergy. In answer to the question 'Is the whole duty regularly supplied?', 347 of the 350 respondents said that it was. The wardens also reported very favourably on the state of repair of their churches, churchyards and parsonage houses. This could be interpreted as a sign of diffidence, or a desire not to attract the notice of the archdeacon who might order expensive repairs, or it may be that they were simply telling the truth. Their responses remained remarkably consistent over the sixty-year period, though it is apparent that the number of churches described as 'under repair' increased in the 1860s. The most noticeable reticence, however, was seen in the wardens' replies to the question 'Is there adultery, fornication or incest?' They were clearly troubled at being asked for information about the sexual activities of their neighbours, and the enquiry was finally dropped from the presentment form in the 1850s. The wardens almost always declined to give a straightforward yes or no, preferring to leave a blank, or to make an ambiguous reply like 'none known', 'I cannot say', or, 'it's feared too many'. Only twice in the presentments sampled did the churchwardens actually name an allegedly fornicating couple; one reported a deceased-wife's-sister marriage in 1835, but was unclear about its moral status. William Taylor, churchwarden of Little Thetford near Ely in 1825, summed up the prevailing mood when he wrote 'cannot account for private

---

[155] Ibid., p. xxv.
[156] LAO CorB5/8/31/1, C. E. Mayo to Kaye, 31 October 1845.
[157] Shaw, *Parochial Lawyer* p. 15.

Immoralitys'.[158] Nineteenth-century churchwardens evidently felt that their scope for legitimate enquiry stopped at the churchyard wall.

Parish clerks and sextons were the lowest officers in the Church, employed for the menial tasks, and usually appointed by the incumbent or officiating minister. The evidence concerning sextons is sparse, and sometimes the two roles of clerk and sexton were combined. The job of the sexton included grave-digging and opening vaults, keeping the church swept and aired, the pews clean, and under the churchwardens' direction, providing water for baptism, candles and other essential items. At service time the sexton was supposed to open pews and keep out dogs and disorderly persons. Women were eligible to serve as sextons, though not as parish clerks; although there is some evidence of women taking on the latter office regardless of the law.[159]

To be technically eligible for the post of parish clerk a man had to be at least twenty and able to read and write. He needed a competent knowledge of liturgy and psalmody, for part of his duties consisted of singing or saying the psalms, and making the prayer book responses with or on behalf of the congregation.[160] In this capacity a clerk had a major influence on the tone of worship.[161] Clerks were supposed to be licensed to their office by the archdeacon, but many were not, thus making impossible any intervention by the archdeacon over matters such as wages. Archidiaconal visitations always seem to have included questions about the parish clerk, and there was general agreement that they were often exploited. In his charge of 1827, Archdeacon Goddard railed against clergy who had, sometimes without even assigning a cause, prohibited their clerks from exercising their functions and receiving their dues. It was inappropriate, he warned, to dismiss clerks on the grounds of incompetence, when their conduct should instead be reported to him:

Indeed when it is considered with how niggardly a hand Country Parishes dole out to the Clerk a pittance utterly insufficient for his maintenance (in some cases scarcely contributing to it) the wonder should be that competent persons should in such Parishes be met with to officiate ... A low salary forms a just presumption against the competency.[162]

158 This data was derived from CUL EDR B15, B16, B17, B18, B19, B20, B21.
159 Shaw, *Parochial Lawyer* p. 247; P. H. Ditchfield, *The Parish Clerk* (London, 1907) p. 203.
160 Shaw, *Parochial Lawyer* pp. 245–6.
161 Nicholas Temperley, *The Music of the English Parish Church* (Cambridge: Cambridge University Press, 1979) vol. 1 *passim*.
162 Charles Goddard, *Charge to the Clergy and Archdeaconry of Lincoln* (1827) p. 37.

Archdeacon Hill reported after his 1828 visitation that he had received very general complaints from parish clerks about the inadequacy of their salaries, and the manner in which they were paid. In Buckinghamshire it had been customary for twice-yearly collections for the parish clerk to be held in the parishes, but as most of the persons applied to failed to give anything, the amounts raised were small. Hill remarked that none of the clerks were licensed, but though thus deprived of powers of intervention, he had, characteristically, not been afraid to make recommendations:

After consulting with the late Bishop [Pelham] I ventured to direct the Churchwardens to pay them a moderate Stipend, rarely exceeding the sum of *three* pounds pr. ann: *in lieu of collections* – & explained to the Ch. wardens that such payment coming from the Church rates wd. be a *fair* and equal collection. This arrangement appears to have given general satisfaction.[163]

Hill felt sufficiently strongly about this issue to suggest in the following year that an Act of Parliament was needed to appoint proper salaries for parish clerks, sextons, bell-ringers and organists.[164] Church rates, of course, could provide a more reliable income than local collections only for as long as they continued to be raised. If the rate was abandoned, the parish clerk's stipend was usually the first item that ceased to be paid, and this was an important contributory factor in their demise.

In Staffordshire salaries paid to parish clerks ranged from fifteen shillings at Kingsley to twenty pounds at Tamworth, and were over ten pounds at fifteen other places. Strict comparisons are difficult, however, because the clerk's income from fees, which were paid for his attendance at the occasional offices, varied enormously from place to place. At St Mowden's, Burton and Lane End fees were the clerks' main or only source of income. At Burton-upon-Trent, with 4,000 parishioners, the clerk received no fixed salary, but presumably managed reasonably well from fees.[165] At Wigginton and Wilnecote voluntary subscriptions were the sole source of the clerks' income,[166] as had been the practice in Buckinghamshire. When fees were paid, their scale was modest. In 1839 in the Nottingham city parishes of St Mary's, St Paul's, St Nicholas' and St Peter's, the clerk received five shillings for

163   LAO CorB5/3/32, J. Hill to Kaye, 7 April 1828.
164   Ibid., Hill to Kaye, 25 June 1829.
165   Robinson, *Visitations of the Archdeaconry of Stafford* p. xxv.
166   Ibid., p. xxvi.

being in attendance at a marriage by licence; sixpence for publishing banns; two shillings and sixpence for attending a marriage by banns (which was the only occasion on which he could command the same fee as the clergyman); one shilling and sixpence at the burial of an adult; one shilling at the burial of an infant; twopence for a churching; fourpence when a certificate was issued.[167] With the exception of the fees for burial, where grave-digging was involved, the sums commanded by sextons tended to be lower than those received by the clerk. In cities and large towns where the occasional offices were in constant use, income from fees would probably have permitted parish clerks to accumulate an adequate income, and the amount of time that they would have had to devote to their parochial duties could well have precluded them from obtaining secular employment. In Nottingham only three of the city's eight parish clerks were listed in the 1848 Post Office Directory as having additional employment – one as a house agent, one as a sheriff's officer and one as a National schoolmaster. In the country, clerks and sextons must have had to find other work.

A country clerk could probably have combined his duties with most types of trade, merely excusing himself now and then for a funeral or a marriage. A sexton could have slipped quite readily from grave-digging to labouring or gardening. The Post Office Directory reveals Nottinghamshire parish clerks combining their duties with shoemaking, schoolteaching, or working in smithies and workshops. At Ingham in Lincolnshire the parish clerk of thirty years standing took out a licence to sell beer in 1835. This caused some offence to certain parishioners, but the vicar defended him. The clerk was doing nothing illegal, nor was he guilty of disorderly conduct. Whilst the vicar admitted that he would not have chosen as parish clerk one who sold beer, 'to dismiss a man, who has grown old and gray in the capacity of clerk, is a different matter'.[168]

The limited evidence suggests that the clergy generally enjoyed reasonably cordial relationships with their clerks. It was certainly a very different relationship from that between clerics and churchwardens, for rancour seems rare,[169] which is perhaps surprising in view of the fact that the clerks were displaced as a result of liturgical changes imposed

---

[167] LAO CorB5/8A/16, G. Wilkins to Kaye, 18 October 1839.
[168] LAO CorB5/4/25/2, M. Hodge to Kaye, 21 April 1835.
[169] It was not unknown however. See Mark Spurrell, *Stow Church Restored 1846–1866* (Lincoln: Lincoln Record Society, 1984) p. xvi.

by the clergy.[170] Clerks tended to accept compliantly their place at the bottom of the ecclesiastical pecking order. Their decline was accelerated by the ending of compulsory church rate, after which they had to rely entirely on fees and voluntary subscriptions, or on the generosity of the incumbent. Changing liturgical tastes in the second half of the century also displaced them from their traditional role in leading the people's responses. The clerk was discarded with the triple-decker pulpit, in which he had traditionally occupied the lowest place, as the reordered chancel became reserved for the clergy and the choir. Writing in the 1880s, F. J. Crowest described an aged clerk who had refused to assist in what he considered 'Puseyite pranks', but had nevertheless been persuaded to head a procession of 'clean-faced boys in white surplices'. Crowest claimed that in many parishes, the presence and aid of the old clerk proved of value 'to many a worried vicar in dealing with the complaints and questionings of a panic-stricken congregation'.[171]

The churchwarden in Shefford and the parish clerk in Nottingham identified above as having served also as schoolmasters, were perhaps not untypical of the period. In the eighteenth century a fair proportion of larger parishes had supported a charity school, but in rural places, dame schools remained common – as at Fifield in Oxfordshire in 1808, where one was kept 'by an old woman, who teaches reading, knitting, a little sewing & the catechism'.[172] The Report of the Select Committee on the Education of the Poor provided a useful survey in 1818. In Oxfordshire, 41 parishes (out of 200 that submitted returns in 1818) had no educational provision of any description, while a further 31 relied on Sunday schools. By 1833, however, the situation had changed dramatically, and only 15 mostly very small Oxfordshire parishes were without schools.[173] The national picture was equally impressive; in 1832, the year before the first State grant to education, 6,730 parishes and chapelries in England were providing some form of church school.[174]

---

[170] Occasionally a clerk might disgrace himself – perhaps by getting drunk – but reported instances are few. At Bawtry, a clerk was alleged to have been drunk at a funeral (LAO CorB5/8/31/6); and at Creeton, a clerk was said to have drunk unconsecrated communion wine with the curate (LAO CorB5/19/2/6). On the positive side may be placed the account of Thomas Evison, the exemplary clerk of Wragby. See Ditchfield, *The Parish Clerk* pp. 281–3.

[171] F. J. Crowest, *Phases of Musical England* (English Publishing Company, 1881) pp. 78–9, cited by Bernard Rainbow, *The Choral Revival in the Anglican Church 1839–1872* (London: Barrie & Jenkins, 1970) p. 284.

[172] Return of Schools, 1808, Bodl MS Oxf. Dioc. Pp. d., 707, cited by Pamela Horn (ed.), *Village Education in Nineteenth-century Oxfordshire* (Oxfordshire Record Society, S1, 1979) p. xiii.

[173] Horn, *Village Education* p. xvii.

[174] Henry James Burgess, *Enterprise in Education: The Story of the Work of the Established Church in the Education of the People Prior to 1870* (London: SPCK, 1958) p. 43.

For most of the nineteenth century the High Church organisation the National Society for Promoting the Education of the Poor in the Principles of the Established Church was the major provider of elementary schooling for the poor. As its name implied, the education that it offered was strongly Anglican in character. It required that schools give instruction on the Prayer Book and the catechism, that pupils attend the parish church on Sunday, and read only those books that had been published by SPCK. Beyond the religious component, the curriculum was generally confined to what was thought suitable for working people. It amounted to the elements of knowledge: reading, writing, arithmetic and sewing for the girls. In the period from 1840 the ideal Anglican parish, with its restored Gothic church, resident incumbent and comfortable parsonage, also had its neat National school, filled with the children of the poor, all apparently learning their catechism and growing up to be useful in their station in life, protected from the dangers of Dissent. The education movement was complementary to the campaign for church extension, and the clear assumption was that the working classes were being educated to worship in the new and enlarged church buildings. Addressing a diocesan education conference at Oxford in 1856, the Tractarian Henry Newland remarked to the assembled schoolmasters: 'When you have manufactured a steady, honest, God-fearing, Church-going population, then you have done your duty as Schoolmasters'.[175]

The explosion of interest in the education of the poor seems to point to a relatively rapid recognition that the provision of schools was too important to be left to chance in the unsupervised hands of the parish clergy. The willingness of Nonconformists to set up schools in areas where educational provision was weak or non-existent began to be perceived by Church people as a challenge to the religious principles of a whole generation. Diocesan structures were harnessed for the new task. A Diocesan Board of Education was established in Lincoln in 1838, and within a year separate archidiaconal and deanery education boards were in existence in other parts of the diocese. In Buckinghamshire the Archidiaconal Board of Education met in Aylesbury on the first Tuesday of every month.[176] It must have been a cumbersome, top heavy body, with thirty-six vice presidents and twenty-one committee members. The rural deans were expected to attend its meetings, and to

[175] Horn, *Village Education* p. xv.
[176] LAO CorB5/3/34/1/12, Statement from the Archidiaconal Board of Education.

use their own deanery education boards to implement at local level the resolutions made by the diocesan and archidiaconal committees.

In Buckinghamshire the Wendover deanery education board was founded on 31 July 1839 by Arthur Isham and his fellow rural dean John Harrison. The deanery very soon boasted a boys school of very high calibre. When Charles Mackenzie inspected it on 22 December 1840, he noted that the timetable included scripture, catechism, Greek, Latin, French, algebra, arithmetic, scripture history, profane history, geography and reading. Mackenzie heard the boys recite passages from English and French authors, and from Virgil, and then enact a scene from the Roman dramatist Terence. 'In all of which they evinced talent and acquaintance with the respective Languages, but were far too rapid in the delivery.'[177] The Wendover deanery school was clearly a show piece with a curriculum far removed from that offered in most National schools. However, the inspectors' reports on other church schools in Buckinghamshire reveal that although the emphasis was firmly on catechism and good behaviour, broader expectations existed.[178]

The impression conveyed by the reports of the inspectors of church schools, themselves clergymen until 1870, was of teachers who were dedicated and competent. The Revd John Allen, inspecting Bedfordshire schools in 1844, commented favourably on the work of many of the teachers in the county, and would typically remark that the master was 'gentle and anxious to do his best' and that the mistress was 'intelligent, pleasing and capable.'[179] Teachers were often very young; in 1871 more than one in three of the male teachers employed in Oxfordshire were under the age of twenty-five, while among the women it was not far short of one in two.[180] After marriage, couples often ran schools together. At Whitchurch in Oxfordshire, Charles and Eliza Soper were employed at the National school for a joint salary of £50 8s a year in 1839, rising to £54 12s in the mid-1840s; Frederick and Sarah Ogilwy succeeded them, and were also paid £54 12s; Frederick and Damaris Batson were paid £63 from 1861 to 1866; Miss Cooke ran the school on her own in 1867 and 1868 and was paid £50; John Eastman and his sister Clara were engaged at a joint salary of £70 plus

[177] LAO CorB5/3/34, Report of an examination of Wendover deanery school by Revd Charles Mackenzie MA, 22 December 1840.

[178] Ibid., miscellaneous inspectors' reports.

[179] David Bushby (ed.), *Bedfordshire Schoolchild: Elementary Education Before 1902* (Bedfordshire Historical Record Society, 67, 1988) pp. 89–92.

[180] Horn, *Village Education* p. xlii.

two-thirds of the government grant in 1868; Barnaby Brown and his wife Jane were paid at the same rate in 1871 and 1872; and from 1872 to 1879 Thomas and Sarah Litchfield received £100 per annum, plus half of the government grant. All these couples received free housing in addition to their stipend.[181] This doubling of the Whitchurch teachers' salary in a 33-year period points to the rising prosperity of the profession. It compares favourably with the fortunes of curates at the same period, for whom the likelihood of a free house was diminishing. A curate continued to enjoy considerably greater social prestige than a schoolmaster, but he might no longer be significantly better placed financially. Schoolmistresses were also expecting a higher standard of living. James Fraser, rector of Ufton Nervet in Berkshire, complained about this trend to Bishop Hamilton in 1861:

Salaries have reached a preposterous height, and under the conditions of the market are certain to fall. You know as well as I, that 10 yrs ago you had no difficulty in planting mistresses out at 25£ a year from all sources – (for not one in three at that day got government augmentation) who now are not content unless they receive £45 or £50, and that, when they are barely of age.[182]

Parochial clergy, as opposed to clerical school inspectors, seem to have been more concerned about teachers' lack of religious conformity than about their abilities in the classroom. Earlier in the century at least, some teachers seem to have shared the laity's flexible approach to denominational identity. At Brill in Buckinghamshire the schoolmaster William Sutton claimed to be a churchman when appointed, but had preached at a Wesleyan Methodist meeting some time after his arrival in 1827. He was remonstrated with, and promised not to reoffend, but after three years of conformity resumed preaching among the Methodists.[183] Legal action was taken to evict Sutton from the school-room, but, in what became a protracted dispute, he did not relinquish control until 1841.[184] This was clearly an exceptional and untypical proceeding, amounting to a major confrontation between the Church and dissent at parish level, and involving many parishioners. In other places an undermining of the Anglican position was likely to be more subtle. At Great Hampden in Buckinghamshire the vicar was taken aback when a teacher remarked in the course of a conversation that he

---

[181] Ibid., pp. lvi–lvii.
[182] PH HAM/4/16/25, J. Fraser to Hamilton, 31 December 1861.
[183] LAO CorB5/3/8/7, J. S. Baron to Kaye, 26 March 1836.
[184] Ibid., Baron to Kaye, 18 September 1841.

'held with adult baptisms and total immersions; and conceived infant baptism to be the cause of much that is objectionable in the lives of professing Xns [Christians]'.[185] At Retford in 1852, ten Sunday school teachers who were reluctant to use the catechism signed a petition refusing to accept its 'non-scriptural' notions that at baptism babies were made 'children of grace', 'Members of Christ', 'Children of God' and 'Inheritors of the Kingdom of Heaven'.[186] Although these teachers clearly had Baptist sympathies, their Evangelical vicar still regarded them as members of his own flock. He commented that he would prefer to 'consult their prejudices rather than lose them from the Church'.[187]

Dissenting schoolteachers who established their own schools in open rivalry to the Church sometimes provided a spur for the clergy. Samuel Oliver, the octogenarian curate of Whaplode in Lincolnshire, gave a vivid portrait of one such teacher in 1835:

About two years ago (more or less) there came a Man into this Parish, named David Hurn, and set himself up as a Schoolmaster; who tells my Sunday Scholars, in his vernacular Fen slang, that 'the Catechism is nought but a pack o' Lies; and that I have no right to teach it in the Church, on Sundays'! – in short, my Lord, I clearly understand him to be a confirmed Infidel! for which reason, more than any other, he is warmly Patronized, and strenuously supported by the great majority of leading People in the Parish.[188]

Oliver responded to Hurn's presence by reviving the office of parish schoolmaster. The post appears to have been vacant for a considerable period, and was precariously dependent upon a will which had directed that the rent from two and a half acres of land be paid to a master 'to teach as many poor boys of the parish to read as will pay 2d a week'.[189]

In the second half of the century teachers were obliged to nail their colours more visibly to the Anglican mast, in response to increasingly less flexible notions of denominational allegiance, and to greater supervision or interference from the clergy. Where there existed a climate of Nonconformist hostility to church schools, teachers had, however, to attempt to conciliate local feeling in order to avoid alienating parents and losing pupils. A teacher at Harrold in Bedfordshire expressed this dilemma in the logbook on 19 November 1863: 'Mr Fever (Butcher)

---

[185] LAO CorB5/3/14/3, C. Lloyd to Kaye, 15 December 1843.
[186] LAO CorB5/8/34, memorial of ten (male) Sunday school teachers, April 1852.
[187] Ibid., C. Hodge to Kaye, 17 April 1852.
[188] LAO CorB5/4/54/1, S. Oliver to Kaye, 15 August 1835.
[189] Ibid.

asked me permission for his boys not to learn the Church Catechism. Granted. Caution – never, if *possible*, sacrifice principle to expediency. It is no gain in reality.' This turned out not to be an isolated case. On 20 April 1866 the teacher wrote: 'There seems almost an impossibility to conduct the school according to the principles of the "Church of England".'[190]

Schoolteachers were expected to show public loyalty to the Church by training the choir, playing the organ or harmonium, or teaching at the Sunday school. There was no question of their being permitted to hold any Nonconformist opinions. Sometimes the demands of the Church may have led to a feeling of exploitation; a Buckinghamshire schoolmaster commented in 1872 that the rural teacher was all too often regarded as 'the parson's fag, squire's door-mat, church scraper, professional singer, sub-curate, land surveyor, drill master, club collector, parish clerk, letter writer, librarian, washerwoman's target, organist, choir master, and youth's instructor'.[191] As teachers rose in status, towards the end of the century, they became more successful at resisting such impositions. By the early years of the twentieth century teachers' agreements in Oxfordshire were stating explicitly that they would not be expected to undertake duties not connected with the work of the school.[192]

THE LAYMAN REDEFINED

From the 1860s onwards there was among some clergy a growing sense of the need for appropriate (which tended to mean clerically-supervised) lay participation in church government. A future bishop of Oxford, J. F. Mackarness, observed at the 1867 Church Congress that 'if you want men to be entirely interested in any institution, you must give them a real voice in its management'.[193] The Church congresses were but one of three initiatives that aimed to give a voice to lay as well as to clerical opinion in the second half of the nineteenth century. The others were the introduction of diocesan conferences in the 1860s, and the creation of a House of Laity to sit in addition to the Houses of Clergy and Bishops in the Convocations of Canterbury and York in the period from 1886 to 1892. The Church Congress had started as a

190 Bushby, *Bedfordshire Schoolchild* p. 186.
191 E. Richardson, *Cloddy in Bucks* (London, 1872) p. iv, cited in Horn, *Village Education* p. xliv.
192 Horn, *Village Education* p. xliv.
193 Ibid.

small meeting held at King's College, Cambridge, in 1861. It was open to the public, with papers and discussions by laity and clergy. It became an annual event, and admitted women from 1863, although they were not permitted to speak in the debates. By the 1880s, however, the congresses had run out of steam, and they were to some extent superseded by the creation of a House of Laity in Convocation.[194]

Bishop Browne of Ely in 1866 and Bishop Selwyn of Lichfield in 1868 began to hold diocesan conferences where the participation of laymen was regarded as important.[195] By 1882 they had spread to all but three dioceses.[196] Both Browne and Selwyn were old-fashioned High Churchmen, with little sympathy for Anglo-Catholics or Evangelicals. They regarded the participation of laymen in diocesan discussions as a natural progression from their inclusion in the newly-revived deanery chapters. It was intended by this means to bring the diocese together as a self-conscious body, and to foster a stronger Anglican identity to which dedicated church people contributed. It marked a further step on the road from national church to denomination, and reflected an increasing wish to distinguish formally between the committed and the nominal churchman.

Bishop Browne in particular became a tireless campaigner for a new role for the laity. He gave eloquent expression to his views in his charge for 1869:

I cannot doubt that great strength would be given to the rector of the parish, if he could have a committee of the Laity to work and to take counsel with continually. For schools and charities, for church rates, for mission societies, for the suppression of vice, for the maintenance of truth and the suppression of error, all ought to be working, and all ought to work together ... A clergyman who stands alone, may perhaps have more of his own way, but he will surely do less to lead others in the way to God ... In theory, churchwardens, sidesmen, vestries and the like were meant in great measure for this very purpose, viz. to work with the clergyman in things spiritual and ecclesiastical. The sidesman has become a thing of the past, the vestry has other thoughts in view, the churchwarden mostly limits his attention to the fabric of the church, and possibly its services. We want to awaken the heart and interest of true Churchmen and true Christians in all that is doing in the church services, in the village, in the school, in the neighbourhood, in the diocese, in the Church at large.[197]

[194]   Chadwick, *The Victorian Church*, part II, p. 362–3.
[195]   Ibid., p. 360; Burns, 'The diocesan revival' pp. 298–305.
[196]   Chadwick, *The Victorian Church*, part II, p. 360.
[197]   E. H. Browne, *Charge to the Clergy of the Diocese of Ely, 1869* (London, 1953).

At the Ely diocesan conferences a range of practical and ecclesiastical topics were debated; theological questions were deemed unsuitable for lay discussion. By 1869, their agenda had included (in the order listed by Browne) the housing of the poor, the gang system, the straw-plait system, prayer, hymnody, middle-class education, dilapidations, women's church work, more frequent reception of Holy Communion and cottage hospitals.[198]

Browne gave further expression to his convictions in 1869, when he licensed six lay readers and admitted Fanny Elizabeth Eagles as the first deaconess to serve in the diocese of Ely.[199] The readers were unpaid volunteers, and nothing is known of their social origins or theological inclinations. The deaconess, however, was full-time and stipendiary. Browne saw her task as being similar to that of a deacon as defined by the ordinal:

To seek out the sick, poor and impotent folk and intimate their names to the curate; [she] should instruct the young, in school or otherwise, minister to those in hospitals, prisons or asylums; and setting aside all unwomanly usurpation of authority in the Church, should seek to edify the souls of Christ's people in the faith.[200]

She was known thereafter as Sister Fanny, but Browne was at pains to emphasise that she was not a nun, and had taken no vows. Nevertheless, she remained a deaconess for the rest of her life, working with deaconesses and other women in Bedford until her death in 1907.

In his visitation questionnaire of 1873, Browne included several questions that were intended to elicit the views of his clergy on the role of the laity at parochial church councils, at the diocesan conference and in Convocation. The range of responses suggests Evangelical enthusiasm for lay participation, and Anglo-Catholic disdain, coupled with an anxiety concerning the degree of commitment of those who might become involved. The incumbent of St Mary's, Bedford, wrote:

I fear that the Laity in the Conferences represent the Rates rather than the religion of the parishes. It would be well if returns could be obtained from the Churchwardens to show how they are assisting the Clergy in promoting Church work and godliness ... I do not see what place the Laity could have in that which is essentially a Convocation of the Clergy.[201]

---

[198] Ibid.
[199] *Ely Diocesan Calendar and Clergy List, 1870* (Ely, 1870) p. 89.
[200] Janet Grierson, *The Deaconess* (London: CIO Publishing, 1981) p. 24.
[201] CUL EDR. C3/25, 1873.

His colleagues at St John's and St Cuthbert's, Bedford, had a more positive appraisal, however, and wished to see the establishment of a House of Laity in Convocation. The incumbent of Clophill expressed his views simply: 'I long for the admission of the laity into Convocation. I also think that the evangelicals are very inadequately represented there.'[202] The Anglo-Catholic vicar of Eaton Bray (who held 364 communion services a year) thought that the diocesan conference, which had admitted laymen since its inception seven years earlier, should be restricted to the clergy. He was scathing about the bishop's suggestion that he should seek the advice and assistance of his parishioners in a parochial council: 'I most humbly but decidedly consider that I am better able to advise my parishioners than they are.'[203] From other parishes there were reports of the total indifference of parishioners to any parochial, diocesan or national schemes. The incumbent of Battleden wrote: 'Tried to have [a parochial council] but the farmers are too indifferent and say they are contented to leave things in my hands.'[204]

It is difficult to gain much sense of popular support for the initiatives of Browne and his like-minded colleagues. Many clergy were unnerved at the implications of lay leadership; Rosemary O'Day has argued that it militated against the clergy developing in the manner of other professions.[205] The efforts of Browne and others seem to suggest an attempt to recapture a lost relationship between clergy and people, one which had become fragmented as the late eighteenth-century parson made the transition from yeoman to gentleman. By about 1780 the typical incumbent was perceived as having become increasingly wealthy, and had withdrawn from the centre of parish life. He had enclosed and ceased to farm his glebe land, and had rebuilt or extended his house, transforming it into an elegant residence. It was not, of course, invariably the case that clergy had benefited from enclosure and the agricultural boom, but those who had were seen as representative of the whole. The incumbent's successor in the early nineteenth century aspired to a similar style, even if he found that financial constraints sometimes made it impossible to live up to the ideal. He was used to dealing with the churchwardens and the parish clerk, but there is generally little sense of his having been at ease with

[202] Ibid.
[203] Ibid.
[204] Ibid.
[205] O'Day, 'The clerical renaissance' pp. 194–6.

the majority of his parishioners. Unless he was connected by social ties, he does not seem to have sought anything beyond purely formal contact. The abandonment of the visitation dinner, when archdeacon, clergy and churchwardens had formerly sat down to enjoy what was intended as a convivial evening, was a potent symbol of the collapsing relationship. Such developments were legitimated both by the Evangelical revival and the Oxford Movement, with their suspicion of what seemed worldly and profane, and their belief in the duty of the faithful to obedient submission. At the same time, Evangelical and Tractarian self-consciousness brought a wholly new sense of the separation of the clerical caste.

The attempts by Browne and others to foster lay participation in diocesan conferences need to be understood in the context of their reappraisal of whether Anglicanism could be forged and sustained by the clergy alone. Browne admitted to having been nervous about how his diocesan conferences would work out: 'I had certainly some little misgiving as to how the clergy would feel when brought face to face with the laity, and how the laity would feel when brought in like manner into public contact with the clergy.'[206] Such an admission seems astonishing in view of the sort of laymen whose acquaintance the clergy were making on such occasions; they were the very men with whom, through links of birth, education and religious feeling, the clergy might have been expected to have had most in common. That they should need any form of reintroduction is suggestive of the extent to which the clergy had become preoccupied with merely clerical concerns.

Those who took part in diocesan conferences were the leading laymen in the diocese; such meetings were not intended to include the inarticulate or the socially inferior. This points to another significant shift in the remoulding of the relations between clergy and laity. The farmers and tradesmen who had held the offices of churchwarden and parish clerk were being displaced from their long-held position as the most important laymen in the Church of England. As has been shown, the clerk had held office as a freehold, and the warden was only removable at a public election. After 1860 the clerk began to disappear almost completely, and the churchwarden became confined to a more limited task in the maintenance of the church fabric. Parish vestries lost almost all their powers under the Local Government Act of 1894. The

---

[206] Chadwick, *The Victorian Church*, part II, p. 360.

Church of England did not succeed in finding any equally important alternative roles for its middle-ranking male members. The lay reader scheme, pioneered by Browne and others, did not have the same appeal. It developed its own internal social hierarchy, with a distinction between parochial readers who were licensed in a single parish, and diocesan readers who were well-educated and commissioned to officiate in any parish at the request of the incumbent.[207] In any case, men did not come forward for clerically-supervised church work in sufficient numbers. By the end of the century most of the church work being performed by lay people was being undertaken by women. They became district visitors and Sunday school teachers in large numbers. A few devoted themselves to the Church full-time as Bible women, deaconesses or religious sisters.

Bishop Campbell of Bangor expressed the sense of a widening gulf in a speech in Convocation in 1884. What was wanted were 'Christian men who can bridge over the gap between the different classes of society; who being in close communication with the clergyman on the one hand and the industrious masses on the other, can interpret each to each'.[208] This seems a clear admission that the clergy had not acquired the ability to communicate with their parishioners. Towards the end of the century, Henry Manning, cardinal archbishop of Westminster, and former Anglican archdeacon, remarked that where the Church of England had gone wrong was in allowing itself to become an institution governed by the conventions of social class. It was an acute analysis from a man who had participated at a high level in two very different Churches.

---

[207] Rhoda Hiscox, *Celebrating Reader Ministry: 125 Years of Lay Ministry in the Church of England* (London: Mowbray, 1991) p. 15.
[208] Ibid., p. 14.

CHAPTER 6

Conclusion

By 1870 the Church of England could no longer claim to be the Church of the English nation. It has been conventional to regard the most significant moments in this transition from national Church to denomination as those that altered the Anglican character of Parliament; the Repeal of the Test and Corporation Acts in 1828, Catholic Emancipation in 1829, the admission of Jews to Parliament in 1858 and of the atheist Charles Bradlaugh in 1886. At the level of local politics, these changes are seen as mirrored by the reform of the Municipal Corporations in 1835 and the ending of compulsory church rate in 1868. Important though these developments were, the process had ramifications beyond those implied by a political realignment. There were other, equally significant steps on the road from national Church to denomination. One came in 1824, when the final parliamentary grant was made for church building; after that, the money had to be raised by Anglicans themselves. Another was the implementation of the Civil Registration Act in 1837, which gave people the freedom to opt out of Anglican rites at birth and marriage. A third was in 1853, when Palmerston ended the issuing of royal letters in support of the National Society, the Society for the Propagation of the Gospel and the Incorporated Church Building Society, on the grounds that they made too close a link between Church and Crown. Bishop Hamilton believed that this action had affected collections for diocesan hospitals, education, the penitentiary, church building and home and foreign missions.[1] It was the first matter he discussed in his first meeting with his archdeacons and rural deans.

As it moved from national Church to denomination, the Church of England had to learn to rely on a narrower base of support. The sharpening of denominational identity was apparent in some urban

[1] PH Ham1/1/4, 15 July 1855.

areas by mid-century, and twenty years later had spread to the countryside. As denominational divisions hardened, the Church became less hospitable to the Wesleyan Methodists who had happily conformed on a regular or occasional basis, and who in turn began to forge a separate identity. Increasingly, clergy began to classify their parishioners according to degrees of commitment to Anglicanism. Parochial charities were no longer regarded as open to all who lived within the parish boundaries, but were redirected to benefit the regular church-goer. Christian philanthropy continued, but it became focused on the so-called 'unchurched masses' who were perceived as outside, not a part of, Christian society. In part, this was a response to the vast expansion of population, and to the loss of a society in which people were acquainted with, and felt a responsibility for, their poorer neighbours.

The narrowing of the definition of Anglicanism had a spiritual as well as a social dimension, and participation in the Eucharist began to be seen as the true badge of church membership by Evangelicals and High Churchmen. Indeed, the spiritual revival associated with Evangelicalism and Tractarianism had the effect of driving a further wedge between the 'godly' and those who did not attain the ideal. The church building began to be used exclusively for worship, forcing out vestry meetings, concerts and other communal activities. The parish church became a resort for the devout rather than a resource for the community, and this made it seem less important in the lives of many parishioners. Nevertheless, the growth of denominational exclusiveness did not have the effect of deterring all who fell short of total commitment. The continued popularity of the Church's rites of passage meant that it retained links with a broad cross-section of society, in a manner that concentration on the Eucharist, or indeed on Sunday church-going, tends to obscure.[2]

On the whole, people did not adjust easily to these changes. The campaign to persuade the faithful to attend worship twice on a Sunday was not particularly successful, perhaps because of the length and repetition in the Prayer Book services, perhaps for other more practical reasons, relating to their own domestic arrangements or work patterns. What had once been large congregations became split and demoralised. Staying away from one service could become the prelude to staying away from both. The expectations of clergy and laity con-

---

[2]   Jeffrey Cox, *The English Churches in a Secular Society: Lambeth 1870–1930* (New York and Oxford: Oxford University Press, 1982) p. 5.

cerning worship did not coincide. Clerical emphasis on the importance of the Eucharist had the effect of deterring the wary. This was not because people were indifferent to the Eucharist, but often they had no tradition of regular reception, and were afraid of its power. Holy Communion was perceived as only for those who were far advanced in spiritual things, or who were unlikely to fall into sin subsequently because they were on the point of death. Such beliefs were deeply ingrained: fears of unworthy reception had a long history and a scriptural warrant. Trying to persuade people to come to communion presented clergy with a considerable challenge. The importance of regular communion was a theme much repeated by the Anglican tract writers, and probably also expounded from many pulpits. In rural areas it was not, however, until the 1860s that most churches provided the opportunity for communion at monthly rather than quarterly intervals. Mattins remained the major service in most parishes on three Sundays out of four. Outside the relatively narrow confines of Evangelicalism and Anglo-Catholicism, people may well have remained as reluctant to go to communion in 1870 as they had been in 1800. Thus both of these movements were in some respects counter-productive, because they emphasised those aspects of religion to which many people were least receptive.

People who drifted away from regular church-going tended to remake a version of Christianity that suited themselves, rather than lapsing from it completely. Elements of Jeffrey Cox's account of religious life in Lambeth after 1870 may already be discerned in the earlier period. Cox argues convincingly that there was little evidence of outright unbelief. Instead, a 'diffusive Christianity' could be detected, 'which comprised a general belief in God, a conviction that God was both just and benevolent although remote from everyday concerns, a certain confidence that "good people" would be taken care of in the life to come, and a belief that the Bible was a uniquely worthwhile book and that children in particular should be exposed to its teachings'.[3] Such beliefs coincided with a decline in a literal understanding of hell, and a growth in the idea that heaven was the universal destination of the dead. Cox's account, regarded by Hugh McLeod as the most significant book on the subject to appear in the 1980s, has found favour with an increasing number of scholars, and has led to a questioning of the once prevalent notion of widespread

---

[3] Ibid., p. 94.

working-class irreligion.[4] McLeod admitted that his own views on the subject were modified by the evidence derived from oral history surveys, in which a startlingly high proportion of those interviewed claimed that their mothers (and sometimes also their fathers) attended church or chapel with some degree of frequency.[5] He suggested that oral history provides graphic illustrations of Cox's arguments concerning the pervasive social influence of the churches, even in places where church-going was low.

In a culture suffused by diffused Christianity, what was it that caused Anglicanism to retain a measure of popularity? Respectability was perhaps a part of the answer. Even tract writers were not afraid to capitalise on the social status that the Church of England was seen to confer. One such tract entitled *Home Made Troubles: A Word for Mothers*, concerns a woman who attends chapel in the hope of soup tickets. In it her husband remarks: 'To think of you going to Chapel, wife ... and we belonging to St Thomas's it ain't hardly respectable ... and it don't seem right to change not for nothing.'[6] In this tract at least, no more substantial reasons were offered in support of the practice of Anglicanism. Cox has noted that working-class mothers in particular were inclined to associate the Church with respectability, and that this was one reason for their insisting upon Anglican rites of passage.[7] Sarah Williams, however, has suggested a modification to Cox's position. Her conclusion, based on research on popular religion in Southwark for the period 1880–1939, emphasised the place of Christian orthodoxy among the complex motivations surrounding the rites of passage. 'The social dimension of the ritual, just like the superstitious elements encompassed by it, did not necessarily preclude a desire to please the Deity. One cannot explain participation in the rituals simply as a desire for social status without reference to the wider range of meanings which were combined in the motivation to act in this way.'[8] Orthodoxy and

---

[4]   Hugh McLeod, *Religion and Irreligion in Victorian England: How Secular was the Working Class?* (Bangor: Headstart History, 1993) p. 8. See also Callum Brown, 'Did urbanization secularize Britain?', *Urban History Year Book* (1988) pp. 1–14 and Jeremy Morris, 'Church and people 33 years on: a historical critique', *Theology*, 94 (1991) pp. 92–101.

[5]   McLeod, *Religion and Irreligion* p. 32. See also Hugh McLeod, 'New perspectives on Victorian working-class religion; the oral evidence', *Oral History*, 14:1 (1986) pp. 31–49.

[6]   Margaret E. Hayes, *Home Made Troubles: A Word for Mothers* (SPCK tract no. 2146, n.d., but probably 1860s).

[7]   Cox, *The English Churches in a Secular Society* p. 98; see also Hugh McLeod, *Class and Religion in the Late Victorian City* (London: Croom Helm, 1974) p. 218 *passim*.

[8]   Sarah Williams, 'Urban religion and the rites of passage' in Hugh McLeod (ed.), *European Religion in the Age of Great Cities 1830–1930* (London: Routledge, 1995) p. 231.

superstition were intertwined. Indeed, Anglicanism was embedded into diffusive Christianity; it was something that could be taken for granted, and (unlike Roman Catholicism or Nonconformity) it was not seen to require explanation or justification.

Hugh McLeod has suggested that in Victorian religion and irreligion, 'the crucial dividing line is that of gender. In all areas of Victorian society, women were more likely than men to be actively involved in a church or a chapel; conversely, men were far more likely than women to join a secularist organisation, and more men than women were agnostics.'[9] That the Church of England drew the bulk of its support from women has been widely asserted, though the precise extent remains difficult to quantify.[10] It is apparent that a majority of SPCK tracts in the later period were aimed explicitly at a female readership. By the end of the century the assistants who worked with Charles Booth on the *Religious Influences* volumes (1902) of his survey of the *Life and Labour of the People in London*, took it for granted that most church-goers in London were women. Some contemporary observers suggested that in Lambeth religiously-inclined men were attracted to Nonconformity, where they might be given real responsibility for running chapel affairs, while women accepted clerical authority within Anglicanism just as they accepted a subordinate position at home.[11] In the earlier part of the nineteenth century fewer comments seem to have been made about the gender balance in church, and it is therefore harder to know anything about the ratio of women to men who attended. Obelkevich detected (albeit on the basis of a limited survey) the possible survival of an older custom in which a man, as head of the household, was a family's 'official representative' – in the community, and at church. He noted that in Massingberd's Lincolnshire parishes of Ormsby and Driby, male labourers attended communion noticeably more frequently than their wives.[12] Obelkevich concluded that appearance at the altar rails was a communal responsibility for the men, but an individual decision for the women, and that the labourer and his wife led independent religious lives.[13] By the end of the century the sense of a man having a communal religious responsibility had been

---

[9] McLeod, *Religion and Irreligion*, pp. 48–9.
[10] Sean Gill, *Women and the Church of England from the Eighteenth Century to the Present* (London: SPCK, 1994) p. 7.
[11] Cox, *The English Churches in a Secular Society* p. 27.
[12] James Obelkevich, *Religion and Rural Society: South Lindsey 1825–1875* (Oxford: Clarendon Press, 1976) pp. 141–2.
[13] Ibid., p. 142.

lost, but a woman generally retained her freedom of individual decision in the matter of church attendance. For those women unable to attend on Sunday there existed a variety of church-sponsored weekday activities that helped them to retain their links with formal religion.[14]

It was argued in the previous chapter that whilst the Church found new opportunities to make use of women – as district visitors in particular – the roles that it made available to men had been diminished. The decline in the authority of the parish vestry was an example. The vestry had been a relatively democratic institution, empowered to legislate on a wide range of civil as well as ecclesiastical matters. All ratepayers could attend, and all could vote, though the number of votes they could cast depended on the value of their property, and no once could cast more than six. Every decision was taken by a majority vote, and not on the instructions of the chairman (who was usually the clergyman) or the churchwardens. Vestries fell victim to the increasing complexity of local government, the powers they had previously exercised being taken over by other, specialised bodies. The end of compulsory church rate in 1868 meant that the parish as a whole became indifferent to ecclesiastical matters, and this had the effect of tilting the balance of power in favour of the incumbent.[15] The parish clerk, a paid employee despite his freehold, was frequently another casualty of the ending of church rate. Church-wardens, meanwhile, found the scope of their civic duties reduced, and that clergy were increasingly taking over their responsibility for the care and maintenance of the church building.

This state of affairs contrasted with the early nineteenth century, when laymen had played a critical role both in influencing and in supporting the Church. Indifference had been less common. In the early years pressure for change had come from every level of society: from the rick-burning Swing rioters and radical propagandists like John Wade, Richard Carlile and William Hone, but also from pillars of the Establishment and loyal sons of the Church like Sir Robert Peel and Lord Henley, who took the initiative in founding and setting the agenda for the Ecclesiastical Commission. As a result, bishops were acutely aware of the hold that laymen had over them. They began to adopt a defensive mentality that was intensely vulnerable to the attacks of radicals and reformers. Kaye hammered the warning home to his

---

[14] Cox, *The English Churches in a Secular Society* pp. 71–3.
[15] Owen Chadwick, *The Victorian Church* 2nd edn (London: A & C Black, 1972), part II, pp. 193–202.

clergy in 1828: if churchmen shrank from the task of pointing out and correcting ecclesiastical abuses, it would be 'taken up and executed with unsparing severity by those who entertain no friendly feeling towards us; who keep their eyes incessantly fixed upon us with the sole intent of discovering and exposing our weaknesses, our failings, our errors'.[16] Blomfield summed up the episcopal mood in a note to Kaye in September 1830: 'Every succeeding shift is giving the drama a more tragic character. The times are awful ... From all that I have heard in different quarters ... I am convinced that if we do not take some step ourselves to improve the present arrangement of Church property, before long it will be done for us.'[17]

By the mid-1830s the threatening storm clouds had dispersed, and the prospect of disestablishment had receded, at least for a while. In 1838 Kaye remarked that it was the measures of the Ecclesiastical Commission, more than any other single factor, which had been responsible in the previous three years for quelling the cry for church reform, and improving public feeling towards the Church.[18] There was some truth in this: both radicals and reformers were placated at the sight of the Church adapting itself to contemporary standards of organisation and management.

While the Ecclesiastical Commission may have helped to dampen down the antagonisms of lay people, it had the reverse effect on the parochial clergy. The impact that the sudden onset of institutional reform had should not be underestimated, nor should the general sense of crisis in the 1830s that had prompted it. Clergy felt excluded from the deliberations of a distant yet powerful Ecclesiastical Commission: in the first five years of its life only bishops were members of the Commission, and even when its membership was enlarged in 1840, more bishops were included, leaving the parochial clergy without an effective voice.[19] From the point of view of the rural clergy, the Commission became synonymous with a betrayal of their interests. They were the men whose lives and careers were changed almost beyond recognition by the parliamentary legislation that the Commission recommended. The centrepiece was the Pluralities Act of 1838,

[16] John Kaye, *Charge* (1828), reprinted in W. F. J. Kaye (ed.), *The Works of John Kaye* (London, 1888), vol. VII, p. 47.

[17] LAO CorB5/5/1/1, C. J. Blomfield to Kaye, 29 September 1830.

[18] Kaye, 'A letter to the Archbishop of Canterbury' (1838) *Works*, vol. VII, pp. 188–9; see also p. 216. Kaye published this open letter as a sort of *apologia* for the Ecclesiastical Commission.

[19] G. F. A. Best, *Temporal Pillars: Queen Anne's Bounty, the Ecclesiastical Commissioners and the Church of England* (Cambridge: Cambridge University Press, 1964) p. 348.

which severely limited the grounds on which an incumbent could hold more than one living and become non-resident. It also revised the regulations concerning the employment of curates in sole charge, provided for the uniting and disuniting of benefices and for the compulsory mortgaging of livings in order to finance the construction or repair of parsonages. This Act lay behind many of the changes in clerical life that took place over the following decades.

The position of curates became less secure. They ceased to be placed in sole charge of parishes in the absence of the incumbent, appointments which could last for many years, and they became instead the assistants, perhaps newly-ordained assistants, to resident incumbents. Thus the usual definition of a 'curate' changed radically between 1800 and 1870. As a newly created body, assistant curates were practically invisible in law, and their stipends were not subject to regulation, unlike those of curates in sole charge. All curates were paid by the incumbents who employed them, but the revenues of many parishes were too small to support one clergyman, let alone two. As the number of men entering the clerical profession reached record proportions, a title for orders with a reasonable stipend became the object of intense ambition. It would seem that a proportion of curates supplemented their clerical stipends with private income, or with support from their family or other benefactors. Others relied on the generosity of their employer to divert some of his own money for their stipend. Still others had to live as economically as possible, perhaps with help from the Church Pastoral Aid Society or the Additional Curates Society, or, after 1866, from the Curates' Augmentation Fund. Both the financial provisions and the institutional structure of the Church of England were quite unsuited for the rapid expansion in the number of assistant curates. To some extent the Church was kept afloat by the private contributions by members of the middle classes.

Finance was not the only difficulty that curates encountered. Insecurity of tenure was another, which affected equally assistant curates and those in sole charge. The death or resignation of his incumbent meant that a curate's appointment was terminated. It did not seem permissible to grant him security of tenure whilst he was being paid as the employee of an incumbent who possessed the freehold of the parish. When the freehold passed to another incumbent, he would not necessarily keep his predecessor's curate, any more than he would feel bound to retain his domestics. This meant that the status of a curate was little better than that of a servant. Yet a curate was expected also to be a gentleman; if he was obliged to groom his own horse, like a curate at Bramcote in Nottinghamshire in 1845, he could find himself at the centre of a local scandal.[20] Although he might be the social and intellectual equal of his employer, as long as a curate remained unbeneficed, he could not hope for any measure of independence.

The transition in the status and duties of curates, and the arrival of a more or less fully resident body of incumbents, was a gradual process. It was characteristic of the church reform movement that, although reformers in the 1830s viewed the problems confronting them with urgency, the solutions which they proposed were slow in their realisation. By 1840 the sense of impending crisis had receded, and reform measures began to be understood as part of a longer-term strategy. Thus, although it has been shown that in the case of the diocese of Lincoln at least, the effects of the Pluralities Act were marked, it was not until the 1870s that the holding of livings in plurality was virtually eradicated. Church reform differed from parallel reform movements – for example those associated with Parliament, the municipal corporations and the poor law – insofar as it involved a redistribution of property, thus striking at the heart of one of the nineteenth century's most cherished values. There was no choice but to respect vested interests, but the wheels of change turned correspondingly slowly.

The one development that did not conform to this pattern was the revival of the office of rural dean. This was principally an innovation of the 1820s, and a sign that bishops and archdeacons were prepared to initiate change independent of the promptings of Parliament. Ostensibly set up to monitor activities in the parishes of non-resident clergy, rural deans were able to exert a variety of subtle pressures. In effect they provided a network of senior incumbents, dedicated to clerical self-regulation and to the promotion of Anglican causes such as church schools. In the absence of any coherent form of clerical career structure, appointment to the office of rural dean, although honorary, gave an opportunity for the public reward of those incumbents whom bishops and archdeacons wished to serve as a model for the rest.

Debates concerning churchmanship have been avoided as an explicit theme in this book, because they seem to have been largely irrelevant to the majority of the lower clergy. There is little evidence to suggest that considerations of churchmanship greatly impinged upon many lay

[20] LAO CorB5/8/20, G. Wilkins to Kaye, 21 February 1845.

people, though of course there were some exceptions. In any case, it may be a flawed notion to suppose that churchmanship can be labelled and pinned down by an historian. The reality of human experience is more complicated, as seen in the examples of the two clergy whose diaries have been used as a source in this study. Francis Massingberd was an Oxford man and a direct contemporary of Newman. When in London, he attended one of the highest of the High Churches, Frederick Oakeley's Margaret Street chapel, and he became devoted to the Eucharist. He was not a Tractarian, however, and continued to be marked by an older, High Church orthodoxy, upholding the principles of the Reformation and a conception of the State as a divinely ordained institution. He claimed to belong to no party. John Rashdall, on the other hand, had clear Evangelical sympathies, and a regard for Nonconformists that was rare, even among clergy of his type. Yet his dancing, socialising and novel reading hardly conform to the conventional picture of the nineteenth-century Evangelical curate. Though he could describe his friend Alfred Tennyson as 'quite ignorant of the "mystery of Godliness"' he admitted to finding his Evangelical brethren usually 'a good deal bigoted'. Like Massingberd, Rashdall transcends stereotypes.

The clergy seem to have experienced higher levels of anxiety than they had previously known, though such intangibles are impossible to quantify. There was an obvious concern about the Church being engulfed in the rising tide of dissent; it was the fear that nonconformity had grown to the point where the Church was in danger of becoming peripheral or superfluous which caused clerical tolerance to evaporate. Even Rashdall claimed that he would have been less accommodating to Methodists in Orby if he had contemplated a longer stay in the parish. Numerous clergy must have felt personally threatened as they witnessed the construction of a new chapel in their own parish. Church people were slow in grasping that at a practical as well as a constitutional level Anglican hegemony had passed away. Many appeared to believe that once people had a resident clergyman offering them two Sunday services in a well-maintained building, and a place for their children in a church school, they would flock back to their Anglican spiritual home, leaving Nonconformity to wither away. It was a false assumption. Roman Catholicism was far less of a threat in rural areas, although Bishop Hamilton gives a rare glimpse into his psychological state when he recorded in his diary in December 1856 his 'great distress' at having dreamt that his chaplain James Fraser had become a

Roman Catholic.[21] As the most notable of the High Church bishops of his day, Hamilton must have lived in fear of the damage that the conversion of any of his subordinates would cause.

More powerful than the threat from rival creeds, however, was the sense of personal unworthiness that haunted those who were the guardians of souls. This anxiety may have been most acute at the time when clergy were in the transitional phase, shifting from seeing themselves as literally responsible for the eternal wellbeing of all their parishioners, to defining their role in terms of a general concern for church people. Francis Massingberd felt responsible for the souls of all who lived in his three parishes, and many of his anxieties seemed to stem from dread at the prospect of the final encounter with the Deity. His apparently quite literal understanding of the coming Day of Judgement infused his spiritual life with an edge of terror. Such fears were common in the first half of the century, when 'What must I do to be saved?' was a pressing question for a large proportion of the population. By 1870 some of the urgency that underpinned the question was beginning to fade, although the question itself did not disappear.

[21] PH Ham1/1/4, 30 December 1856.

Select bibliography

This is a bibiography of the papers and books referred to in the text, excluding standard reference books and periodicals.

I MANUSCRIPT SOURCES

Lincolnshire Archives Office – selections from

CorB5/3/1–37 Buckinghamshire
CorB5/4/1–151 Lincolnshire
CorB5/5/1–17 Leicestershire
CorB5/7/1–5 Bedfordshire
CorB5/8, 8A/1–40 Nottinghamshire
CorB5/9/1–14 visitation and confirmation
CorB5/10/1–22 Ecclesiastical Commissioners
CorB5/13 pluralities
CorB5/14/1–8 ordination
CorB5/16 rural deans
CorB5/18/1–3 requests for patronage
CorB5/19/1–18 clergy discipline cases
CorB5/21/1–3 schools
CorB5/22 miscellaneous
CorB5/29 general bundle relating to Pelham, 1822–4
SPE 18 diocesan specula for the years 1832, 1844, 1853
MASS8/1, MASS8/2 Francis Massingberd's diaries
Miscellaneous Lincolnshire parish registers

Cambridge University Library

Selections from Ely Diocesan Records
EDR C1/4 visitation returns, 1807
EDR C1/6 visitation returns, 1825
EDR C1/8 visitation returns, 1837
EDR C1/9 visitation returns, 1850
EDR C1/12 visitation returns, 1865

EDR C3/25; C3/40 visitation returns, 1873
EDR B15 churchwardens' presentments, 1805
EDR B16 churchwardens' presentments, 1815
EDR B17 churchwardens' presentments, 1825
EDR B18 churchwardens' presentments, 1835
EDR B19 churchwardens' presentments, 1845
EDR B20 churchwardens' presentments, 1855
EDR B21 churchwardens' presentments, 1864
EDR G1/17 Ely Episcopal Act Book, 1832–48

Bodleian Library, Oxford

MS Eng. Misc. e. 351–2 John Rashdall's diaries

Pusey House, Oxford

HAM1/1/4 W. K. Hamilton's daily journal
HAM2/1/1 W. K. Hamilton's diocesan diary
HAM4 Salisbury diocesan correspondence

Lambeth Palace Library

ICBS files and minute books

British Library

Add. MSS 40417
Add. MSS 40418
Add. MSS 40333

2 PRINTED SOURCES, UNPUBLISHED THESES AND ARTICLES

Albers, J., 'Seeds of contention: society, politics and the Church of England in
    Lancashire, 1689–1790' (unpublished PhD thesis, Yale University, 1988)
Alexander, W., *The Holy Bible . . . Principally Designed to Facilitate the Audible and
    Social Reading of Sacred Scriptures* (London, 1828)
Ambler, R. W., *Lincolnshire Returns of the Census of Religious Worship 1851* (Lincoln:
    Lincolnshire Record Society, 72, 1979)
Anderson, O., 'The incidence of civil marriage in England and Wales' *Past
    and Present*, 69 (1975)
[Anon], *Ely Diocesan Calendar and Clergy List* (Ely: 1870)
[Anon], *The Order of Confirmation: With Instructions for them that Come to be Confirmed
    and Prayers to be used Before and After Confirmation* (London: SPCK, 1800)
Armstrong, H. B. J., *Armstrong's Norfolk Diary: Further Passages from the Diary of*

The Reverend Benjamin John Armstrong Vicar of East Dereham 1850–88 (London: Hodder & Stoughton, 1963)

Ashwell, A. R. and Wilberforce, R., *Life of Samuel Wilberforce*, 2 vols. (London, 1880)

Austin, M. R. (ed.), *The Church in Derbyshire in 1823–4: The Parochial Visitation of the Rev Samuel Butler, Archdeacon of Derby in the Diocese of Lichfield and Coventry* (Derbyshire Archaelogical Society, 5, 1974)

Avis, P., 'What is "Anglicanism"?' in Sykes, S., and Booty, J. (eds.), *The Study of Anglicanism* (London: SPCK, 1988)

Balleine, G. R., *A History of the Evangelical Party in the Church of England* (1st edn, 1908; reprinted, 1951)

Baring-Gould, S., *The Church Revival* (London, 1914)

Barrie-Curien, V., 'London clergy in the eighteenth century' in Walsh, J., Haydon, C., and Taylor, S. (eds.), *The Church of England c. 1689–c. 1833: From Toleration to Tractarianism* (Cambridge: Cambridge University Press, 1993)

Barry, J., 'The parish in civic life: Bristol and its churches 1640–1750' in Wright, S. J. (ed.), *Parish, Church and People: Local Studies in Lay Religion 1350–1750* (London: Hutchinson, 1988)

Bebbington, D. W., *Evangelicalism in Modern Britain: A History from the 1730s to the 1980s* (London: Unwin Hyman, 1989)

Best, G. F. A., *Temporal Pillars: Queen Anne's Bounty, the Ecclesiastical Commissioners, and the Church of England* (Cambridge: Cambridge University Press, 1964); *Mid-Victorian Britain 1851–1875* (London: Weidenfeld & Nicolson, 1971)

Biggs, B. J., 'Saints of the soil: early Methodism in agricultural areas', *Proceedings of the Wesley Historical Society*, 48:6 (October 1992)

Blomfield, A., *A Memoir of C. J. Blomfield*, 2 vols. (London, 1863)

Bowen, D., *The Idea of the Victorian Church: A Study of the Church of England 1833–1889* (Montreal: McGill University Press, 1968)

Brabbs, D., *English Country Churches* (London: Weidenfeld & Nicolson, 1985)

Bradley, J., *Religion, Revolution and English Radicalism: Nonconformity in Eighteenth-Century Politics and Society* (Cambridge: Cambridge University Press, 1990)

[Branks, T.], *Heaven our Home* (Edinburgh, 1861)

Brose, O. J., *Church and Parliament: The Reshaping of the Church of England 1828–1860* (Stanford and London: Oxford University Press, 1959)

Brown, C., 'Did urbanization secularize Britain?', *Urban History Yearbook* (1988)

Brown, C. K. F., *A History of the English Clergy, 1800–1900* (London, 1953)

Browne, E. H., *Charge to the Clergy of the Diocese of Ely, 1869* (London: 1869)

Browne, J. H., *Five Letters Addressed to Revd G. Wilkins, Containing Strictures on Some Part of a Publication Entitled 'Body and Soul'* (London, 1823)
    A Sixth Letter to Revd G. Wilkins in Reply to a Chapter in the Second Volume of 'Body and Soul' Entitled 'Evangelism' (London, 1823)

Burgess, H. J., *Enterprise in Education: The Story of the Work of the Established Church in the Education of the People Prior to 1870* (London: SPCK, 1958)

Burgon, J. W., *Lives of Twelve Good Men* (London, 1888)

Burns, R. A., 'The diocesan revival in the Church of England *c.*1825–1865' (unpublished DPhil. thesis, University of Oxford, 1990)

Bushaway, R. W., 'Rite, legitimation and community in southern England 1700–1850: the ideology of custom' in Stapleton, B. (ed.), *Conflict and Community in Southern England* (Stroud, 1992)

Bushby, D. (ed.), *Bedfordshire Schoolchild: Elementary Education Before 1902* (Bedfordshire Historical Record Society, 67, 1988)

Chadwick, O., *The Founding of Cuddesdon* (Oxford: Oxford University Press, 1954)
The Victorian Church 2 vols. (London: A & C Black; part I, 3rd edn, 1971; part II, 2nd edn, 1972)

Church, R. W., *The Oxford Movement: Twelve Years 1833–45* (1st edn, 1891; reprinted, 1970, ed., G. F. A. Best)

Clark, D., *Between Pulpit and Pew: Folk Religion in a North Yorkshire Fishing Village* (Cambridge: Cambridge University Press, 1982)

Clark, J. C. D., *English Society 1688–1832* (Cambridge: Cambridge University Press, 1985)

Cobb, P. G., *The Oxford Movement in Nineteenth Century Bristol* (Bristol: Bristol Branch of the Historical Association, 1988)

Coleman, B. I., 'Anglican church extension and related movements *c.*1800–1860, with special reference to London' (unpublished Cambridge PhD thesis, 1968)
'Southern England in the Census of Religious Worship, 1851', *Southern History*, 5 (1983)

Collinson, P., *The Religion of Protestants: The Church in English Society 1559–1625* (Oxford: Clarendon Press, 1982)

Conybeare, W. J., 'Church parties' *Edinburgh Review*, 99 (1854)

Cox, J., *The English Churches in a Secular Society: Lambeth, 1870–1930* (New York and Oxford: Oxford University Press, 1982)

Cross, C., *Church and People 1450–1660: The Triumph of the Laity in the English Church* (London: Fontana, 1976)

Crowther, M. A., *The Church Embattled: Religious Controversy in Mid-Victorian England* (Newton Abbot: David & Charles, 1970)

Currie, R., 'A micro-theory of Methodist growth' *Proceedings of the Wesley Historical Society*, 36 (October 1967)

Dansey, W., *Horae Decanicae Rurales*, 2 vols. (London, 1835)

Davies, R .E., *Methodism* (London: Epworth Press, 1963)

Davis, R. W., *Political Change and Continuity 1760–1885: A Buckinghamshire Study* (Newton Abbot: David & Charles, 1972)

Dearing, T., *Wesleyan and Tractarian Worship* (London: Epworth/SPCK, 1966)

Deconinck-Brossard, F., 'Eighteenth-century sermons and the age' in Jacob, W. M., and Yates, N. (eds.), *Crown and Mitre: Religion and Society in Northern Europe Since the Reformation* (Woodbridge: Boydell Press, 1993)

Dennis, R., *English Industrial Cities in the Nineteenth Century: A Social Geography* (Cambridge: Cambridge University Press, 1984)

Dewey, C., *The Passing of Barchester* (London: Hambledon Press, 1991)

Ditchfield, P. H., *The Parish Clerk* (London, 1907)

Donald, J. (ed.), *The Letters of Thomas Hayton: Vicar of Long Crendon, Buckinghamshire 1821–1887* (Aylesbury: Buckinghamshire Record Society, 1979)

Drewery, G., 'Victorian church building and restoration in the diocese of York, with special reference to the archdeaconry of Cleveland' (unpublished Cambridge PhD thesis, 1994)

Duffy, E. A., *The Stripping of the Altars: Traditional Religion in England 1400–1580* (New Haven and London: Yale University Press, 1992)

Gash, N., *Sir Robert Peel* (London: Longmans, 1972)

Gilbert, A. D., *Religion and Society in Industrial England: Church, Chapel and Social Change 1740–1914* (London: Longman, 1976)

Gill, S., *Women and the Church of England from the Eighteenth Century to the Present* (London: SPCK, 1994)

Gladstone, W. E., *Manual of Prayers from the Liturgy Arranged for Family Use* (2nd edn, London, 1845)

Goddard, C., *Charge to the Clergy of the Archdeaconry of Lincoln* (1827)

Gregory, J., 'The eighteenth-century Reformation: the pastoral task of Anglican clergy after 1689' in Walsh, J., Haydon, C., and Taylor, S. (eds.), *The Church of England c. 1689–c. 1833: From Toleration to Tractarianism* (Cambridge: Cambridge University Press, 1993)

Grierson, J., *The Deaconess* (London: CIO Publishing, 1981)

Haig, A., *The Victorian Clergy* (London and Sydney: Croom Helm, 1984)

Halcombe, J. J., *The Church and her Curates: A Series of Essays on the Need for More Clergy and the Best Means of Supporting Them* (London: W. Wells Gardner, 1874)

Harding, N. S. (ed.), *Bonney's Church Notes: Being Notes on the Churches in the Archdeaconry of Lincoln 1845–1848* (Lincoln, 1937)

   A Stow Visitation: Being Notes on the Churches in the Archdeaconry of Stow, 1845 by The Venerable W. B. Stonehouse (Lincoln, 1940)

Harford, J. S., *A Life of Thomas Burgess D.D.* (London, 1840)

Hayes, M. E., *Home Made Troubles: A word for Mothers* (SPCK tract no. 2146, n.d., but probably 1860s)

Heeney, B., *A Different Kind of Gentleman: Parish Clergy as Professional Men in Early and Mid-Victorian England* (Connecticut: Archon Books, 1976)

Hempton, D. N., *Methodism and Politics in British Society 1750–1984* (London: Hutchinson, 1984)

   'Popular religion 1800–1986' in Thomas, T. (ed.), *The British: Their Religious Beliefs and Practices 1800–1986* (London and New York: Routledge, 1988)

Hennock, E. P., 'The Anglo-Catholics and Church Extension in Victorian Brighton' in Kitch, M. J., (ed.), *Studies in Sussex Church History* (London: Leopard's Head Press, 1981)

Herring, G. W., 'Tractarianism to Ritualism: a study of some aspects of Tractarianism outside Oxford, from the time of Newman's conversion in 1845 until the first ritual commission in 1867' (unpublished Oxford DPhil. thesis, 1984)

Hilton, B., *The Age of Atonement: The Influence of Evangelicalism on Social and Economic Thought: 1785–1865* (Oxford: Clarendon Press, 1988)

Hiscox, R., *Celebrating Reader Ministry: 125 Years of Lay Ministry in the Church of England* (London: Mowbray, 1991)

Hole, R., *Pulpits, Politics and Public Order in England 1760–1832* (Cambridge: Cambridge University Press, 1989)

Horn, P., *Village Education in Nineteenth-century Oxfordshire* (Oxfordshire Record Society, 51, 1979)

Houghton, W. E., *The Victorian Frame of Mind 1830–1870* (New Haven and London: Yale University Press, 1957)

Huelin, G., *King's College London 1828–1978: A History Commemorating the 150th Anniversary of the Foundation of the College* (London: King's College London, 1978)

Hylson-Smith, K., *Evangelicals in the Church of England 1734–1984* (Edinburgh: T & T Clark, 1988)

Inglis, K. S., *Churches and the Working Classes in Victorian England* (London: Routledge and Kegan Paul, 1963)

'Patterns of religious worship in 1851', *Journal of Ecclesiastical History*, 11 (1960)

Jackson, J., *Charge Delivered to the Clergy of the Diocese of Lincoln, 1855* (1855)

Jacob, W. M., 'Church and borough: King's Lynn 1700–1750' in Jacob, W. M., and Yates, N. (eds.), *Crown and Mitre: Religion and Society in Northern Europe since the Reformation* (Woodbridge: Boydell Press, 1993)

Jagger, P. J., *Clouded Witness: Initiation in the Church of England in the Mid-Victorian Period, 1850–1875* (Allison Park, Pennsylvania, 1982)

Jamieson, R., and Bickersteth, E. H. (eds.), *The Holy Bible with Devotional and Practical Commentary*, 2 vols. (London, 1861)

Kaye, W. F. J. (ed.), *The Works of John Kaye*, 8 vols. (London, 1888)

Keble, J., *The Christian Year* (London, 1828)

Kent, J., *The Unacceptable Face: The Modern Church in the Eyes of the Historian* (London: SCM Press, 1987)

Feelings and festivals: an interpretation of some working-class religious attitudes' in Dyos, H. J., and Wolff, M. (eds.), *The Victorian City: Images and Realities*, 2 vols. (London and Boston: Routledge & Kegan Paul, 1973)

Ker, I. and Gornall, T. (eds.), *The Letters and Diaries of John Henry Newman*, 5 vols. (Oxford: Clarendon Press, 1978–81)

Knight, F. M. R., 'Ministering to the ministers: the discipline of recalcitrant clergy in the diocese of Lincoln 1830–1845' in Sheils, W. J., and Wood, D. (eds.), *The Ministry: Clerical and Lay*, Studies in Church History, 26 (Oxford: Blackwell, 1989)

'Bishop, clergy and people: John Kaye and the diocese of Lincoln 1827–1853' unpublished PhD thesis, University of Cambridge, 1990

'The influence of the Oxford Movement in the parish *c.* 1833–1860: a reassessment' in Rowell, G., and Vaiss, P. (eds.), *From Oxford to the People* (Fowler Wright, 1995)

Laslett, P., *The World We Have Lost – Further Explored* (London: Methuen, 1983)

Maas, J., *Holman Hunt and the Light of the World* (London and Berkeley: Scolar Press, 1984)

McClatchey, D., *Oxfordshire Clergy 1777–1869: A Study of the Established Church and the Role of its Clergy in Local Society* (Oxford: Clarendon Press, 1960)

Machin, G. I. T., *Politics and the Churches in Great Britain 1832 to 1868* (Oxford: Clarendon Press, 1977)

McLeod, H., *Class and Religion in the Late Victorian City* (London: Croom Helm, 1974)

    Religion and Irreligion in Victorian England: How Secular was the Working Class? (Bangor: Headstart History, 1993)

    'New perspectives on Victorian working-class religion: the oral evidence', *Oral History*, 14: 1 (1986)

Maltby, J. D., 'Approaches to the study of religious conformity in late Elizabethan and early Stuart England' (unpublished PhD thesis, University of Cambridge, 1991)

Mather, F. C., *High Church Prophet: Bishop Samuel Horsley (1733–1806) and the Caroline Tradition in the Later Georgian Church* (Oxford: Clarendon Press, 1992)

Meacham, S., *Lord Bishop: The Life of Samuel Wilberforce 1805–1873* (Cambridge, Mass., 1970)

Monro, E., *Parochial Work* (Oxford and London, 1850)

Moore, J. R. (ed.), *Religion in Victorian Britain: Sources* (Manchester: Manchester University Press, 1988)

Morris, J., *Religion and Urban Change: Croydon 1840–1914* (Woodbridge: Boydell Press, 1992)

    'Church and people 33 years on: a historical critique', *Theology*, 94 (1991)

Morrish, P. S., 'History, Celticism and propaganda in the formation of the diocese of Truro', *Southern History*, 5 (1983)

Munson, J., *The Nonconformists: In Search of a Lost Culture* (London: SPCK, 1991)

Newman, J. H., *Apologia Pro Vita Sua* (1st edn, 1864; reprinted 1984, ed., M. Ward)

Newsome, D., *The Parting of Friends: A Study of the Wilberforces and Henry Manning* (London, 1966)

Nockles, P.B., *The Oxford Movement in Context: Anglican High Churchmanship 1760–1857* (Cambridge: Cambridge University Press, 1994)

    'Continuity and change in Anglican High churchmanship in Britain 1792–1850' (unpublished University of Oxford DPhil. thesis, 1982)

    'The Oxford Movement: historical background 1780–1833' in Rowell, G. (ed.), *Tradition Renewed: The Oxford Movement Conference Papers* (London: Darton, Longman & Todd, 1986)

    'Church parties in the pre-Tractarian Church of England 1750–1833: the 'Orthodox' – some problems of definition and identity' in Walsh, J., Haydon, C., and Taylor, S. (eds.), *The Church of England c. 1698–1833: From Toleration to Tractarianism* (Cambridge: Cambridge University Press, 1993)

Norman, E. R., *Church and Society in England 1770–1970* (Oxford: Clarendon Press, 1976)

Obelkevich, J., *Religion and Rural Society: South Lindsey 1825–1875* (Oxford: Clarendon Press, 1976)

O'Day, R., 'The clerical renaissance in Victorian England and Wales' in Parsons, G. (ed.), *Religion in Victorian Britain: Traditions* (Manchester: Manchester University Press, 1988)

Ollard, S. L., *A Short History of the Oxford Movement* (first edition 1915; reprinted London: Faith Press, 1963)

Overton, J. H., *The English Church in the Nineteenth Century (1800–1833)* (London, 1894)

Palliser, D. M., 'Introduction: the parish in perspective' in Wright, S. J. (ed.), *Parish, Church and People: Local Studies in Lay Religion 1350–1750* (London: Hutchinson, 1988)

Parker, S., *Informal Marriage, Cohabitation and the Law, 1750–1989* (Basingstoke: Macmillan, 1990)

Parsons, G. (ed.), *Religion in Victorian Britain*, 4 vols. (Manchester: Manchester University Press, 1988), vol. I, *Traditions*, vol. II, *Controversies*, vol. IV, *Interpretations*

Pelling, H., *Popular Politics and Society in Late Victorian Britain* (London: Macmillan, 1968)

Pugh, R. K., *The Letter-Books of Samuel Wilberforce, 1843–1868* (Oxford: Oxford Record Society, 47, 1969)

Rainbow, B., *The Choral Revival in the Anglican Church 1839–1872* (London: Barrie & Jenkins, 1970)

Roberts, M. J. D., 'Private patronage and the Church of England, 1800–1900', *Journal of Ecclesiastical History* 32: 2 (1981)

Robinson, D. (ed.), *Visitations of the Archdeaconry of Stafford 1829–1841* (London: Stafford Record Society, 1980)

Robinson, J., *The Clergyman's Assistant in the Discharge of Parochial Duties Especially those of a Private Nature* (London, 1805)

Rowell, G., *Hell and the Victorians: A Study of the Nineteenth-Century Theological Controversies Concerning Eternal Punishment and the Future Life* (Oxford: Clarendon Press, 1974)

Royle, E. R., *The Victorian Church in York* (York: Borthwick Papers, 64, 1983)

Russell, A. J., *The Clerical Profession* (London: SPCK, 1980)
'A sociological analysis of a clergyman's role: with special reference to its development in the early nineteenth century' (unpublished DPhil. thesis, University of Oxford, 1970)

Russell, R.C., *Friendly Societies in the Caistor, Binbrook and Brigg Area in the Nineteenth Century* (Nettleton WEA, 1975)

Shaw, J., *The Parochial Lawyer* (London, 1833)

Shaw, T., *A History of Cornish Methodism* (Truro: Bradford Barton, 1967)

Smith, M. A., 'Religion in Industrial Society: the case of Oldham and Saddleworth 1780–1865' (unpublished Oxford University DPhil. thesis, 1987)
'The Reception of Richard Podmore: Anglicanism in Saddleworth 1700-

1830' in Walsh, J., Haydon, C., and Taylor, S., *The Church of England c.1689–c.1833* (Cambridge: Cambridge University Press, 1993)

Snell, K. D. M., *Church and Chapel in the North Midlands: Religious Observance in the Nineteenth Century* (Leicester: Leicester University Press, 1991)

Soloway, R.A., *Prelates and People: Ecclesiastical Social Thought in England 1783–1852* (London: Routledge, 1969)

Somerville, C. J., *Popular Religion in Restoration England* (Gainesville, 1977)

Spaeth, D., 'Parsons and Parishioners: Lay–Clerical Conflict and Popular Piety in Wiltshire Villages, 1660–1740' (unpublished Brown University PhD thesis, 1985)

Spurrell, M., *Stow Church Restored 1846–1866* (Lincoln: Lincolnshire Record Society, 1984)

Symondson, A. (ed.), *The Victorian Crisis of Faith* (London: SPCK, 1970)

Temperley, N., *The Music of the English Parish Church* (Cambridge: Cambridge University Press, 1979)

Thomas, K., *Religion and the Decline of Magic: Studies in Popular Beliefs in Sixteenth- and Seventeenth-Century England* (London: Weidenfeld & Nicolson, 1971)

Thompson, D. M., 'The Churches and Society in Nineteenth-century England: A Rural Perspective' in Cuming, G. J., and Baker, D. (eds.), *Popular Belief and Practice* Studies in Church History 8 (Cambridge: Cambridge University Press, 1972)

Nonconformity in the Nineteenth Century (London: Routledge, 1972)

'Baptism, Church and Society in Britain since 1800' (University of Cambridge Hulsean lectures, 1983-4)

'Historical Survey, 1750–1949' in Owen, D. M. (ed.), *A History of Lincoln Minster* (Cambridge: Cambridge University Press, 1994)

Thompson, K. A., *Bureaucracy and Church Reform: The Organizational Response of the Church of England to Social Change 1800-1965* (Oxford: Clarendon Press, 1970)

Trimmer, S., *The Teacher's Assistant: Consisting of Lectures in Catechetical Form: Being Part of a Plan for Appropriate Instruction for the Children of the Poor* (London: Rivington, 1808)

Urdank, A. M., *Religion and Society in a Cotswold Vale: Nailsworth, Gloucestershire 1780–1865* (Berkeley: University of California Press, 1990)

Varley, E. A., *The Last of the Prince Bishops: William Van Mildert and the High Church Movement of the Early Nineteenth Century* (Cambridge: Cambridge University Press, 1992)

Vickers, J. A., *The Religious Census of Sussex, 1851* (Lewes: Sussex Record Society 75, 1989)

The Religious Census of Hampshire, 1851 (Winchester: Hampshire Record Series XII, 1993)

Vickers, W., *Companion to the Altar* (London: n.d.)

Virgin, P., *The Church in an Age of Negligence: Ecclesiastical Structure and Problems of Church Reform 1700–1840* (Cambridge: James Clarke & Co, 1989)

Walsh, J., and Taylor, S., 'Introduction: the Church and Anglicanism in the "long" eighteenth century' in Walsh, J., Haydon, C., and Taylor, S., *The Church of England c.1689–c.1833: From Toleration to Tractarianism* (Cambridge: Cambridge University Press, 1993)

Walsh, W., *The Secret History of the Oxford Movement* (London, 1897)

Warne, A., *Church and Society in Eighteenth Century Devon* (Newton Abbot: David & Charles, 1969)

Waterman, A. M. C., *Revolution, Economics and Religion: Christian Political Economy, 1798–1833* (Cambridge: Cambridge University Press, 1991)

Watts, M., *Religion in Victorian Nottinghamshire: The Religious Census of 1851*, 2 vols. (Nottingham: University of Nottingham, 1988)

Welch, P. J., 'Blomfield and Peel: A Study in Co-operation between Church and State 1841–46' *Journal of Ecclesiastical History* 12 (1961)

Wenham, J., *Private and Family Prayers* (London, 1855)

'W. F. W.', *Prayers for the Dead, for the Use of Members of the Church of England and Meditations on the Four Last Things* (London: 1845)

Wheeler, M., *Death and the Future Life in Victorian Literature and Theology* (Cambridge: Cambridge University Press, 1990)

White, J. F., *Protestant Worship: Traditions in Transition* (Louisville, Kentucky, 1989)

Wolffe, J. R., *The Protestant Crusade in Great Britain 1829–1860* (Oxford: Clarendon Press, 1991)

Wolfram, S., *In-laws and Outlaws: Kinship and Marriage in England* (London and Sydney: Croom Helm, 1987)

Wright, J. R., 'Anglicanism, *Ecclesia Anglicana*, and Anglican: An Essay on Terminology' in Sykes, S., and Booty, J. (eds.), *The Study of Anglicanism* (London: SPCK, 1988)

Wright, S. J. (ed.), *Parish, Church and People: Local Studies in Lay Religion* (London, 1988)

Yates, N., 'Leeds and the Oxford Movement: A Study of "High Church" Activity in the rural deaneries of Allerton, Armley, Headingley and Whitkirk in the Diocese of Ripon 1836–1934', *Thoresby Society Publications* Vol.55, No.121 (Leeds, 1975)

The Oxford Movement and parish life: St Saviour's Leeds, 1839–1929 Borthwick Papers, No.48 (York: Borthwick Institute, 1975)

Buildings, Faith and Worship: The Liturgical Arrangement of Anglican Churches 1600–1900 (Oxford: Clarendon Press, 1991)

Index